Benjamin Franklin's
AUTOBIOGRAPHY
Introduction by Dixon Wecter

Selected Writings
Edited with an Introduction by
Larzer Ziff

HOLT, RINEHART AND WINSTON, INC.
New York • Chicago • San Francisco • Atlanta
Dallas • Montreal • Toronto • London • Sydney

CONTENTS

INTRODUCTION TO

BENJAMIN FRANKLIN'S

AUTOBIOGRAPHY

BENJAMIN FRANKLIN (1706–1790), printer, publicist, scientist, statesman, and philanthropist, once remarked in the pages of *Poor Richard's Almanac:* "There are three things extremely hard— steel, a diamond, and to know thyself." About human beings he had a curiosity as keen as that with which he studied the other remarkable phenomena of nature, and this interest included himself. But he was not an introvert nor, for all his engaging little symptoms of vanity, was he ever intoxicated by his own importance. He realized, in the words of Poor Richard, that "he that falls in love with himself will have no rivals." Indeed this is the most modest of the world's great autobiographies. A reader who knew nothing else about Franklin would gain little notion of his real stature in diplomacy, government, and science. Of course the story ends around 1757, short of his most illustrious phase. But even so, it passes over his celebrated experiment with the kite in 1752 and omits to mention the honorary degrees and medals which had begun to shower upon him at home and abroad about the same time. The serene homespun simplicity of the *Autobiography*, its dry humor, and the writer's refusal to take too seriously either himself or these memoirs (as he calls them) of a garrulous old man— the approach is unaffected, disarming, wholly relaxed and delightful.

This is the story of a bright but penniless lad who made good in the big city, first Philadelphia and then London—a graduate of what Abraham Lincoln later called "the poor boy's college," the printing shop. Even in the eighteenth century, America was the land of opportunity. The modern reader is interested to observe the easy democracy of colonial society by which Franklin, an unknown but enterprising mechanic in his teens, quickly attracted the notice both of Governor Keith of Pennsylvania and of Governor Burnet of New York. Merely at its surface level, this is a tale of pluck and luck much more sincere and convincing than any found in the pages of Horatio Alger.

Franklin began writing it on a summer's holiday in 1771, as the plain annals of his life, of interest chiefly to his son William. But when he picked up the thread again after an interruption of thirteen busy years while the American Revolution was born, fought for, and won, he had grown less conscious of his son's reading over his shoulder—a Tory son who had gravely strained the filial bond by taking sides with King George—and more aware of his general public and the exemplary effect of what Doctor Franklin had to say. But this did not greatly alter the tone in which his narrative had begun, nor was it his nature to preach what he had not practiced.

Some people, recalling chiefly those passages about young Ben as a hustler trundling his newsprint in a wheelbarrow through the cobbled streets of Philadelphia "to secure my credit and character as a tradesman," keeping a daily score card of his virtues and vices, assume that the Poor Richard of the famous Almanac which Franklin wrote was somehow identical with his creator. Naturally enough, with his abiding desire to improve himself and his fellowmen, Franklin offered his experience in life for whatever practical value it might have. Penning its latter pages in October, 1788, as a very old man near the end of his road, he could still remark to a French friend, La Rochefoucauld, that his dwelling so long upon the years of green manhood was "of more general use to young readers, as exemplifying strongly the effects of prudent and imprudent conduct in the commencement of a life of business." The net result of Franklin's preoccupation with his earlier days, joined to the incomplete story told by the *Autobiography*, has been to direct popular notice to only one of Franklin's many character-facets— that of the industrious apprentice, living by sharp and thrifty maxims, making a fetish of worldly success.

Such oversimplification is unfair to so versatile, well rounded, and in some ways complex a character as Franklin's. Even Poor Richard once recklessly avowed that "An egg today is better than a hen tomorrow," while the real Franklin confessed that frugality was "a virtue I never could acquire myself," although his wife's good management helped to balance his extravagance. Another virtue, orderliness, gave him still more trouble, as he admits in the *Autobiography*. William Strahan, like other friends, complained of Franklin's "natural inactivity" and at times the latter seems to have taken a certain pride in his easygoing ways. As a matter of fact, it is hard to imagine Franklin's roving curiosity ever permitting him to grow indolent, although it frequently seduced him from the routines of business into the pleasant meadows of experiment and speculation. (Whenever bored in a public meeting or legislative body, instead of doodling he drew "magic squares" as mathematical amusements.) And in his eighty-first year, he who had written so many proverbs about improving the shining hour—including the reminder that "there will be sleeping enough in the grave"—reached a different conclusion, as he romped with his grandchildren in a sunny back garden in Philadelphia or played a little cribbage. To a friend he wrote of his occasional self-reproaches over wasted time, until an inner voice reassured him: "You know the soul is immortal; why, then, should you be such a niggard of time, when you have a whole eternity before you?" Plainly enough there were lights, shades, and nuances in the real Franklin which have no place in the maxims of Poor Richard or even in the legendary Franklin of the savings banks and preachers of the gospel of getting-on.

Furthermore, as he implied to La Rochefoucauld, Franklin did not spare himself mention of his "imprudent conduct" as well as the more edifying sort. One or two of these "errata"—as the veteran printer calls them, in the pages that follow—concern business judgment; the rest have to do with his youthful relations with women. It is noteworthy that the two most popular and accessible books of advice to young men which the English-speaking world can claim—Franklin's *Autobiography* and Lord Chesterfield's *Letters*—should appear so frank and tolerant upon the one topic about which Anglo-Saxons are thought to be so reticent. But how could they well be otherwise? Each was addressed to the writer's natural son, and sanctimony would have been transparent.

Franklin's attitude toward life is never prim nor pompous. Instead it appears shrewd, whimsical, or ironic, skeptical of rhetoric and smug conventions, and curiously detached from the passion and heat of prejudice—as if able to bring a cool scientific appraisal to bear upon himself and his neighbors. His youthful career was an education in wariness, if not downright disillusion. His elder brother treated him so unfraternally as to implant in Ben a life-long dislike for tyranny in any form; his first chum, Collins, decamped to the West Indies with a sum of money that had been left in Franklin's hands as a trust; his first patron, Sir William Keith, proved to be a liar and maker of empty promises; a London ironmonger filched his idea for the Franklin stove, making a small fortune from doing what the inventor had refused idealistically to do, namely to patent it; and, in the last year covered by the *Autobiography*, Lord Loudoun's duplicity left him saddled with unpaid debts against the British Crown as the reward of his declining to profiteer. Long years in politics, diplomacy, and public life served to show Franklin, a rational and honest man, how rarely reason and integrity govern the affairs of legislatures, privy councils, and nations. Indeed, Franklin had his moments of skepticism about the human race. "Half the lives you save are not worth saving, as being useless, and almost all the other half ought not to be saved, as being mischievous," he wrote banteringly to his friend Doctor John Fothergill in 1764, trying to persuade him to give up the practice of medicine and enjoy life. "Does your conscience never hint to you the impiety of being in constant warfare against the plans of Providence?" True, life's vicissitudes tinged him with a mild cynicism, but in no sense did they embitter him or even make him petty. The *Autobiography* records the shabby conduct of his youthful friend Ralph, who deserted his mistress for Franklin to support, then returned long enough to rebuke him in a lofty style for having attempted a little familiarity with her and promptly reneged on all his debts to Franklin. Characteristically the latter adds, "I loved him, notwithstanding, for he had many amiable qualities."

Nor did Franklin ever waver in his benevolence toward the race —an attitude which belonged to him both by nature and by nurture in the air of eighteenth-century humanitarianism. He never doubted that "the most acceptable service of God was the doing good to man." Unlike the penny pincher of the Poor Richard legend, as has been suggested, the real Franklin was generous to a fault. As a lad of seventeen, landing at Philadelphia wharf, he pressed his last shilling upon "the people of the boat for my passage" even though he had paid his way by rowing, and after spending the remaining coppers upon his three famous rolls he gave two to a woman and child who had been his fellow passengers. Throughout his life Franklin proffered his time and money freely to every worthy cause. And having won a competence, at the age of forty-two he retired from the printing shop to devote himself to science and presently to disinterested public service, "uninterrupted by the little cares and fatigues of business." For, in the first place, Franklin always preferred knowledge to wealth; in the second he had what his Quaker neighbors called "a concern" for the duties of good citizenship. To his mother he wrote in 1750 that he "would rather have it said 'He lived usefully' than 'He died rich.'"

He was the father of the subscription library in America, sponsored the first volunteer fire company as well as the pioneer fire-insurance company, busied himself about street cleaning and paving and the planting of trees to purify city air, served as deputy postmaster general for the colonies and later organized the present postal system, formed a volunteer militia company, founded the University of Pennsylvania and also the first Pennsylvania charity hospital, and served as the first president of the Pennsylvania Society for Promoting the Abolition of Slavery. Adding to the health, prosperity, comfort, and knowledge of mankind was the essence of Franklin's day-by-day philanthropy and his rule of life. Kindliness, generosity, and sympathy appealed more than did the negative aspects of conduct, the prohibitions of codes and churches.

The inventor of bifocal spectacles, Franklin at times exhibited a kindred duality of vision in immaterial things. The great conciliator of the Federal Convention, he had long since learned to compromise differences of opinion without compromising himself. In politics he was divided between his admiration for firm and efficient government—which made him a devotee of national sovereignty over states' rights—and a suspicion of too much prerogative, whether in terms of proprietary abuses in the affairs of colonial Pennsylvania or the still greater absentee tyranny of the British king. The latter inclination led him to favor a unicameral legislature for his state, to take little stock in the checks-and-balances theory of government so dear to the Federalists, and to espouse an almost universal franchise.

The too rigid application of dogma he always disliked, knowing among other things the background of self-interest that lay behind most rationalizations, as well as man's infinite capacity for deceiving himself. For example, in the sphere of personal habit he was youthfully a vegetarian by principle, but, as he tells us in the *Autobiography*, broke his rule when tempted by the savor of frying fish, and was quick to reason that big fish themselves devour the smaller ones. "So convenient a thing it is to be a *reasonable creature*," he explains slyly, "since it enables one to find a reason for every thing one has a mind to do." In ethics, he tended to reason from practical consequences to first principles—that is, certain actions are called virtues or vices because they benefit or harm the doer—just as in theology he was prone to reason from effects to the First Cause, "the God of Newton."

All his days Franklin took sects, creeds, rites, and sacraments with a grain of salt and a tincture of quiet skepticism. As an ambitious young printer he admits that he had no time for church attendance, "Sunday being my studying day." He once proposed to found a church for men like himself to be called "the Society of the Free and Easy." From this sector of experience his pervasive sense of humor was not absent. As related in the *Autobiography*, in his brief military service during the Indian wars he boosted the poor attendance at devotions, of which the Presbyterian chaplain complained, by persuading him to dole out rum and prayers at the same time. His own prayers, we learn, were addressed to "Powerful Goodness." Franklin once alluded to the "wise and good God, who is the author and owner of our system," as if He were a kindly landlord or senior partner in the firm, approachable with casual and assured familiarity. Franklin's was a reasonable God, an Omnipotence without thunder, overseeing a rational universe in which there was nothing to fear but fear itself. Thus rejecting the Calvanist heritage of his native Boston, he tended in some measure to follow the Quakers of his adopted Philadelphia in stressing the validity of private judgment over the literal Scriptures. Still more clearly did he gain a tinge of freethinking from the French and English Deists of his time, supplanting supernaturalism by natural law. The beauty of holiness—the passion of that other famous American of Franklin's middle years. Jonathan Edwards—played as little part in the sage's make-up as did a sense of poetry. The aesthetic and the spiritual were virtually missing from his many-sided character, so rich and lively in most other perceptions. Franklin, however, did believe in some kind of immortality, as indicated above, for his benevolent God had no intention of extinguishing the intelligence He had created. After the death of his brother John in 1756 Franklin wrote to one of the bereaved family, expressing his belief that our bodies are lent to us so long as they can afford us pleasure, but when the toll of pain outweighs pleasure a kindly God relieves us of them through the ministry of death: "Our friend and we were invited abroad on a party of pleasure, which is to last for ever. His chair was ready first, and he is gone before us. We could not all conveniently start together; and why should you and I be grieved at this, since we are soon to follow, and know where to find him?"

Yet on the whole, speculations about the here and now absorbed him more than those about the hereafter. Natural science, its laws, and phenomena were self-revelations of the God of Newton. Like his contemporaries, he called these investigations "philosophical," and from the little band of like-minded Philadelphians whom Franklin had formed into the Junto in 1727 sprang the still distinguished American Philosophical Society. Toward science he displayed a gusto keener than he ever brought to the humdrum routines of business or the solemn play acting of diplomacy, for, as Carl Becker says, "Nature alone met him on equal terms, with a disinterestedness matching his own." Shortly before his retirement from business, as he intimates all too briefly in the *Autobiography*, the arrival of that latest plaything in Continental science, the Leyden jar, set him off on a course of brilliant experiments which the present-day physicist Robert A. Millikan has called probably the most basic ever performed in electrical research. Franklin early decided that "the electric fire is . . . really an element diffused among matter." In some respects the father of atomic research, Franklin began clearly to anticipate the concept of electrons and protons, which had to wait almost two centuries for verification. He was the first to use, at least in English, such terms as armature, battery, condense, charge, discharge, nonconductor. His flying a kite in an electrical storm held such dangerous possibilities that it might well have made him a martyr to science rather than allowed him to survive as the apostle of prudence. If the hempen cord had grown thoroughly wet before transmission of the charge, his fate would have been that of the Swedish scientist Richmann, who, hearing of the experiment, undertook to duplicate it at St. Petersburg and was killed by the lightning which he lured from the clouds.

Classical-minded admirers called Franklin "the modern Prometheus" who harnessed the celestial fire of electricity for mankind, and helped to wrest liberty for his countrymen from the hand of tyrants. But, beyond the plagues of gout and stone that afflicted his old age (when he speculated about "a balloon sufficiently large to raise me from the ground . . . being led by a string held by a man walking on the ground"), this Prometheus suffered naught for his impiety against the gods nor against King George. The scientific method was as natural to him as breathing. He never grew too sophisticated to enjoy the little tricks and mystifications of science—such as electrocuting a turkey for dinner with his Philadelphia cronies and drinking healths in electrified bumpers, or stilling the waters of a little pond by waving over them his hollow cane filled with oil. As Carl Van Doren observes, Doctor Franklin found electricity a curiosity and left it a science. Thorough, accurate, modest, diffident, cooperative, selfless, more eager to hear contrary evidence than confirmation of his theories—as man and researcher Franklin had innate good manners.

Some of his most winning qualities are not disclosed by the *Autobiography*. His letters, for example, show his unfailing delight in the company of children and young people, and the singular charm which he had for women of all ages and degrees of worldliness. As for men, he made a host of stout friendships on both sides of the Atlantic and of politics, which weathered time's erosion and even the tensions of war. From his own Pennsylvania, Franklin reported to his English friend Peter Collinson in 1756, with undoubted truth: "The people happen to love me. Perhaps that's my fault." He had been their champion against excessive privilege, and at all times the most useful citizen of the commonwealth in promoting the greatest good of the greatest number. Sent to France late in 1776 on a mission of persuasion, he was followed by adoring crowds wherever he went, and Parisian shopkeepers even sold window space where a good view could be had of the passing sage. Going his untroubled way through an amazing net of British spies set to trap him, speaking some of his mind to everybody but never all of his mind to anybody, he was *le bonhomme Richard*, the name the French gave to a famous frigate. Beyond question his personal popularity, and his services as advocate and publicist for the American cause, cemented the Franco-American alliance without which independence could hardly have been won.

Having lent his counsels to the drafting in 1776 of the Declaration of Independence, and in 1787 to that of the Constitution, and having played so versatile a role in the flowering of his America—in journalism, municipal affairs, public health, science, education, philanthropy, domestic politics, and foreign policy—Franklin felt a lifelong curiosity about his land and her people. Even in the days of her agrarian youth he seems dimly to have guessed America's enormous potential for becoming the world's foremost industrial and engineering power. In setting down his observations on flies apparently drowned in wine but revived by sunshine, Franklin on the threshold of his seventies wrote with grave playfulness to his friend Dubourg that "having a very ardent desire to see and observe the state of America a hundred years hence, I should prefer to any ordinary death the being immersed in a cask of Madeira wine with a few friends till that time, to be then recalled to life by the solar warmth of my dear country." Though such resuscitation lay only in the realm of fancy, something of the living Franklin— homely and unpretending, meeting the exactions of life without haste or tension but always with quiet mastery, humorous and a trifle cynical, yet in the truest sense a man of good will and of serene wisdom—is preserved forever in the pages of his *Autobiography*.

San Marino, California
June, 1948

DIXON WECTER

BIBLIOGRAPHICAL NOTE

For the career of Franklin, James Parton's *Life and Times of Benjamin Franklin* (2 vols., 1864) remains invaluable, though cumbersome; Carl Van Doren's *Benjamin Franklin* (1938) stands as the best one-volume biography; and Carl L. Becker's "Benjamin Franklin," in *Dictionary of American Biography*, VI (1931), is a good concise account.

There are a host of specialized books on one or another of Franklin's numerous activities. Of greatest interest to students of history and literature are Bruce I. Granger's *Benjamin Franklin, An American Man of Letters* (1964); I. Bernard Cohen's *Benjamin Franklin, His Contribution to the American Tradition* (1953); Gerald Stourzh's *Benjamin Franklin and American Foreign Policy* (1954); and Paul W. Conner's *Poor Richard's Politics, Benjamin Franklin and His New American* (1966). On the fascinating subject of Franklin and France, see Alfred O. Aldridge's *Franklin and His French Contemporaries* (1957) and Claude Anne Lopez's *Mon Cher Papa, Franklin and the Ladies of Paris* (1966).

The Papers of Benjamin Franklin, ed. Leonard W. Labaree et al., began issuing from the Yale University Press in 1959 and when complete will supersede all existing editions. Until such time *The Writings of Benjamin Franklin,* ed. Albert H. Smyth (10 vols., 1905-1907) is the most reliable edition; it is the source for the selected writings included in this volume. The text of the *Autobiography* is taken from the nineteenth-century version that established the book as a monumental contribution to American folklore as well as a major work of American literature.

INTRODUCTION TO
BENJAMIN FRANKLIN'S
SELECTED WRITINGS

SPEAKING of literary developments at the beginning of the eighteenth century, Matthew Arnold observed that an age of prose was making special demand upon the writer. "The men of letters, whose destiny it may be to bring their nation to the attainment of a fit prose," he said, "must of necessity, whether they work in prose or in verse, give a predominating, and almost exclusive attention to the qualities of regularity, uniformity, precision, balance." In large part, the destiny of which Arnold spoke was fulfilled for the American nation by Benjamin Franklin. He was the first American man of letters, and his great literary gift to his country was a clear, coherent, and emphatic prose style, free of the private passion and ornate rambling of seventeenth-century American rhetoric.

Though Franklin's prose owes its greatest debt to the fact that he developed his talents in an age of accelerating scientific investigation, avid political controversy, and liberal rational religion, its roots are firmly fixed in the Puritan soil of his boyhood. As a member of Cotton Mather's congregation in Boston, he received habits of mind which his genius channeled towards the immediate goals of his day, but the underlying pattern is, nevertheless, Puritan. Writing to Samuel Mather, Franklin told him that Cotton Mather's *Essays to do Good* "gave me such a turn of thinking, as to have an influence on my conduct through life." Characteristically, he went on in the letter to explain the high esteem in which he always held the "doer of good," and in so doing displays within a paragraph a model of his intellectual development. Taking his impulse from his Puritan training, he then secularized his goal, detaching activity from concern about its ultimate cause, the better to affect the world of man. Certainly, if Cotton Mather had heard of the success achieved by his young parishioner, he would have matched his delight at the news with dismay at learning that Franklin esteemed doing to the exclusion of holiness, or that, at least, Franklin held piety and morality to be one and the same so far as man is to judge.

For the first generations of American Puritans, right behavior, good doing, was the effect of a sanctified condition. The deeds mattered little in comparison with the spiritual condition of the doer. Upon this basis, the Mather dynasty erected its system of morality. Benjamin Franklin, the runaway heir of this intellectual tradition, accepted the habits on which it so insisted but measured the value of those habits in terms of their ability to achieve beneficial results rather than in terms of what they revealed about the state of sanctification of the doer. He accepted his inherited zeal for knowledge, but he applied it to the good and the useful rather than to the holy and the absolutely true.

Perhaps the most profound of all Puritan intellectual habits was that of introspection: the soul-harrowing weekly and daily—if not hourly—examination into one's thoughts and activities in order to discover signs of God's disposition. Benjamin Franklin acquired this trait. His chart of virtues in the *Autobiography* has numerous precedents in the diaries of the early New Englanders. Jonathan Edwards, for instance, framed a set of resolutions for self-improvement which he read over to himself weekly in order to review his progress. But how different the ultimate goals which the two men set for their similar activities!

Likewise, Cotton Mather, Jonathan Edwards, and other Puritans were profoundly interested in natural phenomena. Cotton Mather and his father, Increase, for example, long cherished a plan to collect from widely separated correspondents all of the reliable data available on phenomenal occurrences in the colonies, and they hoped that a careful comparison of the dates on which these phenomena occurred, together with a rational distribution of them into categories, would yield general laws. These laws, however, they characterized as the bases of "providences," as laws of God's disposition toward man, especially toward the American saint.

Benjamin Franklin's habit of acute observation of natural occurrences was awakened in this atmosphere. In his letter of August 25, 1755, to Peter Collinson, he tells of riding on horseback over the Maryland countryside with a group of friends and seeing a small whirlwind a short distance off. "The rest of the company stood looking after it," he reports, "but my curiosity being stronger, I followed it." As Carl Van Doren has pointed out, we are here presented with a vignette exemplifying the difference between Franklin and his contemporaries: they were content to glance at the phenomenon, but Franklin's "curiosity being stronger" he investigated it. We should also recognize that Cotton Mather, too, would have ridden after the whirlwind, but the questions he would have asked of it would not have been answerable, as in part Franklin's were, by data on its size and path. That he followed the whirlwind reflects Franklin's Boston beginnings; that he did so in order to gather the specific information he did record, reflects his immense capacity to live in a world few saw coming more clearly than he. As Benjamin Franklin demonstrated, the theology of the Puritans had to be modified if not relinquished before one could be a scientific observer, but the man who was able to retain the insatiable Puritan curiosity about natural phenomena and the profound Puritan concern for behavior while detaching them from a context in which God was a perceivable cause, that man had a large head start on his contemporaries.

In so detaching the appearance of things from questions of their ultimate reality, Franklin was also preparing himself for a distinguished literary career. The demands that science, politics, and society made on an eighteenth-century man were demands, as Matthew Arnold indicated, which had to be met by a prose capable of coping with the immediate in a direct fashion. The prose of the century was developed with so total a concentration on the matter at hand that the age was pre-eminently one in which the private personality of the writer disappeared from his works. Each of

Benjamin Franklin's pieces reflects a sharp recognition of the audience for which it is designed not only in the assumptions which it asks the reader to share and the way in which the thoughts in it are organized, but also in the point of view from which it is presented. Is the object to ridicule the mores which condemn the fallen woman while overlooking the man? Then the speaker is the amiable, good-hearted, yet guilty Polly Baker. Is the object to drive home a collection of proverbs on economy? Then the speaker is Father Abraham, a trim and successful old man who has benefited from the best of such sayings. Is the object to gain permission for the exportation of American grain? Then the speaker is a homespun farmer who matches folksy sayings with shrewd observations on society. Even the signature, "B.F.," is a mask, indicating not that one Benjamin Franklin wrote the piece but that the speaker has something crisp, concise, and rigidly organized to lay before the public and the best voice for the task is the practical printer of Philadelphia. The speaker who places before the Pennsylvanians proposals for the education of their youth informs them that he is offering "Hints towards forming a Plan" and that he is speaking, in effect, for "some publick-spirited Gentlemen." Having thus detached himself from an intense personal concern for the project, he can set it forth in a well-outlined and dispassionate fashion so that the "B.F." at the close indicates the printer rather than the author.

Franklin's brilliant creation of the appropriate *persona* for the literary task at hand is a feature of almost every piece he wrote. His famous apprenticeship, literary as well as commercial, began with his creation of Silence Dogood, and even in the *Autobiography* he is writing through *personae*: in the first part, as father to son, while in the second part he takes on the more general role of the successful citizen. These are the viewpoints which have the greatest application to what he is saying, and the economy of his style brooks no waste—everything is to be utilized, even the character of the speaker who is delivering the piece.

Indeed, so successful is Franklin in his creation of *personae* that his very achievement threatens, at times, to impair his reputation among those readers of literature who should most enjoy him because of their sensitivity to good prose. D. H. Lawrence, for example, allows the father of the *Autobiography*, mixed with a generous dash of Poor Richard, to pass as the complete character of Benjamin Franklin and consequently unleashes his splendid ire against the rhetorical device, taking it for the man. What he has to say about Franklin, then, does not very well apply to the author of Polly Baker's speech. Others who quickly take exception to those of Franklin's *personae* that seem too easily to accept the perfectibility of man overlook the mature resignation of the speech at the close of the Constitutional Convention, or Poor Richard's insistence upon man's incurable selfishness: "If you would have a faithful servant and one that you like, serve yourself"; "In the affairs of this world, men are saved, not by faith, but by the want of it."

While the foes of a narrow morality thus frequently made Franklin their mistaken target, so, too, his masterly use of *personae* exposes him to attack from moralists who conclude that if the author did employ so many and so varied a cast of speakers then he must have been a man with no principles of his own. Franklin anticipated such criticism when he wrote that all good writings should "have a tendency to benefit the reader, by improving his virtue or his knowledge." He recognized, however, that there was a sense in which "that is best wrote, which is best adapted for obtaining the end of the writer." A scant view of Franklin's writings will yield him the latter and lesser of the two laurels he sought, but a broader view of his writings—which includes his letter to Ezra Stiles as well as Silence Dogood, his "Observations Concerning the Increase of Mankind" as well as "The Ephemera"—yields him the greater as well.

From Franklin's careful creation of *personae*, it is but a step to his great skill as a satirist. Satire depends fundamentally on a convincingly unaware speaker so that the reader's outrage of what is being said is heightened by his discovery of the viciousness or gullibility of the speaker. Should the reader learn of the speakers' artificiality too soon, the satire fails because it has been detected as such before it can generate the heat necessary for its proper effect.

However, should the deceit remain undiscovered to the end, then again the satire fails because the reader concentrates his ire on the individual speaker rather than on the point of view being ridiculed. Franklin's ability to create appropriate *personae* removed him to a safe distance from the former of these dangers but constantly exposed him to the latter. Whereas the Americanus who wants to thank England for the felons exported to his country by sending rattlesnakes to St. James Park is a transparent chucklehead, the King of Prussia is so convincingly rendered in his bombastic intentions towards his late colony that we are slow in making the application to George's American policy; indeed many of the original readers lost the intent entirely. When Franklin's audience finally did make the discovery, however, they were by that point in the satire so thoroughly incensed at Frederic's reasoning that their wrath at such a colonial policy was not easily retractable even though they found their own government to be the butt.

Swift's writings were Franklin's guides to satire, and together with other neoclassical writings, Addison's especially, had also given Franklin his clear and simple standard of good writing and his distrust of passionate expression. To this already rigorous measure, science added a severe demand for lucidity. In the following pages, one may trace the effects this demand had upon Franklin's style by, for instance, comparing the letter to Peter Collinson on electricity (July 11, 1747) with that undated letter to Oliver Neave on swimming, written in a later period. The precision demanded of Franklin in the former, so that he would be completely understood without a sacrifice of the complexity of his subject, led him to a rigorous organization of his materials—no step could be omitted in his progress from the known to the unknown—and to the invention of new terms. The effect on his style was such that in time he became capable of explaining in writing literally anything he knew. His correspondence course in the art of swimming is a graceful display of this mastery of practical prose.

To his social writings Franklin attempted to bring the same precision he had applied in his scientific essays, and just as science forced upon him a new vocabulary, so writing for a wide audience quickened his sensitivity to the speech of the people. Distrust of passion did not mean absence of grace, and striving for grace did not mean a lofty diction. An anecdote told in the slaves' dialect could as graciously bring home the point as a rounded peroration.

When the need for a fit prose was felt in America, then, Benjamin Franklin rose to the demand and supplied the great models. His Puritan upbringing had made him introspective and curious; his acute awareness of the immediate situation combined with his sense of economy had depersonalized his style; his reading had engendered in him a taste for the clear, the simple, and the graceful; his scientific interests had made him a worshipper of lucidity; and his recognition of the growing audience of common men had kept him alert to the sound of the people talking. With these qualities developed, he proceeded to apply the products of his genius, for in his America prose was as much servant as master; as a man wrote, so his ideas fared. To the extent that we hold this to be true of prose today, we can recognize Franklin as the first of the select company of American prose masters.

Berkeley, California
July, 1959

LARZER ZIFF

THE AUTOBIOGRAPHY

Twyford, at the Bishop of St. Asaph's, 1771.

DEAR SON:

I have ever had a pleasure in obtaining any little anecdotes of my ancestors. You may remember the inquiries I made among the remains of my relations when you were with me in England, and the journey I undertook for that purpose. Now imagining it may be equally agreeable to you to know the circumstances of *my* life, many of which you are yet unacquainted with, and expecting a week's uninterrupted leisure in my present country retirement, I sit down to write them for you. To which I have besides some other inducements. Having emerged from the poverty and obscurity in which I was born and bred to a state of affluence and some degree of reputation in the world, and having gone so far through life with a considerable share of felicity, the conducing means I made use of, which with the blessing of God so well succeeded, my posterity may like to know, as they may find some of them suitable to their own situations, and therefore fit to be imitated.

That felicity, when I reflected on it, has induced me sometimes to say that were it offered to my choice I should have no objection to a repetition of the same life from its beginning, only asking the advantages authors have in a second edition to correct some faults of the first. So would I, if I might, besides correcting the faults, change some sinister accidents and events of it for others more favorable. But though this were denied, I should still accept the offer. However, since such a repetition is not to be expected, the next thing most

1

like living one's life over again seems to be a *recollection* of that life, and to make that recollection as durable as possible the putting it down in writing.

Hereby, too, I shall indulge the inclination so natural in old men to be talking of themselves and their own past actions; and I shall indulge it without being troublesome to others, who, through respect to age, might think themselves obliged to give me a hearing, since this may be read or not as any one pleases. And lastly (I may as well confess it, since my denial of it will be believed by nobody), perhaps I shall a good deal gratify my own *vanity*. Indeed, I scarce ever heard or saw the introductory words, "Without vanity I may say," etc., but some vain thing immediately followed. Most people dislike vanity in others, whatever share they have of it themselves; but I give it fair quarter wherever I meet with it, being persuaded that it is often productive of good to the possessor, and to others that are within his sphere of action; and therefore, in many cases, it would not be quite absurd if a man were to thank God for his vanity among the other comforts of life.

And now I speak of thanking God, I desire with all humility to acknowledge that I owe the mentioned happiness of my past life to His kind providence, which led me to the means I used and gave them success. My belief of this induces me to *hope*, though I must not *presume*, that the same goodness will still be exercised towards me, in continuing that happiness or in enabling me to bear a fatal reverse, which I may experience as others have done, the complexion of my future fortune being known to Him only in whose power it is to bless to us even our afflictions.

The notes one of my uncles (who had the same kind of curiosity in collecting family anecdotes) once put into my hands furnished me with several particulars relating to our ancestors. From these notes I learned that the family had lived in the same village, Ecton, in Northamptonshire, for three hundred years, and how much longer he knew not (perhaps from the time when the name Franklin, that before was the name of an order of people, was assumed by them for a surname when others took surnames all over the kingdom), on a freehold of about thirty acres, aided by the smith's business, which had continued in the family till his time, the eldest son being always bred to that business—a custom which he and my father both followed as to their eldest sons. When I searched the register at Ecton, I found an account of their births, marriages, and burials from the year 1555 only, there being no register kept in that parish at any time preceding. By that register I perceived that I was the youngest son of the youngest son for five generations back. My grandfather Thomas, who was born in 1598, lived at Ecton till he grew too old to follow business longer, when he went to live with his son John, a dyer at Banbury in Oxfordshire, with whom my father served an appenticeship. There my grandfather died and lies buried. We saw his gravestone in 1758. His eldest son, Thomas, lived in the house at Ecton, and left it with the land to his only child, a daughter, who with her husband, one Fisher of Wellingborough, sold it to Mr. Isted, now lord of the manor there. My grandfather had four sons that grew up, viz.: Thomas, John, Benjamin, and Josiah. I will give you what account I can of them at this distance from my papers, and if these are not lost in my absence, you will among them find many more particulars.

Thomas was bred a smith under his father; but, being ingenious, and encouraged in learning (as all his brothers likewise were) by an Esquire Palmer, then the principal gentleman in that parish, he qualified himself for the business of scrivener; became a considerable man in the county affairs; was a chief mover of all public-spirited undertakings for the county or town of Northampton and his own village, of which many instances were told us; and he was at Ecton much taken notice of and patronized by the then Lord Halifax. He died in 1702, January 6, old style, just four years to a day before I was born. The account we received of his life and character from some old people at Ecton, I remember, struck you as something extraordinary, from its similarity to what you knew of mine. "Had he died on the same day," you said, "one might have supposed a transmigration."

John was bred a dyer, I believe of woolens. Benjamin was bred a silk dyer, serving an apprenticeship at London. He was an ingenious man. I remember him well, for when I was a boy he came over to my father in Boston and lived in the house with us some years. He lived to a great age. His grandson, Samuel Franklin, now lives in Boston. He left behind him two quarto volumes, manuscript, of his own poetry, consisting of little occasional pieces addressed to his friends and relations, of which the following, sent to me, is a specimen. [Franklin adds a note in parenthesis, "Here insert it," but no specimen is given.] He had formed a shorthand of his own, which he taught me, but, never practicing it, I have now forgot it. I was named after this uncle, there being a particular affection between him and my father. He was very pious, a great attender of sermons of the best preachers, which he took down in his shorthand, and had with him many volumes of them. He was also much of a politician; too much, perhaps, for his station. There fell lately into my hands, in London, a collection he had made of all the principal pamphlets relating to public affairs from 1641 to 1717; many of the volumes are wanting, as appears by the numbering, but there still remains eight volumes folio, and twenty-four in quarto and octavo. A dealer in old books met with them, and knowing me by my sometimes buying of him, he brought them to me. It seems my uncle must have left them here when he went to America, which was above fifty years since. There are many of his notes in the margins.

This obscure family of ours was early in the Reformation, and continued Protestants through the reign of Queen Mary, when they were sometimes in danger of trouble on account of their zeal against popery. They had got an English Bible, and to conceal and secure it, it was fastened open with tapes under and within the frame of a joint-stool. When my great-great-grandfather read it to his family, he turned up the joint-stool upon his knees, turning over the leaves then under the tapes. One of the children stood at the door to give notice if he saw the apparitor coming, who was an officer of the spiritual court. In that case the stool was turned down again upon its feet, when the Bible remained concealed under it as before. This anecdote I had from my uncle Benjamin. The family continued all of the Church of England till about the end of Charles II's reign, when some of the ministers that had been outed for nonconformity holding conventicles in Northamptonshire, Benjamin and Josiah adhered to them, and so continued all their lives: the rest of the family remained with the Episcopal church.

Josiah, my father, married young, and carried his wife with three children into New England about 1682. The conventicles having been forbidden by law and frequently disturbed induced some considerable men of his acquaintance to remove to that country, and he was prevailed with to accompany them thither, where they expected to enjoy their mode of religion with freedom. By the same wife he had four children more born there, and by a second wife ten more, in all seventeen; of which I remember thirteen sitting at one time at his table, who all grew up to be men and women, and married; I was the youngest son, and the youngest child but two, and was born in Boston, New England. My mother, the second wife, was Abiah Folger, a daughter of Peter Folger, one of the first settlers of New England, of whom honorable mention is made by Cotton Mather, in his church history of that country, entitled *Magnalia Christi Americana*, as "a godly, learned Englishman," if I remember the words rightly. I have heard that he wrote sundry small occasional pieces, but only one of them was printed, which I saw now many years since. It was written in 1675, in the homespun verse of that time and people, and addressed to those then concerned in the government there. It was in favor of liberty of conscience, and in behalf of the Baptists, Quakers, and other sectaries that had been under persecution, ascribing the Indian wars and other distresses that had befallen the country to that persecution, as so many judgments of God to punish so heinous an offense, and exhorting a repeal of those uncharitable laws. The whole appeared to me as written with a good deal of decent plainness and manly freedom. The six last concluding lines I remember, though I have forgotten the two first of the stanza; but the purport of them was that his censures proceeded from good-will and, therefore, he would be known as the author,

"Because to be a Libeller, (says he)
  I hate it with my Heart.
From *Sherburne Town where now I dwell,
  My Name I do put here,
Without Offense, your real Friend.
  It is Peter Folgier."

My elder brothers were all put apprentices to different trades. I was put to the grammar school at eight years of age, my father intending to devote me, as the tithe of his sons, to the service of the church. My early readiness in learning to read (which must have been very early, as I do not remember when I could not read) and the opinion of all his friends that I should certainly make a good scholar encouraged him in this purpose of his. My uncle Benjamin, too, approved of it, and proposed to give me all his shorthand volumes of sermons, I suppose as a stock to set up with, if I would learn his character. I continued, however, at the grammar school not quite one year, though in that time I had risen gradually from the middle of the class of that year to be the head of it, and farther was removed into the next class above it, in order to go with that into the third at the end of the year. But my father, in the meantime, from a view of the expense of a college education, which having so large a family he could not well afford, and the mean living many so educated were afterwards able to obtain—reasons that he gave to his friends in my hearing—altered his first intention, took me from the grammar school, and sent me to a school for writing and arithmetic, kept by a then famous man, Mr. George Brownell, very successful in his profession generally, and that by mild, encouraging methods. Under him I acquired fair writing pretty soon, but I failed in the arithmetic, and made no progress in it. At ten years old I was taken home to assist my father in his business, which was that of a tallow-chandler and soap-boiler; a business he was not bred to, but had assumed on his arrival in New England, and on finding his dying trade would not maintain his family, being in little

* In the Island of Nantucket.

request. Accordingly, I was employed in cutting wick for the candles, filling the dipping mold and the molds for cast candles, attending the shop, going of errands, etc.

I disliked the trade, and had a strong inclination for the sea, but my father declared against it; however, living near the water, I was much in and about it, learned early to swim well and to manage boats; and when in a boat or canoe with other boys, I was commonly allowed to govern, especially in any case of difficulty; and upon other occasions I was generally a leader among the boys, and sometimes led them into scrapes, of which I will mention one instance, as it shows an early projecting public spirit, though not then justly conducted.

There was a salt-marsh that bounded part of the mill-pond, on the edge of which, at high water, we used to stand to fish for minnows. By much trampling, we had made it a mere quagmire. My proposal was to build a wharf there fit for us to stand upon, and I showed my comrades a large heap of stones which were intended for a new house near the marsh and which would very well suit our purpose. Accordingly, in the evening, when the workmen were gone, I assembled a number of my playfellows, and, working with them diligently like so many emmets, sometimes two or three to a stone, we brought them all away and built our little wharf. The next morning the workmen were surprised at missing the stones, which were found in our wharf. Inquiry was made after the removers; we were discovered and complained of; several of us were corrected by our fathers; and, though I pleaded the usefulness of the work, mine convinced me that nothing was useful which was not honest.

I think you may like to know something of his person and character. He had an excellent constitution of body, was of middle stature, but well set, and very strong; he was ingenious, could draw prettily, was skilled a little in music, and had a clear pleasing voice, so that when he played psalm tunes on his violin and sung withal, as he sometimes did in an evening after the business of the day was over, it was extremely agreeable to hear. He had a mechanical genius too, and, on occasion, was very handy in the use of other tradesmen's tools; but his great excellence lay in a sound under-standing and solid judgment in prudential matters, both in private and public affairs. In the latter, indeed, he was never employed, the numerous family he had to educate and the straitness of his circum-stances keeping him close to his trade; but I remember well his being frequently visited by leading people, who consulted him for his opinion in affairs of the town or of the church he belonged to, and showed a good deal of respect for his judgment and advice: he was also much consulted by private persons about their affairs when any difficulty occurred, and frequently chosen an arbitrator between contending parties. At his table he liked to have as often as he could some sensible friend or neighbor to converse with, and always took care to start some ingenious or useful topic for dis-course, which might tend to improve the minds of his children. By this means he turned our attention to what was good, just, and prudent in the conduct of life; and little or no notice was ever taken of what related to the victuals on the table, whether it was well or ill dressed, in or out of season, of good or bad flavor, preferable or inferior to this or that other thing of the kind, so that I was brought up in such a perfect inattention to those matters as to be quite indifferent what kind of food was set before me, and so unobservant of it that to this day if I am asked I can scarce tell a few hours after dinner what I dined upon. This had been a convenience to me in traveling, where my companions have been sometimes very unhappy for want of a suitable gratifica-tion of their more delicate, because better instructed, tastes and appetites.

My mother had likewise an excellent constitution: she suckled all her ten children. I never knew either my father or mother to have any sickness but that of which they died, he at eighty-nine, and she at eighty-five years of age. They lie buried together at Boston, where I some years since placed a marble stone over their grave, with this inscription:

"JOSIAH FRANKLIN
And ABIAH his Wife,
Lie here interred.

They lived lovingly together in Wedlock
Fifty-five Years.
Without an Estate, or any gainful Employment,
By constant labour and Industry,
With God's Blessing,
They maintained a large Family
Comfortably;
And brought up thirteen Children,
And seven Grandchildren
Reputably.
From this Instance, Reader,
Be encouraged to Diligence in thy Calling,
And Distrust not Providence.
He was a pious and prudent Man,
She a discreet and virtuous Woman.
Their youngest Son,
In filial Regard to their Memory,
Places this Stone.
J. F. born 1655—Died 1744—Ætat 89.
A. F. born 1667—Died 1752——85."

By my rambling digressions I perceive myself to be grown old. I used to write more methodically. But one does not dress for private company as for a public ball. 'Tis perhaps only negligence.

To return: I continued thus employed in my father's business for two years, that is, till I was twelve years old;—and my brother John, who was bred to that business, having left my father, married, and set up for himself at Rhode Island, there was all appearance that I was destined to supply his place and be a tallow-chandler. But my dislike to the trade continuing, my father was under apprehensions that if he did not find one for me more agreeable, I should break away and get to sea, as his son Josiah had done, to his great vexation. He therefore sometimes took me to walk with him, and see joiners, bricklayers, turners, braziers, etc., at their work, that he might observe my inclination and endeavor to fix it on some trade or other on land. It has ever since been a pleasure to me to see good workmen handle their tools; and it has been useful to me, having learned so much by it as to be able to do little jobs myself in my house when a workman could not readily be got, and to construct little machines for my experiments, while the intention of making the experiment was fresh and warm in my mind. My father at last fixed upon the cutler's trade, and my uncle Benjamin's son Samuel, who was bred to that business in London, being about that time established in Boston, I was sent to be with him some time, on liking. But his expectations of a fee with me displeasing my father, I was taken home again.

From a child I was fond of reading, and all the little money that came into my hands was ever laid out in books. Pleased with the *Pilgrim's Progress*, my first collection was of John Bunyan's works in separate little volumes. I afterwards sold them to enable me to buy R. Burton's *Historical Collections;* they were small chapman's books, and cheap, forty or fifty in all. My father's little library consisted chiefly of books in polemic divinity, most of which I read and have since often regretted that at a time when I had such a thirst for knowledge, more proper books had not fallen in my way, since it was now resolved I should not be a clergyman. *Plutarch's Lives* there was, in which I read abundantly, and I still think that time spent to great advantage. There was also a book of Defoe's, called an *Essay on Projects*, and another of Dr. Mather's, called *Essays to do Good*, which perhaps gave me a turn of thinking that had an influence on some of the principal future events of my life.

This bookish inclination at length determined my father to make me a printer, though he had already one son (James) of that profession. In 1717 my brother James returned from England with a press and letters to set up his business in Boston. I liked it much better than that of my father, but still had a hankering for the sea. To prevent the apprehended effect of such an inclination, my father was impatient to have me bound to my brother. I stood out some time, but at last was persuaded, and signed the indentures when I was yet but twelve years old. I was to serve as an apprentice till I was twenty-one years of age, only I was to be allowed journeyman's wages during the last year. In a little time I made great proficiency in the business and became a useful hand to my brother. I now had access to better books. An acquaintance with the apprentices of booksellers enabled me sometimes to borrow a small one, which I was careful to return soon and clean. Often I sat up in my room reading the greatest part of the night, when the book was borrowed in the evening and to be returned early in the morning, lest it should be missed or wanted.

And after some time an ingenious tradesman, Mr. Matthew Adams, who had a pretty collection of books, and who frequented our printing-house, took notice of me, invited me to his library, and very kindly lent me such books as I chose to read. I now took a fancy to poetry, and made some little pieces; my brother, thinking it might turn to account, encouraged me, and put me on composing two occasional ballads. One was called *The Lighthouse Tragedy*, and contained an account of the drowning of Captain Worthilake with his two daughters; the other was a sailor's song, on the taking of Teach (or Blackbeard), the pirate. They were wretched stuff, in the Grub-street-ballad style; and when they were printed he sent me about the town to sell them. The first sold wonderfully, the event being recent, having made a great noise. This flattered my vanity; but my father discouraged me by ridiculing my performances and telling me verse-makers were generally beggars. So I escaped being a poet, most probably a very bad one; but as prose writing has been of great use to me in the course of my life, and was a principal means of my advancement, I shall tell you how, in such a situation, I acquired what little ability I have in that way.

There was another bookish lad in the town, John Collins by name, with whom I was intimately acquainted. We sometimes disputed; and very fond we were of argument, and very desirous of confuting one another, which disputatious turn, by the way, is apt to become a very bad habit, making people often extremely disagreeable in company by the contradiction that is necessary to bring it into practice; and thence, besides souring and spoiling the conversation, is productive of disgusts and, perhaps, enmities where you may have occasion for friendship. I had caught it by reading my father's books of dispute about religion. Persons of good sense, I have since observed, seldom fall into it, except lawyers, university men, and men of all sorts that have been bred at Edinburgh.

A question was once, somehow or other, started between Collins and me of the propriety of educating the female sex in learning, and their abilities for study. He was of opinion that it was improper, and that they were naturally unequal to it. I took the contrary side, perhaps a little for dispute's sake. He was naturally more eloquent, had a ready plenty of words, and sometimes, as I thought, bore me down more by his fluency than by the strength of his reasons. As we parted without settling the point, and were not to see one another again for some time, I sat down to put my arguments in writing, which I copied fair and sent to him. He answered, and I replied. Three or four letters of a side had passed, when my father happened to find my papers and read them. Without entering into the discussion, he took occasion to talk to me about the manner of my writing; observed that, though I had the advantage of my antagonist in correct spelling and pointing (which I owed to the printing-house), I fell far short in elegance of expression, in method, and in perspicuity, of which he convinced me by several instances. I saw the justice of his remarks, and thence grew more attentive to the *manner* in writing, and determined to endeavor at improvement.

About this time I met with an odd volume of the *Spectator*. It was the third. I had never before seen any of them. I bought it, read it over and over, and was much delighted with it. I thought the writing excellent, and wished, if possible, to imitate it. With that view I took some of the papers, and, making short hints of the sentiment in each sentence, laid them by a few days, and then, without looking at the book, tried to complete the papers again by expressing each hinted sentiment at length, and as fully as it had been expressed before, in any suitable words that should come to hand. Then I compared my *Spectator* with the original, discovered some of my faults, and corrected them. But I found I wanted a stock of words, or a readiness in recollecting and using them, which I thought I should have acquired before that time if I had gone on making verses; since the continual occasion for words of the same import, but of different length to suit the measure, or of different sound for the rhyme, would have laid me under a constant necessity of searching for variety and also have tended to fix that variety in my mind and make me master of it. Therefore, I took some of the tales and turned them into verse; and, after a time, when I had pretty well forgotten the prose, turned then back again. I also sometimes jumbled my collections of hints into confusion, and after some weeks endeavored to reduce them into the best order, before I began to form the full sentences and complete the paper. This was to teach me method in the arrangement of thoughts. By comparing my work afterwards with the original, I discovered many faults and amended them; but I sometimes had the pleasure of fancying that in certain particulars of small import I had been lucky enough to improve the method or the language, and this encouraged me to think I might possibly in time come to be a tolerable English writer, of which I was extremely ambitious. My time for these exercises and for reading was at night, after work, or before it began in the morning, or on Sundays, when I contrived to be in the printing-house alone, evading as much as I could the common attendance on public worship which my father used to exact of me when I was under his care, and which indeed I still thought a duty, though I could not, as it seemed to me, afford time to practice it.

When about sixteen years of age I happened to meet with a book, written by one Tryon, recommending a vegetable diet. I determined to go into it. My brother, being yet unmarried, did not keep house, but boarded himself and his apprentices in another family. My refusing to eat flesh occasioned an inconveniency, and I was frequently chid for my singularity. I made myself acquainted with Tryon's manner of preparing some of his dishes, such as boiling potatoes or rice, making hasty pudding, and a few others, and then proposed to my brother, that if he would give me, weekly, half the money he paid for my board, I would board myself. He instantly agreed to it, and I presently found that I could save half what he paid me. This was an additional fund for buying books. But I had another advantage in it. My brother and the rest going from the printing-house to their meals, I remained there alone and dispatching presently my light repast, which often was no more than a biscuit or a slice of bread, a handful of raisins or a tart from the pastry-cook's, and a glass of water, had the rest of the time till their return for study, in which I made the greater progress, from that greater clearness of head and quicker apprehension which usually attend temperance in eating and drinking.

And now it was that, being on some occasion made ashamed of my ignorance in figures, which I had twice failed in learning when at school, I took Cocker's book of arithmetic, and went through the whole by myself with great ease. I also read Seller's and Sturmy's books of navigation, and became acquainted with the little geometry they contain; but never proceeded far in that science. And I read about this time Locke *On Human Understanding*, and the *Art of Thinking*, by Messrs. du Pont Royal.

While I was intent on improving my language, I met with an English grammar (I think it was Greenwood's), at the end of which there were two little sketches of the arts of rhetoric and logic, the latter finishing with a specimen of a dispute in the Socratic method; and soon after I procured Xenophon's *Memorable Things of Socrates*, wherein there are many instances of the same method. I was charmed with it, adopted it, dropped my abrupt contradiction and positive argumentation, and put on the humble inquirer and doubter. And being then, from reading Shaftesbury and Collins, become a real doubter in many points of our religious doctrine, I found this method safest for myself and very embarrassing to those against whom I used it; therefore I took a delight in it, practiced it continually, and grew very artful and expert in drawing people, even of superior knowledge, into concessions, the consequences of which they did not foresee, entangling them in difficulties out of which they could not extricate themselves, and so obtaining victories that neither myself nor my cause always deserved. I continued this method some few years, but gradually left it, retaining only the habit of expressing myself in terms of modest diffidence; never using, when I advanced anything that may possibly be disputed, the words *certainly, undoubtedly*, or any others that give the air of positiveness to an opinion; but rather say, I conceive or apprehend a thing to be so or so; it appears to me, or I should think it so or so, for such and such reasons; or I imagine it to be so; or it is so, if I am not mistaken. This habit, I believe, has been of great advantage to me when I have had occasion to inculcate my opinions and persuade men into measures that I have been from time to time engaged in promoting; and, as the chief ends of conversation are to *inform* or to be *informed*, to *please* or to *persuade*, I wish well-meaning, sensible men would not lessen their power of doing good by a positive, assuming manner that seldom fails to disgust, tends to create opposition and to defeat every one of those purposes for which speech was given to us, to wit, giving or receiving information or pleasure. For if you would *inform*, a positive dogmatical manner in advancing your sentiments may provoke contradiction and prevent a candid attention. If you wish information and improvement from the knowledge of others, and yet at the same time express yourself as firmly fixed in your present opinions, modest, sensible men, who do not love disputation, will probably leave you undisturbed in the possession of your error. And by such a manner, you can seldom hope to recommend yourself in *pleasing* your hearers, or to persuade those whose concurrence you desire. Pope says, judiciously:

> "Men should be taught as if you taught them not,
>   And things unknown propos'd as things forgot";

farther recommending to us

> "To speak, tho' sure, with seeming Diffidence."

And he might have coupled with this line that which he has coupled with another, I think less properly,

> "For want of Modesty is want of Sense."

If you ask why *less properly?* I must repeat the lines,

> "Immodest Words admit of *no* Defence;
>   *For* Want of Modesty is Want of Sense."

15

Now, is not *want of sense* (where a man is so unfortunate as to want it) some apology for his *want of modesty?* and would not the lines stand more justly thus?

> "Immodest Words admit *but this* Defence,
>   That Want of Modesty is Want of Sense."

This, however, I should submit to better judgments.

My brother had, in 1720 or 21, begun to print a newspaper. It was the second that appeared in America, and was called the *New England Courant*. The only one before it was the *Boston News-Letter*. I remember his being dissuaded by some of his friends from the undertaking, as not likely to succeed, one newspaper being, in their judgment, enough for America. At this time (1771) there are not less than five-and-twenty. He went on, however, with the undertaking, and after having worked in composing the types and printing off the sheets, I was employed to carry the papers through the streets to the customers.

He had some ingenious men among his friends, who amused themselves by writing little pieces for this paper, which gained it credit and made it more in demand, and these gentlemen often visited us. Hearing their conversations, and their accounts of the approbation their papers were received with, I was excited to try my hand among them; but, being still a boy, and suspecting that my brother would object to printing anything of mine in his paper if he knew it to be mine, I contrived to disguise my hand and, writing an anonymous paper, I put it in at night under the door of the printing-house. It was found in the morning and communicated to his writing friends when they called in as usual. They read it, commented on it in my hearing, and I had the exquisite pleasure of finding it met with their approbation, and that, in their different guesses at the author, none were named but men of some character among us for learning and ingenuity. I suppose now that I was rather lucky in my judges, and that perhaps they were not really so very good ones as I then esteemed them.

Encouraged, however, by this, I wrote and conveyed in the

same way to the press several more papers which were equally approved; and I kept my secret till my small fund of sense for such performances was pretty well exhausted, and then I discovered it, when I began to be considered a little more by my brother's acquaintance, and in a manner that did not quite please him, as he thought, probably with reason, that it tended to make me too vain. And perhaps this might be one occasion of the differences that we began to have about this time. Though a brother, he considered himself as my master, and me as his apprentice, and accordingly expected the same services from me as he would from another, while I thought he demeaned me too much in some he required of me, who from a brother expected more indulgence. Our disputes were often brought before our father, and I fancy I was either generally in the right, or else a better pleader, because the judgment was generally in my favor. But my brother was passionate, and had often beaten me, which I took extremely amiss; and, thinking my apprenticeship very tedious, I was continually wishing for some opportunity of shortening it, which at length offered in a manner unexpected.*

One of the pieces in our newspaper on some political point, which I have now forgotten, gave offense to the Assembly. He was taken up, censured, and imprisoned for a month, by the speaker's warrant, I suppose because he would not discover his author. I too was taken up and examined before the council; but, though I did not give them any satisfaction, they contented themselves with admonishing me, and dismissed me, considering me, perhaps, as an apprentice who was bound to keep his master's secrets.

During my brother's confinement, which I resented a good deal, notwithstanding our private differences, I had the management of the paper; and I made bold to give our rulers some rubs in it, which my brother took very kindly, while others began to consider me in an unfavorable light, as a young genius that had a

* I fancy his harsh and tyrannical treatment of me might be a means of impressing me with that aversion to arbitrary power that has stuck to me through my whole life.

turn for libeling and satire. My brother's discharge was accompanied with an order of the House (a very odd one), that "James Franklin should no longer print the paper called the *New England Courant.*"

There was a consultation held in our printing-house among his friends what he should do in this case. Some proposed to evade the order by changing the name of the paper; but my brother seeing inconveniences in that, it was finally concluded on as a better way to let it be printed for the future under the name of *Benjamin Franklin;* and to avoid the censure of the Assembly, that might fall on him as still printing it by his apprentice, the contrivance was that my old indenture should be returned to me, with a full discharge on the back of it, to be shown on occasion; but to secure to him the benefit of my service, I was to sign new indentures for the remainder of the term, which were to be kept private. A very flimsy scheme it was; however, it was immediately executed, and the paper went on accordingly under my name for several months.

At length, a fresh difference arising between my brother and me, I took upon me to assert my freedom, presuming that he would not venture to produce the new indentures. It was not fair in me to take this advantage, and this I therefore reckon one of the first errata of my life; but the unfairness of it weighed little with me when under the impressions of resentment for the blows his passion too often urged him to bestow upon me, though he was otherwise not an ill-natured man; perhaps I was too saucy and provoking.

When he found I would leave him, he took care to prevent my getting employment in any other printing-house of the town, by going round and speaking to every master, who accordingly refused to give me work. I then thought of going to New York, as the nearest place where there was a printer; and I was the rather inclined to leave Boston when I reflected that I had already made myself a little obnoxious to the governing party, and, from the arbitrary proceedings of the Assembly in my brother's case, it was likely I might, if I stayed, soon bring myself into scrapes; and farther, that my indiscreet disputations about religion began to make me pointed at with horror by good people as an infidel or atheist. I determined on the point, but my father now siding with my brother, I was sensible that, if I attempted to go openly, means would be used to prevent me. My friend Collins, therefore, undertook to manage a little for me. He agreed with the captain of a New York sloop for my passage, under the notion of my being a young acquaintance of his, that had got a naughty girl with child, whose friends would compel me to marry her, and therefore I could not appear or come away publicly. So I sold some of my books to raise a little money, was taken on board privately, and as we had a fair wind, in three days I found myself in New York, near three hundred miles from home, a boy of but seventeen, without the least recommendation to, or knowledge of, any person in the place, and with very little money in my pocket.

My inclinations for the sea were by this time worn out, or I might now have gratified them. But, having a trade, and supposing myself a pretty good workman, I offered my service to the printer in the place, old Mr. William Bradford, who had been the first printer in Pennsylvania, but removed from thence upon the quarrel of George Keith. He could give me no employment, having little to do and help enough already; but, says he, "My son at Philadelphia has lately lost his principal hand, Aquila Rose, by death; if you go thither, I believe he may employ you." Philadelphia was one hundred miles further; I set out, however, in a boat for Amboy, leaving my chest and things to follow me round by sea.

In crossing the bay, we met with a squall that tore our rotten sails to pieces, prevented our getting into the Kill, and drove us upon Long Island. In our way, a drunken Dutchman, who was a passenger too, fell overboard; when he was sinking, I reached through the water to his shock pate, and drew him up, so that we got him in again. His ducking sobered him a little, and he went to sleep, taking first out of his pocket a book, which he desired I would dry for him. It proved to be my old favorite author, Bunyan's *Pilgrim's Progress*, in Dutch, finely printed on good paper, with copper cuts, a dress better than I had ever seen it wear in its own language. I have since found that it has been translated into most of the languages of Europe, and suppose it has been more generally read than any other book, except perhaps the Bible. Honest John was the first that I know of who mixed narration and dialogue, a method of writing very engaging to the reader, who in the most interesting parts finds himself, as it were, brought into the company and present at the discourse. Defoe in his *Crusoe*, his *Moll Flanders*, *Religious Courtship*, *Family Instructor*, and other pieces, has imitated it with success; and Richardson has done the same in his *Pamela*, etc.

When we drew near the island, we found it was at a place where there could be no landing, there being a great surf on the stony beach. So we dropped anchor, and swung round towards the shore. Some people came down to the water edge and hallowed to us, as we did to them; but the wind was so high, and the surf so loud, that we could not hear so as to understand each other. There were canoes on the shore, and we made signs, and hallowed that they should fetch us; but they either did not understand us, or thought it impracticable, so they went away, and night coming on, we had no remedy but to wait till the wind should abate; and in the mean time the boatman and I concluded to sleep if we could; and so crowded into the scuttle, with the Dutchman, who was still wet, and the spray, beating over the head of our boat, leaked through to us, so that we were soon almost as wet as he. In this manner we lay all night, with very little rest; but, the wind abating the next day, we made a shift to reach Amboy before night, having been thirty hours on the water, without victuals or any drink but a bottle of filthy rum, the water we sailed on being salt.

In the evening I found myself very feverish, and went into bed; but having read somewhere that cold water drank plentifully was good for a fever I followed the prescription, sweat plentifully most of the night; my fever left me, and in the morning, crossing the ferry, I proceeded on my journey on foot, having fifty miles to Burlington, where I was told I should find boats that would carry me the rest of the way to Philadelphia.

It rained very hard all the day; I was thoroughly soaked, and by noon a good deal tired; so I stopped at a poor inn, where I stayed all night, beginning now to wish I had never left home. I cut so miserable a figure, too, that I found, by the questions asked me, I was suspected to be some runaway servant, and in danger of being taken up on that suspicion. However, I proceeded the next day, and got in the evening to an inn, within eight or ten miles of Burlington, kept by one Dr. Brown. He entered into conversation with me while I took some refreshment, and, finding I had read a little, became very sociable and friendly. Our acquaintance continued as long as he lived. He had been, I imagine, an itinerant doctor, for there was no town in England or country in Europe of which he could not give a very particular account. He had some letters, and was ingenious, but much of an unbeliever, and wickedly undertook some years after to travesty the Bible in doggerel verse, as Cotton had done Virgil. By this means he set many of the facts in a very ridiculous light, and might have hurt weak minds if his work had been published; but it never was.

At his house I lay that night, and the next morning reached Burlington, but had the mortification to find that the regular boats were gone a little before my coming, and no other expected to go till Tuesday, this being Saturday; wherefore I returned to an old woman in the town, of whom I had bought gingerbread to eat on the water and asked her advice. She invited me to lodge at her house till a passage by water should offer; and, being tired with my foot traveling, I accepted the invitation. She, understanding I was a printer, would have had me stay at that town and follow my business, being ignorant of the stock necessary to begin with. She was very hospitable, gave me a dinner of ox-cheek with great good will, accepting only of a pot of ale in return; and I thought myself fixed till Tuesday should come. However, walking in the evening by the side of the river, a boat came by, which I found was going towards Philadelphia, with several people in her. They took me in, and, as there was no wind, we rowed all the way; and about midnight, not having yet seen the city, some of the company were confident we must have passed it, and would row no farther; the others knew not where we were; so we put towards the shore, got into a creek, landed near an old fence, with the rails of which we made a fire, the night being cold (in October), and there we remained till daylight. Then one of the company knew the place to be Cooper's Creek, a little above Philadelphia, which we saw as soon as we got out of the creek, and arrived there about eight or nine o'clock on the Sunday morning, and landed at the Market Street wharf.

I have been the more particular in this description of my journey, and shall be so of my first entry into that city, that you may in your mind compare such unlikely beginnings with the figure I have since made there. I was in my working dress, my best clothes being to come round by sea. I was dirty from my journey; my pockets were stuffed out with shirts and stockings; I knew no soul nor where to look for lodging. I was fatigued with traveling, rowing, and want of rest; I was very hungry; and my whole stock of cash consisted of a Dutch dollar and about a shilling in copper. The latter I gave the people of the boat for my passage, who at first refused it, on account of my rowing; but I insisted on their taking it, a man being sometimes more generous when he has but a little money than when he has plenty, perhaps through fear of being thought to have but little.

Then I walked up the street, gazing about, till near the market-house I met a boy with bread. I had made many a meal on bread, and, inquiring where he got it, I went immediately to the baker's he directed me to, in Second Street, and asked for biscuit, intending such as we had in Boston; but they, it seems, were not made in Philadelphia. Then I asked for a three-penny loaf, and was told they had none such. So, not considering or knowing the difference of money, and the greater cheapness nor the names of his bread, I bade him give me three-penny-worth of any sort. He gave me, accordingly three great puffy rolls. I was surprised at the quantity, but took it, and, having no room in my pockets, walked off with a roll under each arm, and eating the other. Thus I went up Market Street as far as Fourth Street, passing by the door of Mr. Read, my future wife's father; when she, standing at the door, saw me, and thought I made, as I certainly did, a most awkward, ridiculous appearance. Then I turned and went down Chestnut Street and part of Walnut Street, eating my roll all the way, and, coming round, found myself again at Market Street wharf, near the boat I came in, to which I went for a draught of the river water; and, being filled with one of my rolls, gave the other two to a woman and her child that came down the river in the boat with us, and were waiting to go farther.

Thus refreshed, I walked again up the street, which by this time had many clean-dressed people in it, who were all walking the same way. I joined them, and thereby was led into the great meeting-house of the Quakers near the market. I sat down among them, and, after looking round awhile and hearing nothing said, being very drowsy through labor and want of rest the preceding night, I fell fast asleep, and continued so till the meeting broke up, when one was kind enough to rouse me. This was, therefore, the first house I was in, or slept in, in Philadelphia.

Walking down again toward the river and looking in the faces of people, I met a young Quaker man, whose countenance I liked and accosting him, requested he would tell me where a stranger could get lodging. We were then near the sign of the Three Mariners. "Here," says he, "is one place that entertains strangers, but it is not a reputable house; if thee wilt walk with me, I'll show thee a better." He brought me to the Crooked Billet in Water Street. Here I got a dinner; and while I was eating it several sly questions were asked me, as it seemed to be suspected from my youth and appearance that I might be some runaway.

After dinner my sleepiness returned, and, being shown to a bed, I lay down without undressing, and slept till six in the evening, was called to supper, went to bed again very early, and slept soundly till next morning. Then I made myself as tidy as I could and went to Andrew Bradford the printer's. I found in the shop the old man his father, whom I had seen at New York, and who, traveling on horseback, had got to Philadelphia before me. He introduced me to his son, who received me civilly, gave me a breakfast, but told me he did not at present want a hand, being lately supplied with one; but there was another printer in town, lately set up, one Keimer, who perhaps might employ me; if not, I should be welcome to lodge at his house, and he would give me a little work to do now and then till fuller business should offer.

The old gentleman said he would go with me to the new printer; and when we found him, "Neighbor," says Bradford, "I have

23

brought to see you a young man of your business; perhaps you may want such a one." He asked me a few questions, put a composing stick in my hand to see how I worked, and then said he would employ me soon, though he had just then nothing for me to do; and, taking old Bradford, whom he had never seen before, to be one of the town's people that had a good will for him, entered into a conversation on his present undertaking and prospects; while Bradford, not discovering that he was the other printer's father, on Keimer's saying he expected soon to get the greatest part of the business into his own hands, drew him on by artful questions, and starting little doubts, to explain all his views, what interest he relied on, and in what manner he intended to proceed. I, who stood by and heard all, saw immediately that one of them was a crafty old sophister, and the other a mere novice. Bradford left me with Keimer, who was greatly surprised when I told him who the old man was.

Keimer's printing-house, I found, consisted of an old shattered press, and one small, worn-out font of English, which he was then using himself, composing an elegy on Aquila Rose, before mentioned, an ingenious young man, of excellent character, much respected in the town, clerk of the Assembly, and a pretty poet. Keimer made verses too, but very indifferently. He could not be said to write them, for his manner was to compose them in the types directly out of his head. So there being no copy, but one pair of cases, and the elegy likely to require all the letter, no one could help him. I endeavored to put his press (which he had not yet used, and of which he understood nothing) into order fit to be worked with; and, promising to come and print off his elegy as soon as he should have got it ready, I returned to Bradford's, who gave me a little job to do for the present, and there I lodged and dieted. A few days after, Keimer sent for me to print off the elegy. And now he had got another pair of cases, and a pamphlet to reprint, on which he set me to work.

These two printers I found poorly qualified for their business. Bradford had not been bred to it, and was very illiterate; and Keimer, though something of a scholar, was a mere compositor, knowing nothing of presswork. He had been one of the French prophets, and could act their enthusiastic agitations. At this time he did not profess any particular religion, but something of all on occasion; was very ignorant of the world, and had, as I afterward found, a good deal of the knave in his composition. He did not like my lodging at Bradford's while I worked with him. He had a house, indeed, but without furniture, so he could not lodge me; but he got me a lodging at Mr. Read's, before mentioned, who was the owner of his house; and, my chest and clothes being come by this time, I made rather a more respectable appearance in the eyes of Miss Read than I had done when she first happened to see me eating my roll in the street.

I began now to have some acquaintance among the young people of the town that were lovers of reading, with whom I spent my evenings very pleasantly; and gaining money by my industry and frugality I lived very agreeably, forgetting Boston as much as I could, and not desiring that any there should know where I resided, except my friend Collins, who was in my secret, and kept it when I wrote to him. At length, an incident happened that sent me back again much sooner than I had intended. I had a brother-in-law, Robert Holmes, master of a sloop that traded between Boston and Delaware. He being at Newcastle, forty miles below Philadelphia, heard there of me, and wrote me a letter mentioning the concern of my friends in Boston at my abrupt departure, assuring me of their good will to me, and that everything would be accommodated to my mind if I would return, to which he exhorted me very earnestly. I wrote an answer to his letter, thanked him for his advice, but stated my reasons for quitting Boston fully and in such a light as to convince him I was not so wrong as he had apprehended.

Sir William Keith, governor of the province, was then at New-castle, and Captain Holmes, happening to be in company with him when my letter came to hand, spoke to him of me, and showed him the letter. The Governor read it, and seemed surprised when he was told my age. He said I appeared a young man of prom-ising parts, and therefore should be encouraged; the printers at

Philadelphia were wretched ones; and if I would set up there he made no doubt I should succeed; for his part, he would procure me the public business, and do me every other service in his power. This my brother-in-law afterwards told me in Boston, but I knew as yet nothing of it; when, one day, Keimer and I being at work together near the window, we saw the Governor and another gentleman (which proved to be Colonel French of Newcastle), finely dressed, come directly across the street to our house, and heard them at the door.

Keimer ran down immediately, thinking it a visit to him; but the Governor inquired for me, came up, and with a condescension and politeness I had been quite unused to, made me many compliments, desired to be acquainted with me, blamed me kindly for not having made myself known to him when I first came to the place, and would have me away with him to the tavern, where he was going with Colonel French to taste, as he said, some excellent Madeira. I was not a little surprised, and Keimer stared like a pig poisoned. I went, however, with the Governor and Colonel French to a tavern at the corner of Third Street, and over the Madeira he proposed my setting up my business, laid before me the probabilities of success, and both he and Colonel French assured me I should have their interest and influence in procuring the public business of both governments. On my doubting whether my father would assist me in it, Sir William said he would give me a letter to him, in which he would state the advantages, and he did not doubt of prevailing with him. So it was concluded I should return to Boston in the first vessel, with the Governor's letter recommending me to my father. In the mean time the intention was to be kept secret, and I went on working with Keimer as usual, the Governor sending for me now and then to dine with him—a very great honor I thought it—and conversing with me in the most affable, familiar, and friendly manner imaginable.

About the end of April, 1724, a little vessel offered for Boston. I took leave of Keimer as going to see my friends. The Governor gave me an ample letter, saying many flattering things of me to my father, and strongly recommended the project of my setting up at

Philadelphia as a thing that must make my fortune. We struck on a shoal in going down the bay, and sprung a leak; we had a blustering time at sea, and were obliged to pump almost continually, at which I took my turn. We arrived safe, however, at Boston in about a fortnight. I had been absent seven months, and my friends had heard nothing of me; for my brother Holmes was not yet returned, and had not written about me. My unexpected appearance surprised the family; all were, however, very glad to see me, and made me welcome, except my brother. I went to see him at his printing-house. I was better dressed than ever while in his service, having a genteel new suit from head to foot, a watch, and my pockets lined with near five pounds sterling in silver. He received me not very frankly, looked me all over, and turned to his work again.

The journeymen were inquisitive where I had been, what sort of a country it was, and how I liked it. I praised it much, and the happy life I led in it, expressing strongly my intention of returning to it; and, one of them asking what kind of money we had there, I produced a handful of silver, and spread it before them, which was a kind of raree-show they had not been used to, paper being the money of Boston. Then I took an opportunity of letting them see my watch; and, lastly (my brother still grum and sullen), I gave them a piece of eight to drink, and took my leave. This visit of mine offended him extremely; for, when my mother some time after spoke to him of a reconciliation, and of her wishes to see us on good terms together, and that we might live for the future as brothers, he said I had insulted him in such a manner before his people that he could never forget or forgive it. In this, however, he was mistaken.

My father received the Governor's letter with some apparent surprise, but said little of it to me for some days, when Captain Holmes returning he showed it to him, asked if he knew Keith, and what kind of man he was; adding his opinion that he must be of small discretion to think of setting a boy up in business who wanted yet three years of being at man's estate. Holmes said what he could in favor of the project, but my father was clear in the impropriety of it, and at last gave a flat denial to it. Then he wrote a civil letter to Sir William, thanking him for the patronage he had so kindly offered me, but declining to assist me as yet in setting up, I being, in his opinion, too young to be trusted with the management of a business so important, and for which the preparation must be so expensive.

My friend and companion Collins, who was a clerk at the post-office, pleased with the account I gave him of my new country, determined to go thither also; and, while I waited for my father's determination, he set out before me by land to Rhode Island, leaving his books, which were a pretty collection of mathematics and natural philosophy, to come with mine and me to New York, where he proposed to wait for me.

My father, though he did not approve Sir William's proposition, was yet pleased that I had been able to obtain so advantageous a character from a person of such note where I had resided, and that I had been so industrious and careful as to equip myself so handsomely in so short a time; therefore, seeing no prospect of an accommodation between my brother and me, he gave his consent to my returning again to Philadelphia, advised me to behave respectfully to the people there, endeavor to obtain the general esteem, and avoid lampooning and libeling, to which he thought I had too much inclination; telling me, that by steady industry and a prudent parsimony I might save enough by the time I was one-and-twenty to set me up; and that, if I came near the matter, he would help me out with the rest. This was all I could obtain, except some small gifts as tokens of his and my mother's love, when I embarked again for New York, now with their approbation and their blessing.

The sloop putting in at Newport, Rhode Island, I visited my brother John, who had been married and settled there some years. He received me very affectionately, for he always loved me. A friend of his, one Vernon, having some money due to him in Pennsylvania, about thirty-five pounds currency, desired I would receive it for him, and keep it till I had his directions what to remit it in. Accordingly, he gave me an order. This afterwards occasioned me a good deal of uneasiness.

At Newport we took in a number of passengers for New York,

among which were two young women companions and a grave, sensible, matron-like Quaker woman, with her attendants. I had shown an obliging readiness to do her some little services, which impressed her, I suppose, with a degree of good will towards me; therefore, when she saw a daily growing familiarity between me and the two young women, which they appeared to encourage, she took me aside, and said, "Young man, I am concerned for thee, as thou has no friend with thee, and seems not to know much of the world, or of the snares youth is exposed to; depend upon it, those are very bad women; I can see it in all their actions; and if thee art not upon thy guard, they will draw thee into some danger; they are strangers to thee, and I advise thee, in a friendly concern for thy welfare, to have no acquaintance with them." As I seemed at first not to think so ill of them as she did, she mentioned some things she had observed and heard that had escaped my notice, but now convinced me she was right. I thanked her for her kind advice, and promised to follow it. When we arrived at New York, they told me where they lived, and invited me to come and see them; but I avoided it, and it was well I did; for the next day the captain missed a silver spoon and some other things, that had been taken out of his cabin, and, knowing that these were a couple of strumpets, he got a warrant to search their lodgings, found the stolen goods, and had the thieves punished. So, though we had escaped a sunken rock, which we scraped upon in the passage, I thought this escape of rather more importance to me.

At New York I found my friend Collins, who had arrived there some time before me. We had been intimate from children, and had read the same books together; but he had the advantage of more time for reading and studying, and a wonderful genius for mathematical learning, in which he far outstripped me. While I lived in Boston, most of my hours of leisure for conversation were spent with him, and he continued a sober as well as an industrious lad; was much respected for his learning by several of the clergy and other gentlemen, and seemed to promise making a good figure in life. But, during my absence, he had acquired a habit of sotting with brandy; and I found by his own account, and what I heard from others, that he had been drunk every day since his arrival at New York, and behaved very oddly. He had gamed too, and lost his money, so that I was obliged to discharge his lodgings, and defray his expenses to and at Philadelphia, which proved extremely inconvenient to me.

The then governor of New York, Burnet (son of Bishop Burnet), hearing from the captain that a young man, one of his passengers, had a great many books, desired he would bring me to see him. I waited upon him accordingly, and should have taken Collins with me but that he was not sober. The Governor treated me with great civility, showed me his library, which was a very large one, and we had a good deal of conversation about books and authors. This was the second governor who had done me the honor to take notice of me; which to a poor boy like me was very pleasing.

We proceeded to Philadelphia. I received on the way Vernon's money, without which we could hardly have finished our journey. Collins wished to be employed in some counting-house; but, whether they discovered his dramming by his breath, or by his behavior, though he had some recommendations, he met with no success in any application, and continued lodging and boarding at the same house with me, and at my expense. Knowing I had that money of Vernon's, he was continually borrowing of me, still promising repayment as soon as he should be in business. At length he had got so much of it that I was distressed to think what I should do in case of being called on to remit it.

His drinking continued, about which we sometimes quarrelled; for, when a little intoxicated, he was very fractious. Once, in a boat on the Delaware with some other young men, he refused to row in his turn. "I will be rowed home," says he. "We will not row you," says I. "You must, or stay all night on the water," says he, "just as you please." The others said, "Let us row; what signifies it?" But, my mind being soured with his other conduct, I continued to refuse. So he swore he would make me row, or throw me overboard; and coming along, stepping on the thwarts, toward me, when he came up and struck at me, I clapped my hand under his crutch, and, rising, pitched him head-foremost into the river. I knew he was a good-swimmer, and so was under little concern about him; but before he could get round to lay hold of the boat, we had with a few strokes pulled her out of his reach; and ever when he drew near the boat, we asked if he would row, striking a few strokes to slide her away from him. He was ready to die with vexation, and obstinately would not promise to row. However, seeing him at last beginning to tire, we lifted him in and brought him home dripping wet in the evening. We hardly exchanged a civil word afterwards, and a West India captain, who had a commission to procure a tutor for the sons of a gentleman at Barbados, happening to meet with him, agreed to carry him thither. He left me then, promising to remit me the first money he should receive in order to discharge the debt; but I never heard of him after.

The breaking into this money of Vernon's was one of the first great errata of my life; and this affair showed that my father was not much out in his judgment when he supposed me too young to manage business of importance. But Sir William, on reading his letter, said he was too prudent. There was great difference in persons; and discretion did not always accompany years, nor was youth always without it. "And since he will not set you up," says he, "I will do it myself. Give me an inventory of the things necessary to be had from England, and I will send for them. You shall repay me when you are able; I am resolved to have a good printer here, and I am sure you must succeed." This was spoken with such an appearance of cordiality, that I had not the least doubt of his meaning what he said. I had hitherto kept the proposition of my setting up a secret in Philadelphia, and I still kept it. Had it been known that I depended on the Governor, probably some friend that knew him better would have advised me not to rely on him, as I afterwards heard it as his known character to be liberal of promises which he never meant to keep. Yet, unsolicited as he was by me, how could I think his generous offers insincere? I believed him one of the best men in the world.

I presented him an inventory of a little printing-house, amounting by my computation to about one hundred pounds sterling. He liked it, but asked me if my being on the spot in England to choose the types and see that everything was good of the kind might not be of some advantage. "Then," says he, "when there, you may make acquaintances, and establish correspondences in the bookselling and stationery way." I agreed that this might be advantageous. "Then," says he, "get yourself ready to go with *Annis*," which was the annual ship, and the only one at that time usually passing between London and Philadelphia. But it would be some months before *Annis* sailed, so I continued working with Keimer, fretting about the money Collins had got from me, and in daily apprehensions of being called upon by Vernon, which, however, did not happen for some years after.

I believe I have omitted mentioning that, in my first voyage from Boston, being becalmed off Block Island, our people set about catching cod, and hauled up a great many. Hitherto I had stuck to my resolution of not eating animal food, and on this occasion I considered, with my master Tryon, the taking every fish as a kind of unprovoked murder, since none of them had, or ever could do us any injury that might justify the slaughter. All this seemed very reasonable. But I had formerly been a great lover of fish, and, when this came hot out of the frying-pan, it smelled admirably well. I balanced some time between principle and inclination, till I recollected that, when the fish were opened, I saw smaller fish taken out of their stomachs; then thought I, "if you eat one another, I don't see why we mayn't eat you." So I dined upon cod very heartily, and continued to eat with other people, returning only now and then occasionally to a vegetable diet. So convenient a thing it is to be a *reasonable creature*, since it enables one to find or make a reason for everything one has a mind to do.

Keimer and I lived on a pretty good familiar footing, and agreed tolerably well, for he suspected nothing of my setting up. He retained a great deal of his old enthusiasms and loved argumentation. We therefore had many disputations. I used to work him so with my Socratic method, and had trepanned him so often by questions apparently so distant from any point we had in hand, and yet by degrees led to the point and brought him into difficulties and contradictions that at last he grew ridiculously cautious, and would hardly answer me the most common question, without asking first, "What do you intend to infer from that?" However, it gave him so high an opinion of my abilities in the confuting way, that he seriously proposed my being his colleague in a project he had of setting up a new sect. He was to preach the doctrines, and I was to confound all opponents. When he came to explain with me upon the doctrines, I found several conundrums which I objected to, unless I might have my way a little too, and introduce some of mine.

Keimer wore his beard at full length, because somewhere in the Mosaic law it is said, "Thou shalt not mar the corners of thy beard." He likewise kept the seventh day Sabbath; and these two points were essentials with him. I disliked both; but agreed to admit them upon condition of his adopting the doctrine of using no animal food. "I doubt," said he, "my constitution will not bear that." I assured him it would, and that he would be the better for it. He was usually a great glutton, and I promised myself some diversion in half starving him. He agreed to try the practice, if I would keep him company. I did so, and we held it for three months. We had our victuals dressed and brought to us regularly by a woman in the neighborhood, who had from me a list of forty dishes, to be prepared for us at different times, in all which there was neither fish, flesh, nor fowl; and the whim suited me the better at this time from the cheapness of it, not costing us above eighteenpence sterling each per week. I have since kept several Lents most strictly, leaving the common diet for that, and that for the common, abruptly, without the least inconvenience, so that I think there is little in the advice of making those changes by easy gradations. I went on pleasantly, but poor Keimer suffered grievously, tired of the project, longed for the flesh-pots of Egypt, and ordered a roast pig. He invited me and two women friends to dine with him; but it being brought too soon upon the table, he could not resist the temptation, and ate it all up before we came.

I had made some courtship during this time to Miss Read. I had a great respect and affection for her, and had some reason to believe she had the same for me; but, as I was about to take a long voyage, and we were both very young, only a little above eighteen, it was thought most prudent by her mother to prevent our going too far at present, as a marriage, if it was to take place, would be more convenient after my return, when I should be, as I expected, set up in my business. Perhaps, too, she thought my expectations not so well founded as I imagined them to be.

My chief acquaintances at this time were Charles Osborne, Joseph Watson, and James Ralph, all lovers of reading. The two first were clerks to an eminent scrivener or conveyancer in the town, Charles Brogden; the other was clerk to a merchant. Watson was a pious, sensible young man, of great integrity; the others rather more lax in their principles of religion, particularly Ralph, who, as well as Collins, had been unsettled by me, for which they both made me suffer. Osborne was sensible, candid, frank, sincere and affectionate to his friends, but in literary matters too fond of criticizing. Ralph was ingenious, genteel in his manners, and extremely eloquent; I think I never knew a prettier talker. Both of them great admirers of poetry, and began to try their hands in little pieces. Many pleasant walks we four had together on Sundays into the woods near Schuylkill, where we read to one another, and conferred on what we read.

Ralph was inclined to pursue the study of poetry, not doubting but he might become eminent in it and make his fortune by it, alleging that the best poets must when they first began to write make as many faults as he did. Osborne dissuaded him, assured him he had no genius for poetry, and advised him to think of nothing beyond the business he was bred to; that, in the mercantile way, though he had no stock, he might, by his diligence and punctuality, recommend himself to employment as a factor, and in time acquire wherewith to trade on his own account. I approved the amusing one's self with poetry now and then, so far as to improve one's language, but no farther.

On this it was proposed that we should each of us, at our next meeting, produce a piece of our own composing, in order to improve by our mutual observations, criticisms, and corrections. As language and expression were what we had in view, we excluded all considerations of invention by agreeing that the task should be a version of the eighteenth Psalm, which describes the descent of a diety. When the time of our meeting drew nigh, Ralph called on me first, and let me know his piece was ready. I told him I had been busy, and, having little inclination, had done nothing. He then showed me his piece for my opinion, and I much approved it, as it appeared to me to have great merit. "Now," says he, "Osborne never will allow the least merit in any thing of mine, but makes a thousand criticisms out of mere envy. He is not so jealous of you; I wish, therefore, you would take this piece, and produce it as yours; I will pretend not to have had time, and so produce nothing. We shall then see what he will say to it." It was agreed, and I immediately transcribed it, that it might appear in my own hand.

We met; Watson's performance was read; there were some beauties in it, but many defects. Osborne's was read; it was much better; Ralph did it justice; remarked some faults but applauded the beauties. He himself had nothing to produce. I was backward; seemed desirous of being excused; had not had sufficient time to correct, etc.; but no excuse could be admitted; produce I must. It was read and repeated; Watson and Osborne gave up the contest, and joined in applauding it immoderately. Ralph only made some criticisms, and proposed some amendments; but I defended my text. Osborne was against Ralph, and told him he was no better a critic than poet, so he dropped the argument. As they two went home together, Osborne expressed himself still more strongly in favor of what he thought my production; having restrained himself before, as he said, lest I should think it flattery. "But who would have imagined," says he, "that Franklin had been capable of such a performance; such a painting, such force, such fire! He has even improved the original. In his common conversation he seems to have no choice of words; he hesitates and blunders; and yet, good God! how he writes!" When we next met, Ralph discovered the trick we had played him, and Osborne was a little laughed at.

This transaction fixed Ralph in his resolution of becoming a poet. I did all I could to dissuade him from it, but he continued scribbling verses till Pope cured him. He became, however, a pretty good prose writer. More of him hereafter. But, as I may not have occasion again to mention the other two, I shall just remark here that Watson died in my arms a few years after much lamented, being the best of our set. Osborne went to the West Indies, where he became an eminent lawyer and made money, but died young. He and I had made a serious agreement that the one who happened first to die should, if possible, make a friendly visit to the other, and acquaint him how he found things in that separate state. But he never fulfilled his promise.

The Governor, seeming to like my company, had me frequently to his house, and his setting me up was always mentioned as a fixed thing. I was to take with me letters recommendatory to a number of his friends, besides the letter of credit to furnish me with the necessary money for purchasing the press and types, paper, etc. For these letters I was appointed to call at different times, when they were to be ready; but a future time was still named. Thus we went on till the ship, whose departure too, had been several times postponed, was on the point of sailing. Then, when I called to take my leave and receive the letters, his secretary, Dr. Bard, came to me and said the Governor was extremely busy in writing, but would be down at Newcastle before the ship, and there the letters would be delivered to me.

Ralph, though married, and having one child, had determined to accompany me in this voyage. It was thought he intended to establish a correspondence and obtain goods to sell on commission; but I found afterwards, that through some discontent with his wife's relations he purposed to leave her on their hands and never return again. Having taken leave of my friends, and interchanged some promises with Miss Read, I left Philadelphia in the ship, which anchored at Newcastle. The Governor was there; but when I went to his lodging, the secretary came to me from him with the civillest message in the world, that he could not then see me, being engaged in business of the utmost importance, but should send the letters to me on board, wished me heartily a good voyage and a speedy return, etc. I returned on board a little puzzled, but still not doubting.

Mr. Andrew Hamilton, a famous lawyer of Philadelphia, had

taken passage in the same ship for himself and son, and with Mr. Denham, a Quaker merchant, and Messrs. Onion and Russel, masters of an iron work in Maryland, had engaged the great cabin; so that Ralph and I were forced to take up with a berth in the steerage and, none on board knowing us, were considered as ordinary persons. But Mr. Hamilton and his son (it was James, since Governor) returned from Newcastle to Philadelphia, the father being recalled by a great fee to plead for a seized ship; and, just before we sailed, Colonel French coming on board and showing me great respect, I was more taken notice of, and with my friend Ralph invited by the other gentlemen to come into the cabin, there being now room. Accordingly, we removed thither.

Understanding that Colonel French had brought on board the Governor's dispatches, I asked the captain for those letters that were to be under my care. He said all were put into the bag together and he could not then come at them but before we landed in England I should have an opportunity of picking them out; so I was satisfied for the present, and we proceeded on our voyage. We had a sociable company in the cabin, and lived uncommonly well, having the addition of all Mr. Hamilton's stores, who had laid in plentifully. In this passage Mr. Denham contracted a friendship for me that continued during his life. The voyage was otherwise not a pleasant one, as we had a great deal of bad weather.

When we came into the Channel, the captain kept his word with me, and gave me an opportunity of examining the bag for the Governor's letters. I found none upon which my name was put as under my care. I picked out six or seven, that, by the handwriting, I thought might be the promised letters, especially as one of them was directed to Basket, the king's printer, and another to some stationer. We arrived in London the 24th of December, 1724. I waited upon the stationer, who came first in my way, delivering the letter as from Governor Keith. "I don't know such a person," says he; but opening the letter, "Oh! this is from Riddlesden. I have lately found him to be a complete rascal, and I will have nothing to do with him, nor receive any letters from him." So putting the letter into my hand, he turned on his heel and left me to serve some customer. I was surprised to find these were not the Governor's letters; and after recollecting and comparing circumstances, I began to doubt his sincerity. I found my friend Denham, and opened the whole affair to him. He let me into Keith's character; told me there was not the least probability that he had written any letters for me; that no one who knew him had the smallest dependence on him; and he laughed at the notion of the Governor's giving me a letter of credit, having, as he said, no credit to give. On my expressing some concern about what I should do, he advised me to endeavor getting some employment in the way of my business. "Among the printers here," says he, "you will improve yourself, and when you return to America, you will set up to greater advantage."

We both of us happened to know, as well as the stationer, that Riddlesden, the attorney, was a very knave. He had half ruined Miss Read's father by persuading him to be bound for him. By this letter it appeared there was a secret scheme on foot to the prejudice of Hamilton (supposed to be then coming over with us); and that Keith was concerned in it with Riddlesden. Denham, who was a friend of Hamilton's, thought he ought to be acquainted with it; so, when he arrived in England, which was soon after, partly from resentment and ill-will to Keith and Riddlesden, and partly from good-will to him, I waited on him, and gave him the letter. He thanked me cordially, the information being of importance to him; and from that time he became my friend, greatly to my advantage afterwards on many occasions.

But what shall we think of a governor's playing such pitiful tricks, and imposing so grossly on a poor ignorant boy! It was a habit he had acquired. He wished to please everybody; and having little to give he gave expectations. He was otherwise an ingenious, sensible man, a pretty good writer, and a good governor for the people, though not for his constituents, the proprietaries, whose instructions he sometimes disregarded. Several of our best laws were of his planning and passed during his administration.

Ralph and I were inseparable companions. We took lodgings together in Little Britain at three shillings and sixpence per week—

as much as we could then afford. He found some relations, but they were poor and unable to assist him. He now let me know his intentions of remaining in London, and that he never meant to return to Philadelphia. He had brought no money with him, the whole he could muster having been expended in paying his passage. I had fifteen pistoles; so he borrowed occasionally of me to subsist while he was looking out for business. He first endeavored to get into the playhouse, believing himself qualified for an actor; but Wilkes, to whom he applied, advised him candidly not to think of that employment, as it was impossible he should succeed in it. Then he proposed to Roberts, a publisher in Paternoster Row, to write for him a weekly paper like the *Spectator*, on certain conditions, which Roberts did not approve. Then he endeavored to get employment as a hackney writer, to copy for the stationers and lawyers about the Temple, but could find no vacancy.

I immediately got into work at Palmer's, then a famous printing-house in Bartholomew Close, and here I continued near a year. I was pretty diligent, but spent with Ralph a good deal of my earnings in going to plays and other places of amusement. We had together consumed all my pistoles, and now just rubbed on from hand to mouth. He seemed quite to forget his wife and child, and I, by degrees, my engagements with Miss Read, to whom I never wrote more than one letter, and that was to let her know I was not likely soon to return. This was another of the great errata of my life, which I should wish to correct if I were to live it over again. In fact, by our expenses, I was constantly kept unable to pay my passage.

At Palmer's I was employed in composing for the second edition of Woollaston's *Religion of Nature*. Some of his reasonings not appearing to me well founded, I wrote a little metaphysical piece in which I made remarks on them. It was entitled *A Dissertation on Liberty and Necessity, Pleasure and Pain*. I inscribed it to my friend Ralph; I printed a small number. It occasioned my being more considered by Mr. Palmer as a young man of some ingenuity, though he seriously expostulated with me upon the principles of my pamphlet, which to him appeared abominable. My printing this pamphlet was another erratum. While I lodged in Little Britain, I made an acquaintance with one Wilcox, a bookseller, whose shop was at the next door. He had an immense collection of second-hand books. Circulating libraries were not then in use; but we agreed that, on certain reasonable terms, which I have now forgotten, I might take, read, and return any of his books. This I esteemed a great advantage, and I made as much use of it as I could.

My pamphlet by some means falling into the hands of one Lyons, a surgeon, author of a book entitled *The Infallibility of Human Judgment*, it occassioned an acquaintance between us. He took great notice of me, called on me often to converse on those subjects, carried me to the Horns, a pale alehouse in —— Lane, Cheapside, and introduced me to Dr. Mandeville, author of the *Fable of the Bees*, who had a club there, of which he was the soul, being a most facetious, entertaining companion. Lyons, too, introduced me to Dr. Pemberton, at Batson's Coffeehouse, who promised to give me an opportunity, some time or other, of seeing Sir Isaac Newton, of which I was extremely desirous; but this never happened.

I had brought over a few curiosities, among which the principal was a purse made of the asbestos, which purifies by fire. Sir Hans Sloane heard of it, came to see me, and invited me to his house in Bloomsbury Square, where he showed me all his curiosities, and persuaded me to let him add that to the number, for which he paid me handsomely.

In our house there lodged a young woman, a milliner, who, I think, had a shop in the Cloisters. She had been genteelly bred, was sensible and lively, and of most pleasing conversation. Ralph read plays to her in the evenings; they grew intimate; she took another lodging, and he followed her. They lived together some time; but he being still out of business, and her income not sufficient to maintain them with her child, he took a resolution of going from London, to try for a country school, which he thought himself well qualified to undertake, as he wrote an excellent hand and was a master of arithmetic and accounts. This, however, he deemed a business below him, and confident of future better fortune, when he should be unwilling to have it known that he once was so meanly employed, he changed his name, and did me the honor to assume mine; for I soon after had a letter from him, acquainting me that he was settled in a small village (in Berkshire, I think it was), where he taught reading and writing to ten or a dozen boys, at sixpence each per week, recommending Mrs. T. to my care, and desiring me to write to him, directing for Mr. Franklin, schoolmaster, at such a place.

He continued to write frequently, sending me large specimens of an epic poem which he was then composing, and desiring my remarks and corrections. These I gave him from time to time, but endeavored rather to discourage his proceeding. One of Young's *Satires* was then just published. I copied and sent him a great part of it, which set in a strong light the folly of pursuing the Muses with any hope of advancement by them. All was in vain; sheets of the poem continued to come by every post. In the meantime, Mrs. T., having on his account lost her friends and business, was often in distresses, and used to send for me and borrow what I could spare to help her out of them. I grew fond of her company, and being at this time under no religious restraints and presuming upon my importance to her, I attempted familiarities (another erratum), which she repulsed with a proper resentment, and acquainted him with my behavior. This made a breach between us; and when he returned again to London, he let me know he thought I had cancelled all the obligations he had been under to me. So I found I was never to expect his repaying me what I lent to him, or advanced for him. This was, however, not then of much consequence, as he was totally unable; and in the loss of his friendship I found myself relieved from a burden. I now began to think of getting a little money beforehand; and expecting better work I left Palmer's to work at Watt's, near Lincoln's Inn Fields, a still greater printing-house. Here I continued all the rest of my stay in London.

At my first admission into this printing-house I took to working at press, imagining I felt a want of the bodily exercise I had been used to in America, where presswork is mixed with composing. I drank only water; the other workmen, near fifty in number, were great guzzlers of beer. On occasion I carried up and down stairs a large form of types in each hand, when others carried but one in both hands. They wondered to see, from this and several instances, that the "Water-American," as they called me, was *stronger* than themselves, who drank *strong* beer! We had an alehouse boy who attended always in the house to supply the workmen. My companion at the press drank every day a pint before breakfast, a pint at breakfast with his bread and cheese, a pint between breakfast and dinner; a pint at dinner, a pint in the afternoon about six o'clock, and another when he had done his day's work. I thought it a detestable custom: but it was necessary, he supposed, to drink *strong* beer, that he might be *strong* to labor. I endeavored to convince him that the bodily strength afforded by beer could only be in proportion to the grain or flour of the barley dissolved in the water of which it was made; that there was more flour in a pennyworth of bread, and therefore, if he would eat that with a pint of water, it would give him more strength than a quart of beer. He drank on, however, and had four or five shillings to pay out of his wages every Saturday night for that muddling liquor; an expense I was free from. And thus these poor devils keep themselves always under.

Watts after some weeks desiring to have me in the composing-room, I left the pressmen; a new *bienvenu* or sum for drink, being five shillings, was demanded of me by the compositors. I thought it an imposition, as I had paid below; the master thought so too, and forbade my paying it. I stood out two or three weeks, was accordingly considered as an excommunicate, and had so many little pieces of private mischief done me, by mixing my sorts, transposing my pages, breaking my matter, etc., etc., and if I were ever so little out of the room, and all ascribed to the chapel ghost, which they said ever haunted those not regularly admitted, that, notwithstanding the master's protection, I found myself obliged to comply and pay the money, convinced of the folly of being on ill terms with those one is to live with continually.

I was now on a fair footing with them, and soon acquired considerable influence. I proposed some reasonable alterations in their chapel* laws, and carried them against all opposition. From my example, a great part of them left their muddling breakfast of beer and bread and cheese, finding they could with me be supplied from a neighboring house with a large porringer of hot water-gruel, sprinkled with pepper, crumbed with bread, and a bit of butter in it, for the price of a pint of beer, viz., three halfpence. This was a more comfortable as well as cheaper breakfast, and kept their heads clearer. Those who continued sotting with beer all day, were often, by not paying, out of credit at the alehouse, and used to make interest with me to get beer; their *light*, as they phrased it, *being out*. I watched the paytable on Saturday night, and collected what I stood engaged for them, having to pay sometimes near thirty shillings a week on their accounts. This, and my being esteemed a pretty good Riggite, that is, a jocular verbal satirist, supported my consequence in the society. My constant attendance (I never making a St. Monday) recommended me to the master; and my uncommon quickness at composing occasioned my being put upon all work of dispatch, which was generally better paid. So I went on now very agreeably.

My lodging in Little Britain being too remote, I found another in Duke Street, opposite to the Romish Chapel. It was two pair of stairs backwards, at an Italian warehouse. A widow lady kept the house: she had a daughter and a maid servant and a journeyman, who attended the warehouse but lodged abroad. After sending to inquire my character at the house where I last lodged she agreed to take me in at the same rate, three shillings sixpence per week; cheaper, as she said, from the protection she expected in having a man lodge in the house. She was a widow, an elderly woman; had been bred a Protestant, being a clergyman's daughter, but was converted to the Catholic religion by her husband, whose memory she much revered; had lived much among people of distinction, and knew a thousand anecdotes of them as far back as the times of Charles II. She was lame in her knees with the gout, and therefore seldom stirred out of her room, so sometimes wanted company;

* A printing house is always called a chapel by the workmen. [FRANKLIN'S NOTE.]

and hers was so highly amusing to me, that I was sure to spend an evening with her whenever she desired it. Our supper was only half an anchovy each, on a very little strip of bread and butter, and half a pint of ale between us; but the entertainment was in her conversation. My always keeping good hours, and giving little trouble in the family, made her unwilling to part with me; so that, when I talked of a lodging I had heard of, nearer my business, for two shillings a week, which, intent as I now was on saving money, made some difference, she bid me not think of it, for she would abate me two shillings a week for the future: so I remained with her at one shilling and sixpence as long as I stayed in London.

In a garret of her house there lived a maiden lady of seventy, in the most retired manner, of whom my landlady gave me this account; that she was a Roman Catholic, had been sent abroad when young, and lodged in a nunnery with an intent of becoming a nun; but, the country not agreeing with her, she returned to England, where, there being no nunnery, she had vowed to lead the life of a nun, as near as might be done in those circumstances. Accordingly, she had given all her estate to charitable uses, reserving only twelve pounds a year to live on, and out of this sum she still gave a great deal in charity, living herself on water-gruel only, and using no fire but to boil it. She had lived many years in that garret, being permitted to remain there gratis by successive Catholic tenants of the house below, as they deemed it a blessing to have her there. A priest visited her to confess her every day. "I have asked her," says my landlady, "how she, as she lived, could possibly find so much employment for a confessor?" "Oh," said she, "it is impossible to avoid *vain thoughts*." I was permitted once to visit her. She was cheerful and polite, and conversed pleasantly. The room was clean, but had no other furniture than a mattress, a table with a crucifix and book, a stool which she gave me to sit on, and a picture, over the chimney, of Saint Veronica displaying her handkerchief with the miraculous figure of Christ's bleeding face on it, which she explained to me with great seriousness. She looked pale, but was never sick; and I give it as another instance on how small an income life and health may be supported.

At Watt's printing-house I contracted an acquaintance with an ingenious young man, one Wygate, who, having wealthy relations, had been better educated than most printers; was a tolerable Latinist, spoke French, and loved reading. I taught him and a friend of his to swim at twice going into the river, and they soon became good swimmers. They introduced me to some gentlemen from the country who went to Chelsea by water to see the College and Don Saltero's curiosities. In our return, at the request of the company, whose curiosity Wygate had excited, I stripped and leaped into the river, and swam from near Chelsea to Blackfriar's, performing on the way many feats of activity, both upon and under water, that surprised and pleased those to whom they were novelties.

I had from a child been ever delighted with this exercise, had studied and practiced all Thevenot's motions and positions, added some of my own, aiming at the graceful and easy as well as the useful. All these I took this occasion of exhibiting to the company, and was much flattered by their admiration; and Wygate, who was desirous of becoming a master, grew more and more attached to me on that account, as well as from the similarity of our studies. He at length proposed to me travelling all over Europe together, supporting ourselves everywhere by working at our business. I was once inclined to it; but, mentioning it to my good friend Mr. Denham, with whom I often spent an hour when I had leisure, he dissuaded me from it, advising me to think only of returning to Pennsylvania, which he was now about to do.

I must record one trait of this good man's character. He had formerly been in business at Bristol, but failed in debt to a number of people, compounded, and went to America. There, by a close application to business as a merchant, he acquired a plentiful fortune in a few years. Returning to England in the ship with me, he invited his old creditors to an entertainment, at which he thanked them for the easy composition they had favored him with, and, when they expected nothing but the treat, every man at the first remove found under his plate an order on a banker for the full amount of the unpaid remainder with interest.

He now told me he was about to return to Philadelphia, and

should carry over a great quantity of goods in order to open a store there. He proposed to take me over as his clerk, to keep his books, in which he would instruct me, copy his letters, and attend the store. He added that as soon as I should be acquainted with mercantile business, he would promote me by sending me with a cargo of flour and bread, etc., to the West Indies, and procure me commissions from others which would be profitable; and if I managed well would establish me handsomely. The thing pleased me; for I was grown tired of London, remembered with pleasure the happy months I had spent in Pennsylvania, and wished again to see it; therefore I immediately agreed on the terms of fifty pounds a year, Pennsylvania money; less, indeed, than my present gettings as a compositor, but affording a better prospect.

I now took leave of printing, as I thought, for ever, and was daily employed in my new business, going about with Mr. Denham among the tradesmen to purchase various articles, and seeing them packed up, doing errands, calling upon workmen to dispatch, etc.; and, when all was on board, I had a few days' leisure. On one of these days, I was, to my surprise, sent for by a great man I knew only by name, a Sir William Wyndham, and I waited upon him. He had heard by some means or other of my swimming from Chelsea to Blackfriar's, and of my teaching Wygate and another young man to swim in a few hours. He had two sons, about to set out on their travels; he wished to have them first taught swimming, and proposed to gratify me handsomely if I would teach them. They were not yet come to town, and my stay was uncertain, so I could not undertake it; but from this incident I thought it likely that if I were to remain in England and open a swimming-school, I might get a good deal of money; and it struck me so strongly, that, had the overture been sooner made me, probably I should not so soon have returned to America. After many years, you and I had something of more importance to do with one of these sons of Sir William Wyndham, become Earl of Egremont, which I shall mention in its place.

Thus I spent about eighteen months in London; most part of the time I worked hard at my business, and spent but little upon myself except in seeing plays and in books. My friend Ralph had kept me poor; he owed me about twenty-seven pounds, which I was now never likely to receive; a great sum out of my small earnings! I loved him, notwithstanding, for he had many amiable qualities, though I had by no means improved my fortune; but I had picked up some very ingenious acquaintance, whose conversation was of great advantage to me; and I had read considerably.

We sailed from Gravesend on the 23rd of July, 1726. For the incidents of the voyage, I refer you to my Journal, where you will find them all minutely related. Perhaps the most important part of that journal is the *plan* to be found in it, which I formed at sea, for regulating my future conduct in life. It is the more remarkable, as being formed when I was so young, and yet being pretty faithfully adhered to quite through to old age.

We landed in Philadelphia on the 11th of October, where I found sundry alterations. Keith was no longer governor, being superseded by Major Gordon. I met him walking the streets as a common citizen. He seemed a little ashamed at seeing me, but passed without saying anything. I should have been as much ashamed at seeing Miss Read, had not her friends, despairing with reason of my return after the receipt of my letter, persuaded her to marry another, one Rogers, a potter, which was done in my absence. With him, however, she was never happy, and soon parted from him, refusing to cohabit with him or bear his name, it being now said that he had another wife. He was a worthless fellow, though an excellent workman, which was the temptation to her friends. He got into debt, ran away in 1727 or 28, and went to the West Indies, and died there. Keimer had got a better house, a shop well supplied with stationery, plenty of new types, a number of hands, though none good, and seemed to have a great deal of business.

Mr. Denham took a store in Water Street, where we opened our goods; I attended the business diligently, studied accounts, and grew, in a little time, expert at selling. We lodged and boarded together; he counseled me as a father, having a sincere regard for me. I respected and loved him, and we might have gone on together very happily; but, in the beginning of February, 1726/7, when I had just passed my twenty-first year, we both were taken ill. My distemper was a pleurisy, which very nearly carried me off. I suffered a good deal, gave up the point in my own mind, and was rather disappointed when I found myself recovering, regretting, in some degree, that I must now, some time or other, have all that disagreeable work to do over again. I forget what his distemper was; it held him a long time, and at length carried him off. He left me a small legacy in a nuncupative will, as a token of his kindness for me, and he left me once more to the wide world; for the store was taken into the care of his executors, and my employment under him ended.

My brother-in-law, Holmes, being now at Philadelphia, advised my return to my business; and Keimer tempted me, with an offer of large wages by the year, to come and take the management of his printing-house, that he might better attend his stationer's shop. I had heard a bad character of him in London from his wife and her friends, and was not fond of having any more to do with him. I tried for farther employment as a merchant's clerk; but not readily meeting with any I closed again with Keimer. I found in his house these hands: Hugh Meredith, a Welsh Pennsylvanian, thirty years of age, bred to country work; honest, sensible, had a great deal of solid observation, was something of a reader, but given to drink. Stephen Potts, a young countryman of full age, bred to the same, of uncommon natural parts, and great wit and humor, but a little idle. These he had agreed with at extreme low wages per week, to be raised a shilling every three months, as they would deserve by improving in their business, and the expectation of these high wages, to come on hereafter, was what he had drawn them in with. Meredith was to work at press, Potts at book-binding, which he, by agreement, was to teach them, though he knew neither one nor the other. John ——, a wild Irishman, brought up to no business, whose service, for four years, Keimer had purchased from the captain of a ship; he too, was to be made a pressman. George Webb, an Oxford scholar, whose time for four years he had likewise bought, intending him for a compositor, of whom more presently; and David Harry, a country boy, whom he had taken apprentice.

I soon perceived that the intention of engaging me at wages so much higher than he had been used to give was to have these raw, cheap hands formed through me; and, as soon as I had instructed them, then they being all articled to him, he should be able to do without me. I went on, however, very cheerfully, put his printing-house in order, which had been in great confusion, and brought his hands by degrees to mind their business and to do it better.

It was an odd thing to find an Oxford scholar in the situation of a bought servant. He was not more than eighteen years of age, and gave me this account of himself: that he was born in Gloucester, educated at a grammar school there, had been distinguished among the scholars for some apparent superiority in performing his part when they exhibited plays; belonged to the Witty Club there, and had written some pieces in prose and verse, which were printed in the Gloucester newspapers. Thence he was sent to Oxford, where he continued about a year, but not well satisfied, wishing of all things to see London and become a player. At length, receiving his quarterly allowance of fifteen guineas, instead of discharging his debts he walked out of town, hid his gown in a furze bush, and footed it to London, where having no friends to advise him, he fell into bad company, soon spent his guineas, found no means of being introduced among the players, grew necessitous, pawned his clothes, and wanted bread. Walking the street very hungry, and not knowing what to do with himself, a crimp's bill was put into his hand, offering immediate entertainment and encouragement to such as would bind themselves to serve in America. He went directly, signed the indentures, was put into the ship, and came over, never writing a line to acquaint his friends what was become of him. He was lively, witty, good-natured, and a pleasant companion, but idle, thoughtless, and imprudent to the last degree.

John, the Irishman, soon ran away; with the rest I began to live very agreeably, for they all respected me the more, as they found Keimer incapable of instructing them, and that from me they learned something daily. We never worked on Saturday, that being Keimer's Sabbath, so I had two days for reading. My acquaintance with ingenious people in the town increased. Keimer himself treated me with great civility and apparent regard, and nothing now made me uneasy but my debt to Vernon, which I was yet unable to pay, being hitherto but a poor economist. He, however, kindly made no demand of it.

Our printing-house often wanted sorts, and there was no letter-founder in America; I had seen types cast at James's in London, but without much attention to the manner; however, I now contrived a mold, made use of the letters we had as puncheons, struck the matrices in lead, and thus supplied in a pretty tolerable way all deficiencies. I also engraved several things on occasion; I made the ink; I was warehouseman and everything, and, in short, quite a factotum.

But, however serviceable I might be, I found that my services became every day of less importance, as the other hands improved in the business; and when Keimer paid my second quarter's wages, he let me know that he felt them too heavy, and thought I should make an abatement. He grew by degrees less civil, put on more of the master, frequently found fault, was captious, and seemed ready for an outbreaking. I went on, nevertheless, with a good deal of patience, thinking that his encumbered circumstances were partly the cause. At length a trifle snapped our connection; for a great noise happening near the courthouse, I put my head out of the window to see what was the matter. Keimer, being in the street, looked up and saw me, called out to me in a loud voice and angry tone to mind my business, adding some reproachful words, that nettled me the more for their publicity, all the neighbors who were looking out on the same occasion being witnesses how I was treated. He came up immediately into the printing-house, continued the quarrel, high words passed on both sides, he gave me the quarter's warning we had stipulated, expressing a wish that he had not been obliged to so long a warning. I told him his wish was unnecessary, for I would leave him that instant; and so, taking my hat, walked out of doors, desiring Meredith, whom I saw below, to take care of some things I left, and bring them to my lodgings.

Meredith came accordingly in the evening, when we talked my affair over. He had conceived a great regard for me, and was very unwilling that I should leave the house while he remained in it. He dissuaded me from returning to my native country, which I began to think of; he reminded me that Keimer was in debt for all he possessed; that his creditors began to be uneasy; that he kept his shop miserably, sold often without profit for ready money, and often trusted without keeping accounts; that he must therefore fail, which would make a vacancy I might profit of. I objected my want of money. He then let me know that his father had a high opinion of me, and, from some discourse that had passed between them, he was sure would advance money to set us up, if I would enter into partnership with him. "My time," says he, "will be out with Keimer in the spring; by that time we may have our press and types in from London. I am sensible I am no workman; if you like it, your skill in the business shall be set against the stock I furnish, and we will share the profits equally."

The proposal was agreeable, and I consented; his father was in town and approved of it; the more as he saw I had great influence with his son, had prevailed on him to abstain long from dram-drinking, and he hoped might break him off that wretched habit entirely, when we came to be so closely connected. I gave an inventory to the father, who carried it to a merchant; the things were sent for. The secret was to be kept till they should arrive, and in the meantime I was to get work, if I could, at the other printing-house. But I found no vacancy there, and so remained idle a few days, when Keimer, on a prospect of being employed to print some paper money in New Jersey, which would require cuts and various types that I only could supply, and apprehending Bradford might engage me and get the job from him, sent me a very civil message, that old friends should not part for a few words, the effect of sudden passion, and wishing me to return. Meredith persuaded me to comply, as it would give more opportunity for his improvement under my daily instructions; so I returned, and we went on more smoothly than for some time before. The New Jersey job was obtained, I contrived a copperplate press for it, the first that had been seen in the country; I cut several ornaments and checks for the bills. We went together to Burlington, where I executed the whole to satisfaction; and he received so large a sum for the work as to be enabled thereby to keep his head much longer above water.

At Burlington I made an acquaintance with many principal people of the province. Several of them had been appointed by the Assembly a committee to attend the press, and take care that no more bills were printed than the law directed. They were therefore, by turns, constantly with us, and generally he who attended brought with him a friend or two for company. My mind having been much more improved by reading than Keimer's, I suppose it was for that reason my conversation seemed to be more valued. They had me to their houses, introduced me to their friends, and showed me much civility; while he, though the master, was a little neglected. In truth, he was an odd fish; ignorant of common life, fond of rudely opposing received opinions, slovenly to extreme dirtiness, enthusiàstic in some points of religion, and a little knavish withal.

We continued there near three months; and by that time I could reckon among my acquired friends Judge Allen, Samuel Bustill, the secretary of the Province, Isaac Pearson, Joseph Cooper, and several of the Smiths, members of Assembly, and Isaac Decow, the surveyor-general. The latter was a shrewd, sagacious old man, who told me that he began for himself, when young, by wheeling clay for the brickmakers, learned to write after he was of age, carried the chain for surveyors, who taught him surveying, and he had now by his industry acquired a good estate; and says he, "I foresee that you will soon work this man out of his business, and make a fortune in it at Philadelphia." He had not then the least intimation of my intention to set up there or anywhere. These friends were afterwards of great use to me, as I occasionally was to some of them. They all continued their regard for me as long as they lived.

Before I enter upon my public appearance in business, it may be well to let you know the then state of my mind with regard to my principles and morals, that you may see how far those influenced the future events of my life. My parents had early given me religious impressions, and brought me through my childhood piously in the dissenting way. But I was scarce fifteen, when, after doubting by turns of several points, as I found them disputed in the different books I read, I began to doubt of Revelation itself. Some books against deism fell into my hands; they were said to be the substance of sermons preached at Boyle's lectures. It happened that they wrought an effect on me quite contrary to what was intended by them; for the arguments of the deists, which were quoted to be refuted, appeared to me much stronger than the refutations; in short, I soon became a thorough deist. My arguments perverted some others, particularly Collins and Ralph; but each of them having afterwards wronged me greatly without the least compunction, and recollecting Keith's conduct towards me (who was another free-thinker), and my own towards Vernon and Miss Read, which at times gave me great trouble, I began to suspect that this doctrine, though it might be true, was not very useful. My London pamphlet, which had for its motto these lines of Dryden:

"Whatever is, is right. Though purblind Man
    Sees but a Part of the Chain, the nearest Link,
    His Eyes not carrying to the equal Beam,
    That poises all, above."

and from the attributes of God, his infinite wisdom, goodness, and power, concluded that nothing could possibly be wrong in the world, and that vice and virtue were empty distinctions, no such things existing, appeared now not so clever a performance as I once thought it; and I doubted whether some error had not insinuated itself unperceived into my argument, so as to infect all that followed, as is common in metaphysical reasonings.

I grew convinced that *truth, sincerity* and *integrity* in dealings between man and man were of the utmost importance to the felicity of life; and I formed written resolutions (which still remain in my journal book), to practice them ever while I lived. Revelation had indeed no weight with me as such; but I entertained an opinion that, though certain actions might not be bad *because* they were forbidden by it, or good *because* it commanded them, yet probably these actions might be forbidden *because* they were bad for us, or commanded *because* they were beneficial to us in their own natures, all the circumstances of things considered. And this persuasion, with the kind hand of Providence or some guardian angel, or accidental favorable circumstances and situations, or all together, preserved me through this dangerous time of youth, and the hazardous situations I was sometimes in among strangers, remote from the eye and advice of my father, without any *willful* gross immorality or injustice, that might have been expected from my want of religion. I say *willful*, because the instances I have mentioned had something of *necessity* in them, from my youth, inexperience, and the knavery of others. I had therefore a tolerable character to begin the world with; I valued it properly, and determined to preserve it.

We had not been long returned to Philadelphia before the new types arrived from London. We settled with Keimer, and left him by his consent before he heard of it. We found a house to hire near the market, and took it. To lessen the rent, which was then but twenty-four pounds a year, though I have since known it to let for seventy, we took in Thomas Godfrey, a glazier, and his family, who were to pay a considerable part of it to us, and we to board with them. We had scarce opened our letters and put our press in order, before George House, an acquaintance of mine, brought a countryman to us, whom he had met in the street inquiring for a printer. All our cash was now expended in the variety of particulars we had been obliged to procure, and this countryman's five shillings, being our first-fruits, and coming so seasonably, gave me more pleasure than any crown I have since earned; and from the gratitude I felt towards House, has made me often more ready than perhaps I should otherwise have been to assist young beginners.

There are croakers in every country, always boding its ruin. Such a one then lived in Philadelphia; a person of note, an elderly man, with a wise look and a very grave manner of speaking; his name was Samuel Mickle. This gentleman, a stranger to me, stopped one day at my door, and asked me if I was the young man who had lately opened a new printing-house. Being answered in the affirmative, he said he was sorry for me, because it was an expensive undertaking, and the expense would be lost; for Philadelphia was a sinking place, the people already half-bankrupts, or near being so; all appearances to the contrary, such as new buildings and the rise of rents, being to his certain knowledge fallacious; for they were, in fact, among the things that would soon ruin us. And he gave me such a detail of misfortunes now existing, or that were soon to exist, that he left me half melancholy. Had I known him before I engaged in this business, probably I never should have done it. This man continued to live in this decaying place, and to declaim in the same strain, refusing for many years to buy a house there, because all was going to destruction; and at last I had the pleasure of seeing him give five times as much for one as he might have bought it for when he first began his croaking.

I should have mentioned before that in the autumn of the preceding year, I had formed most of my ingenious acquaintance into a club of mutual improvement, which we called the Junto; we met on Friday evenings. The rules that I drew up required that every member, in his turn, should produce one or more queries on any point of morals, politics, or natural philosophy, to be discussed by the company; and once in three months produce and read an essay of his own writing, on any subject he pleased. Our debates were to be under the direction of a president, and to be conducted in the sincere spirit of inquiry after truth, without fondness for dispute, or desire of victory; and, to prevent warmth, all expressions of positiveness in opinions, or direct contradiction, were after some time made contraband, and prohibited under small pecuniary penalties.

The first members were Joseph Breintnal, a copier of deeds for the scriveners, a good-natured, friendly, middle-aged man, a great lover of poetry, reading all he could meet with, and writing some that was tolerable; very ingenious in many little nick-nackeries, and of sensible conversation. Thomas Godfrey, a self-taught mathematician, great in his way, and afterwards inventor of what is now called Hadley's quadrant. But he knew little out of his way, and was not a pleasing companion; as, like most great mathematicians I have met with, he expected universal precision in everything said, or was forever denying or distinguishing upon trifles, to the disturbance of all conversation. He soon left us. Nicholas Scull, a surveyor, afterwards surveyor-general, who loved books, and sometimes made a few verses. William Parsons, bred a shoemaker, but loving reading, had acquired a considerable share of mathematics, which he first studied with a view to astrology, that he afterwards laughed at. He also became surveyor-general. William Maugridge, a joiner, a most exquisite mechanic, and a solid, sensible man. Hugh Meredith, Stephen Potts, and George Webb I have characterized before. Robert Grace, a young gentleman of some fortune, generous, lively, and witty; a lover of punning and of his friends. And William Coleman, then a merchant's clerk, about my age, who had the coolest, clearest head, the best heart, and the exactest morals of almost any man I ever met with. He became afterwards a merchant of great note, and one of our provincial judges. Our friendship continued without interruption to his death, upwards of forty years. And the club continued almost as long, and was the best school of philosophy and politics that then existed in the province; for our queries, which were read the week preceding their discussion, put us on reading with attention upon the several subjects, that we might speak more to the purpose, and here, too, we acquired better habits of conversation, everything being studied in our rules which might prevent our disgusting each other. From hence the long continuance of the club, which I shall have frequent occasion to speak farther of hereafter.

But my giving this account of it here is to show something of the interest I had, every one of these exerting themselves in recommending business to us. Breintnal particularly procured us from the Quakers the printing fortysheets of their history, the rest being to be done by Keimer; and upon this we worked exceeding hard, for the price was low. It was a folio, pro patria size, in pica, with long primer notes. I composed of it a sheet a day, and Meredith worked it off at press; it was often eleven at night, and sometimes later, before I had finished my distribution for the next day's work, for the little jobs sent in by our other friends now and then put us back. But so determined I was to continue doing a sheet a day of the folio that one night, when, having imposed my forms, I thought my day's work over, one of them by accident was broken, and two pages reduced to pi, I immediately distributed and composed it over again before I went to bed. And this industry, visible to our neighbors, began to give us character and credit; particularly I was told that mention being made of the new printing-office at the merchants' everynight club, the general opinion was that it must fail, there being already two printers in the place, Keimer and Bradford; but Dr. Baird (whom you and I saw many years after at his native place, St. Andrew's in Scotland) gave a contrary opinion: "For the industry of that Franklin," says he, "is superior to anything I ever saw of the kind; I see him still at work when I go home from club, and he is at work again before his neighbors are out of bed." This struck the rest, and we soon after had offers from one of them to supply us with stationery; but as yet we did not choose to engage in shop business.

I mention this industry the more particularly and the more freely, though it seems to be talking in my own praise, that those of my posterity who shall read it may know the use of that virtue, when they see its effects in my favor throughout this relation.

George Webb, who had found a female friend that lent him wherewith to purchase his time of Keimer, now came to offer himself as a journeyman to us. We could not then employ him; but I foolishly let him know, as a secret, that I soon intended to begin a newspaper, and might then have work for him. My hopes of success, as I told him, were founded on this, that the then only newspaper, printed by Bradford, was a paltry thing, wretchedly managed, no way entertaining, and yet was profitable to him; I therefore thought a good paper could scarcely fail of good encouragement. I requested Webb not to mention it; but he told it to Keimer, who immediately, to be beforehand with me, published proposals for printing one himself, on which Webb was to be employed. I resented this; and to counteract them, as I could not yet begin our paper, I wrote several pieces of entertainment for Bradford's paper, under the title of the Busy Body, which Breintnal continued some months. By this means the attention of the public was fixed on that paper, and Keimer's proposals, which we burlesqued and ridiculed, were disregarded. He began his paper, however, and after carrying it on three quarters of a year, with at most only ninety subscribers, he offered it me for a trifle; and I, having been ready some time to go on with it, took it in hand directly; and it proved in a few years extremely profitable to me.

I perceive that I am apt to speak in the singular number, though our partnership still continued; the reason may be that in fact the whole management of the business lay upon me. Meredith was no compositor, a poor pressman, and seldom sober. My friends lamented my connection with him, but I was to make the best of it.

Our first papers made a quite different appearance from any before in the province; a better type, and better printed; but some spirited remarks of my writing on the dispute then going on between Governor Burnet and the Massachusetts Assembly struck the principal people, occasioned the paper and the manager of it to be much talked of, and in a few weeks brought them all to be our subscribers. Their example was followed by many, and our number went on growing continually. This was one of the first good effects of my having learned a little to scribble; another was that the leading men, seeing a newspaper now in the hands of one who could also handle a pen, thought it convenient to oblige and encourage me. Bradford still printed the votes, and laws, and other public business. He had printed an Address of the House to the Governor, in a coarse, blundering manner. We reprinted it elegantly and correctly, and sent one to every member. They were sensible of the difference: it strengthened the hands of our friends in the House, and they voted us their printers for the year ensuing.

Among my friends in the House I must not forget Mr. Hamilton, before mentioned, who was then returned from England, and had a seat in it. He interested himself for me strongly in that instance, as he did in many others afterward, continuing his patronage till his death.*

Mr. Vernon about this time put me in mind of the debt I owed

* I got his son once £500. [FRANKLIN'S NOTE.]

him, but did not press me. I wrote him an ingenuous letter of acknowledgments, craved his forbearance a little longer, which he allowed me, and as soon as I was able, I paid the principal with interest, and many thanks; so that erratum was in some degree corrected.

But now another difficulty came upon me, which I had never the least reason to expect. Mr. Meredith's father, who was to have paid for our printing-house, according to the expectations given me, was able to advance only one hundred pounds currency, which had been paid; and a hundred more was due to the merchant, who grew impatient, and sued us all. We gave bail but saw that if the money could not be raised in time, the suit must soon come to a judgment and execution, and our hopeful prospects must with us be ruined, as the press and letters must be sold for payment, perhaps at half price.

In this distress two true friends, whose kindness I have never forgotten, nor ever shall forget while I can remember anything, came to me separately, unknown to each other, and, without any application from me, offering each of them to advance me all the money that should be necessary to enable me to take the whole business upon myself, if that should be practicable; but they did not like my continuing the partnership with Meredith, who, as they said, was often seen drunk in the streets, and playing at low games in alehouses, much to our discredit. These two friends were William Coleman and Robert Grace. I told them I could not propose a separation while any prospect remained of the Meredith's fulfilling their part of our agreement, because I thought myself under great obligations to them for what they had done, and would do if they could. But if they finally failed in their performance, and our partnership must be dissolved, I should then think myself at liberty to accept the assistance of my friends.

Thus the matter rested for some time, when I said to my partner, "Perhaps your father is dissatisfied at the part you have undertaken in this affair of ours, and is unwilling to advance for you and me what he would for you alone. If that is the case, tell me, and I will resign the whole to you, and go about my business." "No," says he," my father has really been disappointed, and is really unable; and I am unwilling to distress him farther. I see this is a business I am not fit for, I was bred a farmer, and it was a folly in me to come to town, and put myself, at thirty years of age, an apprentice to learn a new trade. Many of our Welsh people are going to settle in North Carolina, where land is cheap. I am inclined to go with them, and follow my old employment. You may find friends to assist you. If you will take the debts of the company upon you; return to my father the hundred pound he has advanced; pay my little personal debts; and give me thirty pounds and a new saddle, I will relinquish the partnership, and leave the whole in your hands." I agreed to this proposal: it was drawn up in writing, signed, and sealed immediately. I gave him what he demanded, and he went soon after to Carolina, from whence he sent me next year two long letters, containing the best account that had been given of that country, the climate, the soil, husbandry, etc., for in those matters he was very judicious. I printed them in the papers, and they gave great satisfaction to the public.

As soon as he was gone, I recurred to my two friends; and because I would not give an unkind preference to either, I took half of what each had offered and I wanted of one, and half of the other; paid off the company debts, and went on with the business in my own name, advertising that the partnership was dissolved. I think this was in or about the year 1729.

About this time there was a cry among the people for more paper money, only fifteen thousand pounds being extant in the province, and that soon to be sunk. The wealthy inhabitants opposed any addition, being against all paper currency, from an apprehension that it would depreciate, as it had done in New England, to the prejudice of all creditors. We had discussed this point in our Junto, where I as on the side of an addition, being persuaded that the first small sum struck in 1723 had done much good by increasing the trade, employment, and number of inhabitants in the province, since I now saw all the old houses inhabited, and many new ones building: whereas I remembered well, that when I first walked about the streets of Philadelphia, eating my roll, I saw most of the houses in Walnut Street, between Second and Front streets, with bills on their doors to be let; and many likewise in Chestnut Street and other streets, which made me then think the inhabitants of the city were deserting it one after another.

Our debates possessed me so fully of the subject, that I wrote and printed an anonymous pamphlet on it, entitled *The Nature and Necessity of a Paper Currency*. It was well received by the common people in general; but the rich men disliked it, for it increased and strengthened the clamor for more money; and they happened to have no writers among them that were able to answer it, their opposition slackened, and the point was carried by a majority in the House. My friends there, who conceived I had been of some service, thought fit to reward me by employing me in printing the money, a very profitable job and a great help to me. This was another advantage gained by my being able to write.

The utility of this currency became by time and experience so evident as never afterwards to be much disputed; so that it grew soon to fifty-five thousand pounds, and in 1739 to eighty thousand pounds, since which it arose during war to upwards of three hundred and fifty thousand pounds—trade, building, and inhabitants all the while increasing—though I now think there are limits beyond which the quantity may be hurtful.

I soon after obtained through my friend Hamilton the printing of the Newcastle paper money, another profitable job as I then thought it, small things appearing great to those in small circumstances; and these, to me, were really great advantages, as they were great encouragements. He procured for me, also, the printing of the laws and votes of that government, which continued in my hands as long as I followed the business.

I now opened a little stationer's shop. I had in it blanks of all sorts, the correctest that ever appeared among us, being assisted in that by my friend Breintnal. I had also paper, parchment, chapmen's books, etc. One Whitemash, a compositor I had known in London, an excellent workman, now came to me, and worked with me constantly and diligently; and J took an apprentice, the son of Aquila Rose.

I began now gradually to pay off the debt I was under for the printing-house. In order to secure my credit and character as a tradesman, I took care not only to be in *reality* industrious and frugal, but to avoid all *appearances* of the contrary. I dressed plainly; I was seen at no places of idle diversion. I never went out afishing or shooting; a book, indeed, sometimes debauched me from my work, but that was seldom, snug, and gave no scandal; and, to show that I was not above my business, I sometimes brought home the paper I purchased at the stores through the streets on a wheelbarrow. Thus being esteemed an industrious, thriving young man, and paying duly for what I bought, the merchants who imported stationery solicited my custom; others proposed supplying me with books; I went on swimmingly. In the meantime, Keimer's credit and business declining daily, he was at last forced to sell his printing-house to satisfy his creditors. He went to Barbados, and there lived some years in very poor circumstances.

His apprentice, David Harry, whom I had instructed while I worked with him, set up in his place at Philadelphia, having bought his materials. I was at first apprehensive of a powerful rival in Harry, as his friends were very able, and had a good deal of interest. I therefore proposed a partnership to him, which he, fortunately for me, rejected with scorn. He was very proud, dressed like a gentleman, lived expensively, took much diversion and pleasure abroad, ran in debt, and neglected his business; upon which, all business left him; and, finding nothing to do, he followed Keimer to Barbados, taking the printing-house with him. There this apprentice employed his former master as a journeyman; they quarreled often; Harry went continually behindhand, and at length was forced to sell his types and return to his country work in Pennsylvania. The person that bought them employed Keimer to use them, but in a few years he died.

There remained now no competitor with me at Philadelphia but the old one, Bradford, who was rich and easy, did a little printing now and then by straggling hands, but was not very anxious about it. However, as he kept the post-office, it was imagined he had better opportunities of obtaining news; his paper was thought a better distributer of advertisements than mine, and therefore had many more, which was a profitable thing to him, and a disadvantage to me; for, though I did indeed receive and send papers by the post, yet the public opinion was otherwise, for what I did send was by bribing the riders, who took them privately, Bradford being unkind enough to forbid it, which occasioned some resentment on my part; and I thought so meanly of him for it, that when I afterward came into his situation I took care never to imitate it.

I had hitherto continued to board with Godfrey, who lived in part of my house with his wife and children, and had one side of the shop for his glazier's business, though he worked little, being always absorbed in his mathematics. Mrs. Godfrey projected a match for me with a relation's daughter, took opportunities of bringing us often together, till a serious courtship on my part ensued, the girl being in herself very deserving. The old folks encouraged me by continual invitations to supper, and by leaving us together, till at length it was time to explain. Mrs. Godfrey managed our little treaty. I let her know that I expected as much money with their daughter as would pay off my remaining debt for the printing-house, which I believe was not then above a hundred pounds. She brought me word they had no such sum to spare; I said they might mortgage their house in the loan-office. The answer to this after some days was that they did not approve the match; that, on inquiry of Bradford, they had been informed the printing business was not a profitable one, the types would soon be worn out, and more wanted, that S. Keimer and D. Harry had failed one after the other, and I should probably soon follow them; and therefore I was forbidden the house, and the daughter shut up.

Whether this was a real change of sentiment or only artifice, on a supposition of our being too far engaged in affection to retract, and therefore that we should steal a marriage, which would leave them at liberty to give or withhold what they pleased, I know not; but I suspected the latter, resented it, and went no more. Mrs. Godfrey brought me afterwards some more favorable accounts of their disposition, and would have drawn me on again; but I declared absolutely my resolution to have nothing more to do with that family. This was resented by the Godfreys; we differed, and they removed, leaving me the whole house, and I resolved to take no more inmates.

But this affair having turned my thoughts to marriage, I looked around me and made overtures of acquaintance in other places; but soon found that, the business of a printer being generally thought a poor one, I was not to expect money with a wife, unless with such a one as I should not otherwise think agreeable. In the meantime that hard-to-be-governed passion of youth hurried me frequently into intrigues with low women that fell in my way, which were attended with some expense and great inconvenience, besides a continual risk to my health by a distemper, which of all things I dreaded, though by great good luck I escaped it.

A friendly correspondence as neighbors and old acquaintances had continued between me and Mrs. Read's family, who all had a regard for me from the time of my first lodging in their house. I was often invited there and consulted in their affairs, wherein I sometimes was of service. I pitied poor Miss Read's unfortunate situation, who was generally dejected, seldom cheerful, and avoided company. I considered my giddiness and inconstancy when in London as in a great degree the cause of her unhappiness, though the mother was good enough to think the fault more her own than mine, as she had prevented our marrying before I went thither, and persuaded the other match in my absence. Our mutual affection was revived, but there were now great objections to our union. That match was indeed looked upon as invalid, a preceding wife being said to be living in England; but this could not easily be proved, because of the distance; and though there was a report of his death, it was not certain. Then, though it should be true, he had left many debts, which his successor might be called upon to pay. We ventured, however, over all these difficulties, and I took her to wife, September 1st, 1730. None of the inconveniences happened that we had apprehended; she proved a good and faithful helpmate, assisted me much by attending the shop; we throve together, and have ever mutually endeavored to make each other happy. Thus I corrected that great erratum as well as I could.

About this time our club meeting not at a tavern but in a little room of Mr. Grace's, set apart for that purpose, a proposition was made by me, that, since our books were often referred to in our disquisitions upon the queries, it might be convenient to us to have them altogether where we met, that upon occasion they might be consulted; and by thus clubbing our books to a common library, we should, while we liked to keep them together, have each of us the advantage of using the books of all the other members, which would be nearly as beneficial as if each owned the whole. It was liked and agreed to, and we filled one end of the room with such books as we could best spare. The number was not so great as we expected; and though they had been of great use, yet some inconveniences occurring for want of due care of them, the collection, after about a year, was separated, and each took his books home again.

And now I set on foot my first project of a public nature, that for a subscription library. I drew up the proposals, got them put into form by our great scrivener, Brockden, and, by the help of my friends in the Junto, procured fifty subscribers of forty shillings each to begin with, and ten shillings a year for fifty years, the term our company was to continue. We afterwards obtained a charter, the company being increased to one hundred. This was the mother of all the North American subscription libraries, now so numerous. It is become a great thing itself, and continually increasing. These libraries have improved the general conversation of the Americans, made the common tradesmen and farmers as intelligent as most gentlemen from other countries, and perhaps have contributed in some degree to the stand so generally made throughout the colonies in defence of their privileges.

Memo. Thus far was written with the intention expressed in the beginning and therefore contains several little family anecdotes of no importance to others. What follows was written many years after, in compliance with the advice contained in these letters, and accordingly intended for the public. The affairs of the Revolution occasioned the interruption.

Letter from Mr. Abel James, with Notes of my Life
(received in Paris).

"MY DEAR AND HONORED FRIEND:

I have often been desirous of writing to thee, but could not be reconciled to the thought that the letter might fall into the hands of the British, lest some printer or busy-body should publish some part of the contents, and give our friend pain, and myself censure.

"Some time since there fell into my hands, to my great joy, about twenty-three sheets in thy own handwriting, containing an account of the parentage and life of thyself, directed to thy son, ending in the year 1730, with which there were notes, likewise in thy writing; a copy of which I enclose, in hopes it may be a means, if thou continued it up to a later period, that the first and latter part may be put together; and if it is not yet continued, I hope thee will not delay it. Life is uncertain, as the preacher tells us; and what will the world say if kind, humane, and benevolent Ben. Franklin should leave his friends and the world deprived of so pleasing and profitable work; a work which would be useful and entertaining not only to a few, but to millions? The influence writings under that class have on the minds of youth is very great, and has nowhere appeared to me so plain, as in our public friend's journals. It almost insensibly leads the youth into the resolution of endeavoring to become as good and eminent as the journalist. Should thine, for instance, when published (and I think it could not fail of it), lead the youth to equal the industry and temperance of thy early youth, what a blessing with that class would such a work be! I know of no character living, nor many of them put together, who has so much in his power as thyself to promote a greater spirit of industry and early attention to business, frugality, and temperance with the American youth. Not that I think the work would have no other merit and use in the world, far from it; but the first is of such vast importance that I know nothing that can equal it."

The foregoing letter and the minutes accompanying it being shown to a friend, I received from him the following:

Letter from Mr. Benjamin Vaughan

"Paris, January 31, 1783.

"MY DEAREST SIR:

When I had read over your sheets of minutes of the principal incidents of your life, recovered for you by your Quaker acquaintance. I told you I would send you a letter expressing my reasons why I thought it would be useful to complete and publish it as he desired. Various concerns have for some time past prevented this letter being written, and I do not know whether it was worth any expectation; happening to be at leisure, however, at present, I shall by writing, at least interest and instruct myself; but as the terms I am inclined to use may tend to offend a person of your manners, I shall only tell you how I would address any other person, who was as good and as great as yourself, but less diffident. I would say to him, Sir, I solicit the history of your life from the following motives: Your history is so remarkable, that if you do not give it, somebody else will certainly give it; and perhaps so as nearly to do as much harm, as your own management of the thing might do good. It will moreover present a table of the internal circumstances of your country, which will very much tend to invite to it settlers of virtuous and manly minds. And considering the eagerness with which such information is sought by them, and the extent of your reputation, I do not know of a more efficacious advertisement than your biography would give. All that has happened to you is also connected with the detail of the manners and situation of a rising people; and in this respect I do not think that the writings of Cæsar and Tacitus can be more interesting to a true judge of human nature and society. But these, sir, are small reasons, in my opinion, compared with the chance which your life will give for the forming of future great men; and in conjunction with your Art of Virtue (which you design to publish) of improving the features of private character, and consequently of aiding all happiness, both public and domestic. The two works I allude to, sir, will in particular give a noble rule and example of self-education. School and other education constantly proceed upon false principles, and show a clumsy apparatus pointed at a false mark; but your apparatus is simple, and the mark a true one; and while parents and young persons are left destitute of other just means of estimating and becoming prepared for a reasonable course in life, your discovery that the thing is in many a man's private power, will be invaluable! Influence upon the private character, late in life, is not only an influence late in life, but a weak influence. It is in youth that we plant our chief habits and prejudices; it is in youth that we take our party as to profession, pursuits and matrimony. In youth, therefore, the turn is given; in youth the education even of the next generation is given; in youth the private and public character is determined; and the term of life extending but from youth to age, life ought to begin well from youth, and more especially before we take our party as to our principal objects. But your biography will not merely teach self-education, but the education of a wise man; and the wisest man will receive lights and improve his progress, by seeing detailed the conduct of another wise man. And why are weaker men to be deprived of such helps, when we see our race has been blundering on in the dark, almost without a guide in this particular, from the farthest trace of time? Show then, sir, how much is to be done, both to sons and fathers; and invite all wise men to become like yourself, and other men to become wise. When we see how cruel statesmen and warriors can be to the human race, and how absurd distinguished men can be to their acquaintance, it will be instructive to observe the instances multiply of pacific, acquiescing manners; and to find how compatible it is to be great and domestic, enviable and yet good-humored.

"The little private incidents which you will also have to relate, will have considerable use, as we want, above all things, rules of prudence in ordinary affairs; and it will be curious to see how you have acted in these. It will be so far a sort of key to life, and explain many things that all men ought to have once explained to them, to give them a chance of becoming wise by foresight. The nearest thing to having experience of one's own, is to have other people's affairs brought before us in a shape that is interesting; this is sure to happen from your pen; our affairs and management will have an air of simplicity or importance that will not fail to strike; and I am convinced you have conducted them with as much originality as if you had been conducting discussions in politics or philosophy; and what more worthy of experiments and system (its importance and its errors considered) than human life?

"Some men have been virtuous blindly, others have speculated fantastically, and others have been shrewd to bad purposes; but you, sir, I am sure, will give under your hand, nothing but what is at the same moment, wise, practical and good. Your account of yourself (for I suppose the parallel I am drawing for Dr. Franklin, will hold not only in point of character, but of private history) will show that you are ashamed of no origin; a thing the more important, as you prove how little necessary all origin is to happiness, virtue, or greatness. As no end likewise happens without a means, so we shall find, sir, that even you yourself framed a plan by which you became considerable; but at the same time we may see that though the event is flattering, the means are as simple as wisdom could make them; that is, depending upon nature, virtue, thought and habit. Another thing demonstrated will be the propriety of every man's waiting for his time for appearing upon the stage of the world. Our sensations being very much fixed to the moment, we are apt to forget that more moments are to follow the first, and consequently that man should arrange his conduct so as to suit the whole of a life. Your attribution appears to have been applied to your life, and the passing moments of it have been enlivened with content and enjoyment, instead of being tormented with foolish impatience or regrets. Such a conduct is easy for those who make virtue and themselves in countenance by examples of other truly great men, of whom patience is so often the characteristic. Your Quaker correspondent, sir (for here again I will suppose the subject of my letter resembling

Dr. Franklin), praised your frugality, diligence and temperance, which is considered as a pattern for all youth; but it is singular that he should have forgotten your modesty and your disinterestedness, without which you never could have waited for your advancement, or found your situation in the meantime comfortable; which is a strong lesson to show the poverty of glory and the importance of regulating our minds. If this correspondent had known the nature of your reputation as well as I do, he would have said, Your former writings and measures would secure attention to your Biography, and Art of Virtue; and your Biography and Art of Virtue, in return, would secure attention to them. This is an advantage attendant upon a various character, and which brings all that belongs to it into greater play; and it is the more useful, as perhaps more persons are at a loss for the means of improving their minds and characters, than they are for the time or the inclination to do it. But there is one concluding reflection, sir, that will show the use of your life as a mere piece of biography. This style of writing seems a little gone out of vogue, and yet it is a very useful one; and your specimen of it may be particularly serviceable, as it will make a subject of comparison with the lives of various public cut-throats and intriguers, and with absurd monastic self-tormentors or vain literary triflers. If it encourages more writings of the same kind with your own, and induces more men to spend lives fit to be written, it will be worth all Plutarch's Lives put together. But being tired of figuring to myself a character of which every feature suits only one man in the world, without giving him the praise of it, I shall end my letter, my dear Dr. Franklin, with a personal application to your proper self. I am earnestly desirous, then, my dear sir, that you should let the world into the traits of your genuine character, as civil broils may otherwise tend to disguise or traduce it. Considering your great age, the caution of your character, and your peculiar style of thinking, it is not likely that any one besides yourself can be sufficiently master of the facts of your life, or the intentions of your mind. Besides all this, the immense revolution of the present period will necessarily turn our attention towards the author of it, and when virtuous principles have been pretended in it, it will be highly important to show that such have really influenced; and, as your own character will be the principal one to receive a scrutiny, it is proper (even for its effects upon your vast and rising country, as well as upon England and upon Europe) that it should stand respectable and eternal. For the furtherance of human happiness, I have always maintained that it is necessary to prove that man is not even at present a vicious and detestable animal; and still more to prove that good management may greatly amend him; and it is for much the same reason, that I am anxious to see the opinion established, that there are fair characters existing among the individuals of the race; for the moment that all men, without exception, shall be conceived abandoned, good people will cease efforts deemed to be hopeless, and perhaps think of taking their share in the scramble of life, or at least of making it comfortable principally for themselves. Take then, my dear sir, this work most speedily into hand: show yourself good as you are good; temperate as you are temperate; and above all things, prove yourself as one, who from your infancy have loved justice, liberty and concord, in a way that has made it natural and consistent for you to have acted, as we have seen you act in the last seventeen years of your life. Let Englishmen be made not only to respect, but even to love you. When they think well of individuals in your native country, they will go nearer to thinking well of your country; and when your countrymen see themselves well thought of by Englishmen, they will go nearer to thinking well of England. Extend your views even further; do not stop at those who speak the English tongue, but after having settled so many points in nature and politics, think of bettering the whole race of men. As I have not read any part of the life in question, but know only the character that lived it, I write somewhat at hazard. I am sure, however, that the life and the treatise I allude to (on the Art of Virtue) will necessarily fulfil the chief of my expectations; and still more so if you take up the measure of suiting these performances to the several views above stated. Should they even prove unsuccessful in all that a sanguine admirer of yours hopes from them, you will at least have framed pieces to interest the human mind; and whoever gives a feeling of pleasure that is innocent to man, has added so much to the fair side of a life otherwise too much darkened by anxiety and too much injured by pain. In the hope, therefore, that you will listen to the prayer addressed to you in this letter, I beg to subscribe myself, my dearest sir, etc., etc.,

"Signed,   BENJ. VAUGHAN."

CONTINUATION

of the Account of my Life, begun at Passy,
near Paris.

1784

It is some time since I received the above letters, but I have been too busy till now to think of complying with the request they contain. It might, too, be much better done if I were at home among my papers, which would aid my memory and help to ascertain dates; but my return being uncertain, and having just now a little leisure, I will endeavor to recollect and write what I can; if I live to get home, it may there be corrected and improved.

Not having any copy here of what is already written, I know not whether an account is given of the means I used to establish the Philadelphia public library, which, from a small beginning, is now become so considerable, though I remember to have come down to near the time of that transaction (1730). I will therefore begin here with an account of it, which may be struck out if found to have been already given.

At the time I established myself in Pennsylvania, there was not a good bookseller's shop in any of the colonies to the southward of Boston. In New York and Philadelphia the printers were indeed stationers; they sold only paper, etc., almanacs, ballads, and a few common school-books. Those who loved reading were obliged to send for their books from England; the members of the Junto had each a few. We had left the alehouse, where we first met, and hired a room to hold our club in. I proposed that we should all of us bring our books to that room, where they would not only be ready to consult in our conferences, but become a common benefit, each of us being at liberty to borrow such as he wished to read at home. This was accordingly done, and for some time contented us.

Finding the advantage of this little collection, I proposed to render the benefit from books more common, by commencing a public subscription library. I drew a sketch of the plan and rules that would be necessary, and got a skilful conveyancer, Mr. Charles Brockden, to put the whole in form of articles of agreement to be subscribed, by which each subscriber engaged to pay a certain sum down for the first purchase of books and an annual contribution for increasing them. So few were the readers at that time in Philadelphia, and the majority of us so poor, that I was not able, with great industry, to find more than fifty persons, mostly young tradesmen, willing to pay down for this purpose forty shillings each, and ten shillings per annum. On this little fund we began. The books were imported; the library was opened one day in the week for lending to the subscribers, on their promissory notes to pay double the value if not duly returned. The institution soon manifested its utility, was imitated by other towns, and in other provinces. The libraries were augmented by donations; reading became fashionable; and our people, having no public amusements to divert their attention from study, became better acquainted with books, and in a few years were observed by strangers to be better instructed and more intelligent than people of the same rank generally are in other countries.

When we were about to sign the above-mentioned articles, which were to be binding on us, our heirs, etc., for fifty years, Mr. Brockden, the scrivener, said to us, "You are young men, but it is scarcely probable that any of you will live to see the expiration of the term fixed in the instrument." A number of us, however, are yet living; but the instrument was after a few years rendered null by a charter that incorporated and gave perpetuity to the company.

The objections and reluctances I met with in soliciting the subscriptions, made me soon feel the impropriety of presenting one's self as the proposer of any useful project that might be supposed to raise one's reputation in the smallest degree above that of one's neighbors, when one has need of their assistance to accomplish that project. I therefore put myself as much as I could out of sight, and stated it as a scheme of a *number of friends*, who had requested me to go about and propose it to such as they thought lovers of reading. In this way my affair went on more smoothly, and I ever after practiced it on such occasions; and, from my frequent successes, can heartily recommend it. The present little sacrifice of your vanity will afterwards be amply repaid. If it remains a while uncertain to whom the merit belongs, some one more vain than yourself will be encouraged to claim it, and then even envy will be disposed to do you justice by plucking those assumed feathers, and restoring them to their right owner.

This library afforded me the means of improvement by constant study, for which I set apart an hour or two each day, and thus repaired in some degree the loss of the learned education my father once intended for me. Reading was the only amusement I allowed myself. I spent no time in taverns, games, or frolics of any kind; and my industry in my business continued as indefatigable as it was necessary. I was indebted for my printing-house; I had a young family coming on to be educated, and I had to contend with, for business, two printers who were established in the place before me. My circumstances, however, grew daily easier. My original habits of frugality continuing, and my father having, among his instructions to me when a boy, frequently repeated a proverb of Solomon, "Seest thou a man diligent in his calling; he shall stand before kings, he shall not stand before mean men," I from thence considered industry as a means of obtaining wealth and distinction, which encouraged me, though I did not think that I should ever literally *stand before kings*, which, however, has since happened; for I have stood before *five*, and even had the honor of sitting down with one—the King of Denmark—to dinner.

We have an English proverb that says, "He that would thrive, must ask his wife." It was lucky for me that I had one as much disposed to industry and frugality as myself. She assisted me cheerfully in my business, folding and stitching pamphlets, tending

shop, purchasing old linen rags for the paper-makers, etc., etc.
We kept no idle servants, our table was plain and simple, our
furniture of the cheapest. For instance, my breakfast was a long
time bread and milk (no tea), and I ate it out of a twopenny earthen
porringer, with a pewter spoon. But mark how luxury will enter
families, and make a progress, in spite of principle: being called
one morning to breakfast, I found it in a china bowl, with a spoon
of silver! They had been bought for me without my knowledge
by my wife, and had cost her the enormous sum of three-and-
twenty shillings, for which she had no other excuse or apology to
make, but that she thought *her* husband deserved a silver spoon
and china bowl as well as any of his neighbors. This was the first
appearance of plate and china in our house, which afterward, in a
course of years, as our wealth increased, augmented gradually to
several hundred pounds in value.

I had been religiously educated as a Presbyterian; and though
some of the dogmas of that persuasion, such as *the eternal decrees
of God, election, reprobation, etc.,* appeared to me unintelligible,
others doubtful, and I early absented myself from the public
assemblies of the sect, Sunday being my studying day, I never was
without some religious principles. I never doubted, for instance,
the existence of the Deity; that he made the world, and governed it
by his Providence; that the most acceptable service of God was the
doing good to man; that our souls are immortal; and that all crime
will be punished, and virtue rewarded, either here or hereafter.
These I esteemed the essentials of every religion; and, being to be
found in all the religions we had in our country, I respected them
all, though with different degrees of respect, as I found them more
or less mixed with other articles, which, without any tendency to
inspire, promote, or confirm morality, served principally to divide
us, and make us unfriendly to one another. This respect to all, with
an opinion that the worst had some good effects, induced me to
avoid all discourse that might tend to lessen the good opinion
another might have of his own religion; and as our province
increased in people, and new places of worship were continually
wanted, and generally erected by voluntary contribution, my mite

for such purpose, whatever might be the sect, was never refused.

Though I seldom attended any public worship, I had still an opinion of its propriety, and of its utility when rightly conducted, and I regularly paid my annual subscription for the support of the only Presbyterian minister or meeting we had in Philadelphia. He used to visit me sometimes as a friend, and admonish me to attend his administrations, and I was now and then prevailed on to do so, once for five Sundays successively. Had he been in my opinion a good preacher, perhaps I might have continued, notwithstanding the occasion I had for the Sunday's leisure in my course of study; but his discourses were chiefly either polemic arguments, or explications of the peculiar doctrines of our sect, and were all to me very dry, uninteresting, and unedifying, since not a single moral principle was inculcated or enforced, their aim seeming to be rather to make us Presbyterians than good citizens.

At length he took for his text that verse of the fourth chapter of Philippians, "Finally, brethren, whatsoever things are true, honest, just, pure, lovely, or of good report, if there be any virtue, or any praise, think on these things." And I imagined, in a sermon on such a text, we could not miss of having some morality. But he confined himself to five points only, as meant by the apostle, viz.: 1. Keeping holy the Sabbath day. 2. Being diligent in reading the holy Scriptures. 3. Attending duly the public worship. 4. Partaking of the Sacrament. 5. Paying a due respect to God's ministers. These might be all good things; but, as they were not the kind of good things that I expected from that text, I despaired of ever meeting with them from any other, was disgusted, and attended his preaching no more. I had some years before composed a little liturgy, or form of prayer, for my own private use (viz., in 1728), entitled, *Articles of Belief and Acts of Religion*. I returned to the use of this, and went no more to the public assemblies. My conduct might be blameable but I leave it, without attempting further to excuse it; my present purpose being to relate facts and not to make apologies for them.

It was about this time I conceived the bold and arduous project of arriving at moral perfection. I wished to live without committing any fault at any time; I would conquer all that either natural inclination, custom, or company might lead me into. As I knew, or thought I knew, what was right and wrong, I did not see why I might not always do the one and avoid the other. But I soon found I had undertaken a task of more difficulty than I had imagined. While my care was employed in guarding against one fault, I was often surprised by another; habit took the advantage of inattention; inclination was sometimes too strong for reason. I concluded, at length, that the mere speculative conviction that it was our interest to be completely virtuous was not sufficient to prevent our slipping; and that the contrary habits must be broken, and good ones acquired and established, before we can have any dependence on a steady, uniform rectitude of conduct. For this purpose I therefore contrived the following method.

In the various enumerations of the moral virtues I had met with in my reading, I found the catalogue more or less numerous, as different writers included more or fewer ideas under the same name. Temperance, for example, was by some confined to eating and drinking, while by others it was extended to mean the moderating every other pleasure, appetite, inclination, or passion, bodily or mental, even to our avarice and ambition. I proposed to myself, for the sake of clearness, to use rather more names, with fewer ideas annexed to each, than a few names with more ideas; and I included under thirteen names of virtues all that at that time occurred to me as necessary or desirable, and annexed to each a short precept, which fully expressed the extent I gave to its meaning.

These names of virtues, with their precepts, were:

1. TEMPERANCE.
Eat not to dullness; drink not to elevation.

2. SILENCE.
Speak not but what may benefit others or yourself; avoid trifling conversation.

3. ORDER.
Let all your things have their places; let each part of your business have its time.

4. RESOLUTION.
Resolve to perform what you ought; perform without fail what you resolve.

5. FRUGALITY.
Make no expense but to do good to others or yourself; *i.e.,* waste nothing.

6. INDUSTRY.
Lose no time; be always employed in something useful; cut off all unnecessary actions.

7. SINCERITY.
Use no hurtful deceit; think innocently and justly, and, if you speak, speak accordingly.

8. JUSTICE.
Wrong none by doing injuries, or omitting the benefits that are your duty.

9. MODERATION.
Avoid extremes; forbear resenting injuries so much as you think they deserve.

10. CLEANLINESS.
Tolerate no uncleanliness in body, clothes, or habitation.

11. TRANQUILLITY.
Be not disturbed at trifles, or at accidents common or unavoidable.

12. CHASTITY.
Rarely use venery but for health or offspring, never to dullness, weakness, or the injury of your own or another's peace or reputation.

13. HUMILITY.
Imitate Jesus and Socrates.

My intention being to acquire the *habitude* of all these virtues, I judged it would be well not to distract my attention by attempting the whole at once, but to fix it on one of them at a time; and, when I should be master of that, then to proceed to another, and so on, till I should have gone through the thirteen; and, as the previous acquisition of some might facilitate the acquisition of certain others, I arranged them with that view, as they stand above. *Temperance* first, as it tends to procure that coolness and clearness of head, which is so necessary where constant vigilance was to be kept up, and guard maintained against the unremitting attraction of ancient habits, and the force of perpetual temptations. This being acquired and established, *Silence* would be more easy; and my desire being to gain knowledge at the same time that I improved in virtue, and considering that in conversation it was obtained rather by the use of the ears than of the tongue, and therefore wishing to break a habit I was getting into of prattling, punning, and joking, which only made me acceptable to trifling company, I gave *Silence* the second place. This and the next, *Order*, I expected would allow me more time for attending to my project and my studies. *Resolution*, once become habitual, would keep me firm in my endeavors to obtain all the subsequent virtues; *Frugality* and *Industry* freeing me from my remaining debt, and producing affluence and independence, would make more easy the practice of *Sincerity* and *Justice*, etc., etc. Conceiving then, that, agreeably to the advice of Pythagoras in his Golden Verses, daily examination would be necessary, I contrived the following method for conducting that examination.

I made a little book, in which I allotted a page for each of the virtues. I ruled each page with red ink, so as to have seven columns, one for each day of the week, marking each column with a letter for the day. I crossed these columns with thirteen red lines, marking the beginning of each line with the first letter of one of the virtues, on which line, and in its proper column, I might mark, by a little black spot, every fault I found upon examination to have been committed respecting that virtue upon that day.

I determined to give a week's strict attention to each of the virtues successively. Thus, in the first week, my great guard was to avoid every the least offence against *Temperance,* leaving the other virtues to their ordinary chance, only marking every evening the faults of the day. Thus, if in the first week I could keep my first line, marked T, clear of spots, I supposed the habit of that virtue so much strengthened, and its opposite weakened, that I might venture extending my attention to include the next, and for the following week keep both lines clear of spots. Proceeding thus to the last, I could go through a course complete in thirteen weeks, and four courses in a year. And like him who, having a garden to weed, does not attempt to eradicate all the bad herbs at once, which would exceed his reach and his strength, but works on one of the beds at a time, and, having accomplished the first, proceeds to a second, so I should have, I hoped, the encouraging pleasure of seeing on my pages the progress I made in virtue, by clearing successively my lines of their spots, till in the end, by a number of courses, I should be happy in viewing a clean book, after a thirteen weeks' daily examination.

Form of the pages.

TEMPERANCE.							
EAT NOT TO DULLNESS; DRINK NOT TO ELEVATION.							
	S.	M.	T.	W.	T.	F.	S.
T.							
S.	*	*		*		*	
O.	* *	*	*		*	*	*
R.			*			*	
F.		*			*		
I.			*				
S.							
J.							
M.							
C.							
T.							
C.							
H.							

This my little book had for its motto these lines from Addison's *Cato*:

> "Here will I hold. If there's a power above us
> (And that there is, all nature cries aloud
> Thro' all her works), He must delight in virtue;
> And that which he delights in must be happy."

Another from Cicero,

"O vitæ Philosophia dux! O virtutum indagatrix expultrixque vitiorum! Unus dies, bene et ex præceptis tuis actus, peccanti immortalitati est anteponendus."

Another from the Proverbs of Solomon, speaking of wisdom or virtue:

"Length of days is in her right hand, and in her left hand riches and honour. Her ways are ways of pleasantness, and all her paths are peace." iii. 16, 17.

And conceiving God to be the fountain of wisdom, I thought it right and necessary to solicit his assistance for obtaining it; to this end I formed the following little prayer, which was prefixed to my tables of examination, for daily use.

"O powerful Goodness! bountiful Father! merciful Guide! Increase in me that wisdom which discovers my truest interest. Strengthen my resolutions to perform what that wisdom dictates. Accept my kind offices to thy other children as the only return in my power for thy continual favors to me."

I used also sometimes a little prayer which I took from Thomson's Poems, viz.:

> "Father of light and life, thou Good Supreme!
> O teach me what is good; teach me Thyself!
> Save me from folly, vanity, and vice,
> From every low pursuit; and fill my soul
> With knowledge, conscious peace, and virtue pure;
> Sacred, substantial, never-fading bliss!"

The precept of *Order* requiring that *every part of my business should have its allotted time,* one page in my little book contained the following scheme of employment for the twenty-four hours of a natural day.

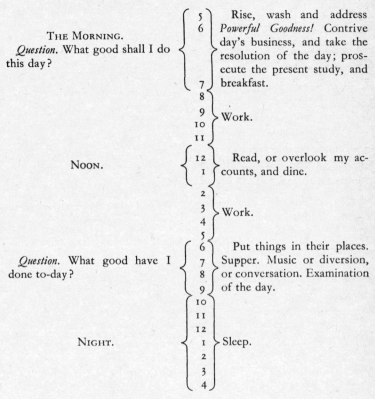

THE MORNING. *Question.* What good shall I do this day?	5 6 7	Rise, wash and address *Powerful Goodness!* Contrive day's business, and take the resolution of the day; prosecute the present study, and breakfast.
	8 9 10 11	Work.
NOON.	12 1	Read, or overlook my accounts, and dine.
	2 3 4 5	Work.
Question. What good have I done to-day?	6 7 8 9	Put things in their places. Supper. Music or diversion, or conversation. Examination of the day.
NIGHT.	10 11 12 1 2 3 4	Sleep.

I entered upon the execution of this plan for self-examination, and continued it with occasional intermissions for some time. I was surprised to find myself so much fuller of faults than I had imagined; but I had the satisfaction of seeing them diminish. To avoid the trouble of renewing now and then my little book, which, by scraping out the marks on the paper of old faults to make room for new ones in a new course, became full of holes, I transferred my tables and precepts to the ivory leaves of a memorandum book, on which the lines were drawn with red ink, that made a durable stain, and on those lines I marked my faults with a black-lead pencil, which marks I could easily wipe out with a wet sponge. After a while I went through one course only in a year, and afterward only one in several years, till at length I omitted them entirely, being employed in voyages and business abroad, with a multiplicity of affairs that interfered; but I always carried my little book with me.

My scheme of ORDER gave me the most trouble; and I found that, though it might be practicable where a man's business was such as to leave him the disposition of his time, that of a journeyman printer, for instance, it was not possible to be exactly observed by a master; who must mix with the world, and often receive people of business at their own hours. *Order,* too, with regard to places for things, papers, etc., I found extremely difficult to acquire. I had not been early accustomed to it, and, having an exceeding good memory, I was not so sensible of the inconvenience attending want of method. This article, therefore, cost me so much painful attention, and my faults in it vexed me so much, and I made so little progress in amendment, and had such frequent relapses, that I was almost ready to give up the attempt and content myself with a faulty character in that respect, like the man who, in buying an ax of a smith, my neighbor, desired to have the whole of its surface as bright as the edge. The smith consented to grind it bright for him if he would turn the wheel; he turned, while the smith pressed the broad face of the ax hard and heavily on the stone, which made the turning of it very fatiguing. The man came every now and then from the wheel to see how the work went on, and at length would take his ax as it was, without farther grinding. "No," said the smith, "turn on, turn on; we shall have it bright by-and-by; as yet, it is only speckled." "Yes," says the man, "but I think I like a speckled ax best." And I believe this may have been the case with many, who having for want of some such means as I employed found the difficulty of obtaining good and breaking bad habits in other points of vice and virtue, have given up the struggle, and concluded that *"a speckled ax was best"*; for something that pretended to be reason, was every now and then suggesting to me that such extreme nicety as I exacted of myself might be a kind of foppery in morals, which, if it were known, would make me ridiculous; that a perfect character might be attended with the inconvenience of being envied and hated; and that a benevolent man should allow a few faults in himself, to keep his friends in countenance.

In truth, I found myself incorrigible with respect to Order; and now I am grown old, and my memory bad, I feel very sensibly the want of it. But on the whole, though I never arrived at the perfection I had been so ambitious of obtaining, but fell far short of it, yet I was, by the endeavor, a better and happier man than I otherwise should have been if I had not attempted it; as those who aim at perfect writing by imitating the engraved copies, though they never reach the wished-for excellence of those copies, their hand is mended by the endeavor, and is tolerable while it continues fair and legible.

It may be well my posterity should be informed that to this little artifice, with the blessing of God, their ancestor owed the constant felicity of his life, down to his 79th year, in which this is written. What reverses may attend the remainder is in the hand of Providence; but if they arrive the reflection on past happiness enjoyed ought to help his bearing them with more resignation. To Temperance he ascribes his long-continued health and what is still left to him of a good constitution; to Industry and Frugality, the early easiness of his circumstances and acquisition of his fortune, with all that knowledge that enabled him to be a useful citizen, and obtained for him some degree of reputation among the learned; to Sincerity and Justice, the confidence of his country, and the honorable employs it conferred upon him; and to the joint influence of the whole mass of the virtues, even in the imperfect state he was able to acquire them, all that evenness of temper, and that cheerfulness in conversation, which makes his company still sought for, and agreeable even to his younger acquaintance. I hope, therefore, that some of my descendants may follow the example and reap the benefit.

It will be remarked that, though my scheme was not wholly

without religion, there was in it no mark of any of the distinguishing tenets of any particular sect. I had purposely avoided them; for, being fully persuaded of the utility and excellency of my method, and that it might be serviceable to people in all religions, and intending some time or other to publish it, I would not have anything in it that should prejudice anyone, of any sect, against it. I purposed writing a little comment on each virtue, in which I would have shown the advantages of possessing it, and the mischiefs attending its opposite vice; and I should have called my book "The Art of Virtue,"* because it would have shown the means and manner of obtaining virtue, which would have distinguished it from the mere exhortation to be good, that does not instruct and indicate the means, but is like the apostle's man of verbal charity, who only without showing to the naked and hungry how or where they might get clothes or victuals, exhorted them to be fed and clothed.—James ii. 15, 16.

But it so happened that my intention of writing and publishing this comment was never fulfilled. I did, indeed, from time to time, put down short hints of the sentiments, reasonings, etc., to be made use of in it, some of which I have still by me; but the necessary close attention to private business in the earlier part of my life, and public business since, have occasioned my postponing it; for, it being connected in my mind with *a great and extensive project,* that required the whole man to execute, and which an unforeseen succession of employs prevented my attending to, it has hitherto remained unfinished.

In this piece it was my design to explain and enforce this doctrine, that vicious actions are not hurtful because they are forbidden, but forbidden because they are hurtful, the nature of man alone considered; that it was, therefore, every one's interest to be virtuous who wished to be happy even in this world; and I should, from this circumstance (there being always in the world a number of rich merchants, nobility, states, and princes, who have need of honest instruments for the management of their affairs, and such being so

*Nothing so likely to make a man's fortune as virtue. [FRANKLIN'S NOTE.]

rare), have endeavored to convince young persons that no qualities were so likely to make a poor man's fortune as those of probity and integrity.

My list of virtues contained at first but twelve; but a Quaker friend having kindly informed me that I was generally thought proud; that my pride showed itself frequently in conversation; that I was not content with being in the right when discussing any point, but was overbearing, and rather insolent, of which he convinced me by mentioning several instances; I determined endeavoring to cure myself, if I could, of this vice or folly among the rest, and I added *Humility* to my list, giving an extensive meaning to the word.

I cannot boast of much success in acquiring the *reality* of this virtue, but I had a good deal with regard to the *appearance* of it. I made it a rule to forbear all direct contradiction to the sentiments of others, and all positive assertion of my own. I even forbid myself, agreeably to the old laws of our Junto, the use of every word or expression in the language that imported a fixed opinion, such as *certainly, undoubtedly,* etc., and I adopted, instead of them, *I conceive, I apprehend,* or *I imagine* a thing to be so or so; or it *so appears to me at present.* When another asserted something that I thought an error, I denied myself the pleasure of contradicting him abruptly, and of showing immediately some absurdity in his proposition; and in answering I began by observing that in certain cases or circumstances his opinion would be right, but in the present case there *appeared* or *seemed* to me some difference, etc. I soon found the advantage of this change in my manner; the conversations I engaged in went on more pleasantly. The modest way in which I proposed my opinions procured them a readier reception and less contradiction; I had less mortification when I was found to be in the wrong, and I more easily prevailed with others to give up their mistakes and join with me when I happened to be in the right.

And this mode, which I at first put on with some violence to natural inclination, became at length so easy, and so habitual to me, that perhaps for these fifty years past no one has ever heard a dogmatical expression escape me. And to this habit (after my character of integrity) I think it principally owing that I had early so much weight with my fellow-citizens when I proposed new institutions, or alterations in the old, and so much influence in public councils when I became a member; for I was but a bad speaker, never eloquent, subject to much hesitation in my choice of words, hardly correct in language, and yet I generally carried my points.

In reality, there is, perhaps, no one of our natural passions so hard to subdue as *pride*. Disguise it, struggle with it, beat it down, stifle it, mortify it as much as one pleases, it is still alive, and will every now and then peep out and show itself; you will see it, perhaps, often in this history; for, even if I could conceive that I had completely overcome it, I should probably be proud of my humility.

Thus far written at Passy, 1784.

I am now about to write at home, August, 1788, but cannot have the help expected from my papers, many of them being lost in the war. I have, however, found the following.

Having mentioned *a great and extensive project* which I had conceived, it seems proper that some account should be here given of that project and its object. Its first rise in my mind appears in the following little paper, accidentally preserved, viz.:

Observations on my reading history, in library, May 19th, 1731.

"That the great affairs of the world, the wars, revolutions, etc., are carried on and affected by parties.

"That the view of these parties is their present general interest, or what they take to be such.

"That the different views of these different parties occasion all confusion.

"That while a party is carrying on a general design, each man has his particular private interest in view.

"That as soon as a party had gained its general point, each member becomes intent upon his particular interest; which, thwarting others, breaks that party into divisions, and occasions more confusion.

"That few in public affairs act from a mere view of the good of their country, whatever they may pretend; and, though their actings bring real good to their country, yet men primarily considered that their own and their country's interest was united, and did not act from a principle of benevolence.

"That fewer still, in public affairs, act with a view to the good of mankind.

"There seems to me at present to be great occasion for raising a United Party for Virtue, by forming the virtuous and good men of all nations into a regular body, to be governed by suitable good and wise rules, which good and wise men may probably be more unanimous in their obedience to, than common people are to common laws.

"I at present think that whoever attempts this aright, and is well qualified, cannot fail of pleasing God, and of meeting with success.   B. F."

Revolving this project in my mind, as to be undertaken hereafter, when my circumstances should afford me the necessary leisure, I put down from time to time, on pieces of paper, such thoughts as occurred to me respecting it. Most of these are lost; but I find one purporting to be the substance of an intended creed, containing, as I thought, the essentials of every known religion, and being free of every thing that might shock the professors of any religion. It is expressed in these words, viz.:

"That there is one God, who made all things.

"That he governs the world by his providence.

"That he ought to be worshipped by adoration, prayer, and thanksgiving.

"But that the most acceptable service of God is doing good to man.

"That the soul is immortal.

"And that God will certainly reward virtue and punish vice, either here or hereafter."

My ideas at that time were, that the sect should be begun and spread at first among young and single men only; that each person to be initiated should not only declare his assent to such creed, but should have exercised himself within the thirteen weeks' examination and practice of the virtues, as in the before-mentioned model; that the existence of such a society should be kept a secret, till it was become considerable, to prevent solicitations for the admission of improper persons, but that the members should each of them search among his acquaintance for ingenuous, well-disposed youths, to whom, with prudent caution, the scheme should be gradually communicated; that the members should engage to afford their advice, assistance, and support to each other in promoting one another's interests, business, and advancement in life; that, for distinction, we should be called *The Society of the Free and Easy:* free, as being, by the general practice and habit of the virtues, free from the dominion of vice; and particularly by the practice of industry and frugality, free from debt, which exposes a man to confinement, and a species of slavery to his creditors.

This is as much as I can now recollect of the project, except that I communicated it in part to two young men, who adopted it with some enthusiasm; but my then narrow circumstances, and the necessity I was under of sticking close to my business, occasioned my postponing the further prosecution of it at that time; and my multifarious occupations, public and private, induced me to continue postponing, so that it has been omitted till I have no longer strength or activity left sufficient for such an enterprise; though I am still of opinion that it was a practicable scheme, and might have been very useful, by forming a great number of good citizens; and I was not discouraged by the seeming magnitude of the undertaking, as I have always thought that one man of tolerable abilities may work great changes, and accomplish great affairs among mankind, if he first forms a good plan, and cutting off all amusements or other employments that would divert his attention makes the execution of that same plan his sole study and business.

In 1732 I first published my almanac, under the name of *Richard Saunders;* it was continued by me about twenty-five years, commonly called *Poor Richard's Almanack.* I endeavored to make it both entertaining and useful, and it accordingly came to be in such demand that I reaped considerable profit from it, vending annually near ten thousand. And observing that it was generally read, scarce any neighborhood in the province being without it, I considered it as a proper vehicle for conveying instruction among the common people, who bought scarcely any other books; I therefore filled all the little spaces that occurred between the remarkable days in the calendar with proverbial sentences, chiefly such as inculcated industry and frugality, as the means of procuring wealth, and thereby securing virtue; it being more difficult for a man in want, to act always honestly, as, to use here one of those proverbs, *it is hard for an empty sack to stand upright.*

These proverbs, which contained the wisdom of many ages and nations, I assembled and formed into a connected discourse prefixed to the Almanac of 1757, as the harangue of a wise old man to the people attending an auction. The bringing all these scattered counsels thus into a focus enabled them to make greater impression. The piece, being universally approved, was copied in all the newspapers of the continent; reprinted in Britain on a broadside, to be stuck up in houses; two translations were made of it in French, and great numbers bought by the clergy and gentry, to distribute gratis among their poor parishioners and tenants. In Pennsylvania, as it discouraged useless expense in foreign super-fluities, some thought it had its share of influence in producing that growing plenty of money which was observable for several years after its publication.

I considered my newspaper, also, as another means of communi-cating instruction, and in that view frequently reprinted in it extracts from the *Spectator,* and other moral writers; and sometimes pub-lished little pieces of my own, which had been first composed for reading in our Junto. Of these are a Socratic dialogue, tending to prove that, whatever might be his parts and abilities, a vicious man could not properly be called a man of sense; and a discourse on self-denial, showing that virtue was not secure till its practice became a habitude, and was free from the opposition of contrary inclinations. These may be found in the papers about the beginning of 1735.

In the conduct of my newspaper, I carefully excluded all libeling and personal abuse, which is of late years become so disgraceful to our country. Whenever I was solicited to insert anything of that kind, and the writers pleaded, as they generally did, the liberty of the press, and that a newspaper was like a stage-coach, in which any one who would pay had a right to a place, my answer was, that I would print the piece separately if desired, and the author might have as many copies as he pleased to distribute himself, but that I would not take upon me to spread his detraction; and that, having contracted with my subscribers to furnish them with what might be either useful or entertaining, I could not fill their papers with private altercation, in which they had no concern, without doing them manifest injustice. Now, many of our printers make no scruple of gratifying the malice of individuals by false accusations of the fairest characters among ourselves, augmenting animosity even to the producing of duels; and are, moreover, so indiscreet as to print scurrilous reflections on the government of neighboring states, and even on the conduct of our best national allies, which may be attended with the most pernicious consequences. These things I mention as a caution to young printers, and that they may be encouraged not to pollute their presses and disgrace their profession by such infamous practices, but refuse steadily, as they may see by my example that such a course of conduct will not, on the whole, be injurious to their interests.

In 1733 I sent one of my journeymen to Charleston, South Carolina, where a printer was wanting. I furnished him with a press and letters, on an agreement of partnership, by which I was to receive one-third of the profits of the business, paying one-third of the expense. He was a man of learning, and honest but ignorant in matters of account; and though he sometimes made me remittances, I could get no account from him, nor any satisfactory state of our partnership while he lived. On his decease, the business was continued by his widow, who, being born and bred in Holland, where, as I have been informed, the knowledge of accounts makes a part of female education, she not only sent me as clear a state as she could find of the transactions past, but continued to account with the greatest regularity and exactness every quarter afterwards, and managed the business with such success, that she not only brought up reputably a family of children, but, at the expiration of the term, was able to purchase of me the printing-house, and establish her son in it.

I mention this affair chiefly for the sake of recommending that branch of education for our young females, as likely to be of more use to them and their children, in case of widowhood, than either music or dancing, by preserving them from losses by imposition of crafty men, and enabling them to continue, perhaps, a profitable mercantile house, with established correspondence, till a son is grown up fit to undertake and go on with it, to the lasting advantage and enriching of the family.

About the year 1734 there arrived among us from Ireland a young Presbyterian preacher, named Hemphill, who delivered with a good voice, and apparently extempore, most excellent discourses, which drew together considerable numbers of different persuasions, who joined in admiring them. Among the rest, I became one of his constant hearers, his sermons pleasing me, as they had little of the dogmatical kind, but inculcated strongly the practice of virtue, or what in the religious style are called good works. Those, however, of our congregation, who considered themselves as orthodox Presbyterians, disapproved his doctrine, and were joined by most of the old clergy, who arraigned him of heterodoxy before the synod, in order to have him silenced. I became his zealous partisan, and contributed all I could to raise a party in his favor, and we combated for him a while with some hopes of success. There was much scribbling pro and con upon the occasion; and finding that, though an elegant preacher, he was but a poor writer, I lent him my pen and wrote for him two or three pamphlets, and one piece in the *Gazette* of April, 1735. Those pamphlets, as is generally the case with controversial writings, though eagerly read at the time, were soon out of vogue, and I question whether a single copy of them now exists.

During the contest an unlucky occurrence hurt his cause exceedingly. One of our adversaries having heard him preach a sermon that was much admired, thought he had somewhere read the sermon before, or at least a part of it. On search, he found that part quoted at length, in one of the British reviews, from a discourse of Dr. Foster's. This detection gave many of our party disgust, who accordingly abandoned his cause, and occasioned our more speedy discomfiture in the synod. I stuck by him, however, as I rather approved his giving us good sermons composed by others, than bad ones of his own manufacture, though the latter was the practice of our common teachers. He afterward acknowledged to me that none of those he preached were his own: adding, that his memory was such as enabled him to retain and repeat any sermon after one reading only. On our defeat, he left us in search elsewhere of better fortune, and I quitted the congregation, never joining it after, though I continued many years my subscription for the support of its ministers.

I had begun in 1733 to study languages; I soon made myself so much a master of the French as to be able to read the books with ease. I then undertook the Italian. An acquaintance, who was also learning it, used often to tempt me to play chess with him. Finding this took up too much of the time I had to spare for study, I at length refused to play any more, unless on this condition, that the victor in every game should have a right to impose a task, either in parts of the grammar to be got by heart, or in translations, etc., which tasks the vanquished was to perform upon honor, before our next meeting. As we played pretty equally, we thus beat one another into that language. I afterwards with a little painstaking, acquired as much of the Spanish as to read their books also.

I have already mentioned that I had only one year's instruction in a Latin school, and that when very young, after which I neglected that language entirely. But, when I had attained an acquaintance with the French, Italian, and Spanish, I was surprised to find, on looking over a Latin Testament, that I understood so much more of that language than I had imagined, which encouraged me to apply myself again to the study of it, and I met with more success, as those preceding languages had greatly smoothed my way.

From these circumstances, I have thought that there is some inconsistency in our common mode of teaching languages. We are told that it is proper to begin first with the Latin, and, having acquired that, it will be more easy to attain those modern languages which are derived from it; and yet we do not begin with the Greek, in order more easily to acquire the Latin. It is true that, if you can clamber and get to the top of a staircase without using the steps, you will more easily gain them in descending; but certainly, if you begin with the lowest you will with more ease ascend to the top; and I would therefore offer it to the consideration of those who superintend the education of our youth, whether, since many of those who begin with the Latin quit the same after spending some years without having made any great proficiency, and what they have learned becomes almost useless, so that their time has been lost, it would not have been better to have begun with the French, proceeding to the Italian, etc.; for, though after spending the same time they should quit the study of languages and never arrive at the Latin, they would, however, have acquired another tongue or two that, being in modern use, might be serviceable to them in common life.

After ten years' absence from Boston, and having become easy in my circumstances, I made a journey thither to visit my relations, which I could not sooner well afford. In returning, I called at Newport to see my brother, then settled there with his printing-house. Our former differences were forgotten, and our meeting was very cordial and affectionate. He was fast declining in his health, and requested of me that, in case of his death which he apprehended not far distant, I would take home his son, then but ten years of age, and bring him up to the printing business. This I accordingly performed, sending him a few years to school before I took him into the office. His mother carried on the business till he was grown up, when I assisted him with an assortment of new types, those of his father being in a manner worn out. Thus it was that I made my brother ample amends for the service I had deprived him of by leaving him so early.

In 1736 I lost one of my sons, a fine boy of four years old, by the smallpox, taken in the common way. I long regretted bitterly, and still regret that I had not given it to him by inoculation. This I mention for the sake of parents who omit that operation, on the supposition that they should never forgive themselves if a child died under it; my example showing that the regret may be the same either way, and that, therefore, the safer should be chosen.

Our club, the Junto, was found so useful, and afforded such satisfaction to the members, that several were desirous of introducing their friends, which could not well be done without exceeding what we had settled as a convenient number, viz., twelve. We had from the beginning made it a rule to keep our institution a secret, which was pretty well observed; the intention was to avoid applications of improper persons for admittance, some of whom, perhaps, we might find it difficult to refuse. I was one of those who were against any addition to our number, but, instead of it, made in writing a proposal, that every member separately should endeavor to form a subordinate club, with the same rules respecting queries, etc., and without informing them of the connection with the Junto. The advantages proposed were, the improvement of so many more young citizens by the use of our institutions; our better acquaintance with the general sentiments of the inhabitants on any occasion, as the Junto member might propose what queries we should desire, and was to report to the Junto what passed in his separate club; the promotion of our particular interests in business by more extensive recommendation, and the increase of our influence in public affairs, and our power of doing good by spreading through the several clubs the sentiments of the Junto.

The project was approved, and every member undertook to form his club, but they did not all succeed. Five or six only were completed, which were called by different names, as the Vine, the Union, the Band, etc. They were useful to themselves, and afforded us a good deal of amusement, information, and instruction, besides answering, in some considerable degree, our views of influencing the public opinion on particular occasions, of which I shall give some instances in course of time as they happened.

My first promotion was my being chosen, in 1736, clerk of the General Assembly. The choice was made that year without opposition; but the year following, when I was again proposed (the choice like that of the members, being annual), a new member made a long speech against me, in order to favor some other candidate. I was, however, chosen, which was the more agreeable to me, as, besides the pay for the immediate service as clerk, the place gave me a better opportunity of keeping up an interest among the members, which secured to me the business of printing the votes, laws, paper money, and other occasional jobs for the public, that, on the whole, were very profitable.

I therefore did not like the opposition of this new member, who was a gentleman of fortune and education, with talents that were likely to give him, in time, great influence in the House, which, indeed, afterwards happened. I did not, however, aim at gaining his favor by paying any servile respect to him, but after some time, took this other method. Having heard that he had in his library a certain very scarce and curious book, I wrote a note to him, expressing my desire of perusing that book, and requesting he would do me the favor of lending it to me for a few days. He sent it immediately, and I returned it in about a week with another note, expressing strongly my sense of the favor. When we next met in the House, he spoke to me (which he had never done before), and with great civility; and he ever after manifested a readiness to serve me on all occasions, so that we became great friends, and our friendship continued to his death. This is another instance of the truth of an old maxim I had learned, which says, "He that has once done you a kindness will be more ready to do you another, than he whom you yourself have obliged." And it shows how much more profitable it is prudently to remove than to resent, return, and continue inimical proceedings.

In 1737 Colonel Spotswood, late governor of Virginia, and then postmaster-general, being dissatisfied with the conduct of his deputy at Philadelphia respecting some negligence in rendering and inexactitude of his accounts, took from him the commission and offered it to me. I accepted it readily, and found it of great advantage; for though the salary was small, it facilitated the correspondence that improved my newspaper, increased the number demanded, as well as the advertisements to be inserted, so that it came to afford me a considerable income. My old competitor's newspaper declined proportionately, and I was satisfied without retaliating his refusal, while postmaster, to permit my papers being carried by the riders. Thus he suffered greatly from his neglect in due accounting; and I mention it as a lesson to those young men who may be employed in managing affairs for others, that they should always render accounts and make remittances with great clearness and punctuality. The character of observing such a conduct is the most powerful of all recommendations to new employments and increase of business.

I began now to turn my thoughts a little to public affairs, beginning, however, with small matters. The city watch was one of the first things that I conceived to want regulation. It was managed by the constables of the respective wards in turn; the constable warned a number of housekeepers to attend him for the night. Those who chose never to attend, paid him six shillings a year to be excused, which was supposed to be for hiring substitutes, but was, in reality, much more than was necessary for that purpose, and made the constableship a place of profit; and the constable, for a little drink, often got such ragamuffins about him as a watch that respectable housekeepers did not choose to mix with. Walking the rounds, too, was often neglected, and most of the nights spent in tippling. I thereupon wrote a paper to be read in Junto, representing these irregularities, but insisting more particularly on the inequality of this six-shilling tax of the constables, respecting the circumstances of those who paid it, since a poor widow housekeeper, all whose property to be guarded by the watch did not perhaps exceed the value of fifty pounds, paid as much as the wealthiest merchant, who had thousands of pounds' worth of goods in his stores.

On the whole, I proposed as a more effectual watch, the hiring of proper men to serve constantly in that business; and as a more equitable way of supporting the charge, the levying a tax that should be proportioned to the property. This idea, being approved by the Junto, was communicated to the other clubs, but as arising in each of them; and though the plan was not immediately carried into execution, yet by preparing the minds of people for the change, it paved the way for the law obtained a few years after, when the members of our clubs were grown into more influence.

About this time I wrote a paper (first to be read in Junto, but it was afterwards published) on the different accidents and carelessnesses by which houses were set on fire, with cautions against them, and means proposed of avoiding them. This was much spoken of as a useful piece, and gave rise to a project, which soon followed it, of forming a company for the more ready extinguishing of fires, and mutual assistance in removing and securing of goods when in danger. Associates in this scheme were presently found, amounting to thirty. Our articles of agreement obliged every member to keep always in good order, and fit for use, a certain number of leather buckets, with strong bags and baskets (for packing and transporting of goods), which were to be brought to every fire; and we agreed to meet once a month to spend a social evening together, in discoursing and communicating such ideas as occurred to us upon the subject of fires, as might be useful in our conduct on such occasions.

The utility of this institution soon appeared, and many more desiring to be admitted than we thought convenient for one company, they were advised to form another, which was accordingly done; and this went on, one new company being formed after another, till they became so numerous as to include most of the inhabitants who were men of property; and now, at the time of my writing this, though upward of fifty years since its establishment, that which I first formed, called the Union Fire Company, still subsists and flourishes, though the first members are all deceased but myself and one, who is older by a year than I am. The small fines that have been paid by members for absence at the monthly meetings have been applied to the purchase of fire-engines, ladders, fire-hooks, and other useful implements for each company, so that I question whether there is a city in the world better provided with the means of putting a stop to beginning conflagrations; and, in fact, since these institutions, the city has never lost by fire more than one or two houses at a time, and the flames have often been extinguished before the house in which they began has been half consumed.

In 1739 arrived among us from Ireland the Reverend Mr. Whitefield, who had made himself remarkable there as an itinerant preacher. He was at first permitted to preach in some of our churches; but the clergy taking a dislike to him soon refused him their pulpits, and he was obliged to preach in the fields. The multitudes of all sects and denominations that attended his sermons were enormous, and it was matter of speculation to me, who was one of the number, to observe the extraordinary influence of his oratory on his hearers, and how much they admired and respected him, notwithstanding his common abuse of them, by assuring them they were naturally *half beasts and half devils*. It was wonderful to see the change soon made in the manners of our inhabitants. From being thoughtless or indifferent about religion, it seemed as if all the world were growing religious, so that one could not walk through the town in an evening without hearing psalms sung in different families of every street.

And it being found inconvenient to assemble in the open air, subject to its inclemencies, the building of a house to meet in was no sooner proposed, and persons appointed to receive contributions, but sufficient sums were soon received to procure the ground and erect the building, which was one hundred feet long and seventy broad, about the size of Westminster Hall; and the work was carried on with such spirit as to be finished in a much shorter time than could have been expected. Both house and ground were vested in trustees, expressly for the use of any preacher of any religious persuasion who might desire to say something to the people at Philadelphia; the design in building not being to accommodate any particular sect, but the inhabitants in general; so that even if the Mufti of Constantinople were to send a missionary to preach Mohammedanism to us, he would find a pulpit at his service.

Mr. Whitefield, in leaving us, went preaching all the way through the colonies to Georgia. The settlement of that province had lately been begun, but, instead of being made with hardy, industrious husbandmen, accustomed to labor, the only people fit for such an enterprise, it was with families of broken shop-keepers and other insolvent debtors, many of indolent and idle habits, taken out of the jails, who, being set down in the woods, unqualified for clearing land, and unable to endure the hardships of a new settlement, perished in numbers, leaving many helpless children unprovided for. The sight of their miserable situation inspired the benevolent heart of Mr. Whitefield with the idea of building an Orphan House there, in which they might be supported and educated. Returning northward, he preached up this charity, and made large collections, for his eloquence had a wonderful power over the hearts and purses of his hearers, of which I myself was an instance.

I did not disapprove of the design, but, as Georgia was then destitute of materials and workmen, and it was proposed to send them from Philadelphia at a great expense, I thought it would have been better to have built the house here, and brought the children to it. This I advised; but he was resolute in his first project, rejected my counsel, and I therefore refused to contribute. I happened soon after to attend one of his sermons, in the course of which I perceived he intended to finish with a collection, and I silently resolved he should get nothing from me. I had in my pocket a handful of copper money, three or four silver dollars, and five pistoles in gold. As he proceeded I began to soften, and concluded to give the coppers. Another stroke of his oratory made me ashamed of that, and determined me to give the silver; and he finished so admirably, that I emptied my pocket wholly into the collector's dish, gold and all. At this sermon there was also one of our club, who, being of my sentiments respecting the building in Georgia, and suspecting a collection might be intended, had, by precaution, emptied his pockets before he came from home. Towards the conclusion of the discourse, however, he felt a strong desire to give, and applied to a neighbor, who stood near him, to borrow some money for the purpose. The application was unfortunately [made] to perhaps the only man in the company who had the firmness not to be affected by the preacher. His answer was, "At any other time, Friend Hopkinson, I would lend to thee freely; but not now, for thee seems to be out of thy right senses."

Some of Mr. Whitefield's enemies affected to suppose that he would apply these collections to his own private emolument; but I, who was intimately acquainted with him (being employed in printing his Sermons and Journals, etc.), never had the least suspicion of his integrity, but am to this day decidedly of opinion that he was in all his conduct a perfectly *honest man;* and methinks my testimony in his favor ought to have the more weight, as we had no religious connection. He used, indeed, sometimes to pray for my conversion, but never had the satisfaction of believing that his prayers were heard. Ours was a mere civil friendship, sincere on both sides, and lasted to his death.

The following instance will show something of the terms on which we stood. Upon one of his arrivals from England at Boston, he wrote to me that he should come soon to Philadelphia, but knew not where he could lodge when there, as he understood his old friend and host, Mr. Benezet, was removed to Germantown. My answer was, "You know my house; if you can make shift with its scanty accommodations, you will be most heartily welcome." He replied, that if I made that kind offer for Christ's sake, I should not miss of a reward. And I returned, "Don't let me be mistaken; it was not for Christ's sake, but for your sake." One of our common acquaintance jocosely remarked that, knowing it to be the custom of the saints, when they received any favor, to shift the burden of the obligation from off their own shoulders, and place it in heaven, I had contrived to fix it on earth.

The last time I saw Mr. Whitefield was in London, when he consulted me about his Orphan House concern, and his purpose of appropriating it to the establishment of a college.

He had a loud and clear voice, and articulated his words and sentences so perfectly, that he might be heard and understood at a great distance, especially as his auditories, however numerous, observed the most exact silence. He preached one evening from the top of the Courthouse steps, which are in the middle of Market Street, and on the west side of Second Street, which crosses it at right angles. Both streets were filled with his hearers to a considerable distance. Being among the hindmost in Market Street, I had the curiosity to learn how far he could be heard, by retiring backwards down the street towards the river; and I found his voice distinct till I came near Front Street, when some noise in that street obscured it. Imagining then a semi-circle, of which my distance should be the radius, and that it were filled with auditors, to each of whom I allowed two square feet, I computed that he might well be heard by more than thirty thousand. This reconciled me to the newspaper accounts of his having preached to twenty-five thousand people in the fields, and to the ancient histories of generals haranguing whole armies, of which I had sometimes doubted.

By hearing him often, I came to distinguish easily between sermons newly composed, and those which he had often preached in the course of his travels. His delivery of the latter was so improved by frequent repetitions that every accent, every emphasis, every modulation of voice, was so perfectly well turned and well placed that, without being interested in the subject, one could not help being pleased with the discourse; a pleasure of much the same kind with that received from an excellent piece of music. This is an advantage itinerant preachers have over those who are stationary, as the latter can not well improve their delivery of a sermon by so many rehearsals.

His writing and printing from time to time gave great advantage to his enemies; unguarded expressions, and even erroneous opinions delivered in preaching, might have been afterwards explained or qualified by supposing others that might have accompanied them, or they might have been denied; but *litera scripta manet.* Critics attacked his writing violently, and with so much appearance of reason as to diminish the number of his votaries and prevent their increase; so that I am of opinion if he had never written anything, he would have left behind him a much more numerous and important sect, and his reputation might in that case have been still growing, even after his death, as there being nothing of his writing on which to found a censure and give him a lower character, his proselytes would be left at liberty to feign for him as great a variety of excellences as their enthusiastic admiration might wish him to have possessed.

My business was now continually augmenting, and my circumstances growing daily easier, my newspaper having become very profitable, as being for a time almost the only one in this and the neighboring provinces. I experienced, too, the truth of the observation, "that after getting the first hundred pound, it is more easy to get the second," money itself being of a prolific nature.

The partnership at Carolina having succeeded, I was encouraged to engage in others, and to promote several of my workmen, who had behaved well, by establishing them with printing-houses in different colonies, on the same terms with that in Carolina. Most of them did well, being enabled at the end of our term, six years, to purchase the types of me, and go on working for themselves, by which means several families were raised. Partnerships often finish in quarrels; but I was happy in this, that mine were all carried on and ended amicably, owing, I think, a good deal to the precaution of having very explicitly settled, in our articles, everything to be done by or expected from each partner, so that there was nothing to dispute, which precaution I would therefore recommend to all who enter into partnerships; for, whatever esteem partners may have for, and confidence in each other at the time of the contract, little jealousies and disgusts may arise, with ideas of inequality in the care and burden of the business, etc., which are attended often with breach of friendship and of the connection, perhaps with lawsuits and other disagreeable consequences.

I had, on the whole, abundant reason to be satisfied with my being established in Pennsylvania. There were, however, two things that I regretted, there being no provision for defense, nor for a complete education of youth; no militia, nor any college. I therefore, in 1743, drew up a proposal for establishing an academy; and at that time, thinking the Reverend Mr. Peters, who was out of employ, a fit person to superintend such an institution, I communicated the project to him; but he, having more profitable views in the service of the proprietaries, which succeeded, declined the undertaking; and, not knowing another at that time suitable for such a trust, I let the scheme lie a while dormant. I succeeded better the next year, 1744, in proposing and establishing a Philosophical Society. The paper I wrote for that purpose will be found among my writings, when collected.

With respect to defense, Spain having been several years at war against Great Britain, and being at length joined by France, which brought us into great danger; and the labored and long-continued endeavor of our governor, Thomas, to prevail with our Quaker Assembly to pass a militia law, and make other provisions for the security of the province, having proved abortive, I determined to try what might be done by a voluntary association of the people. To promote this, I first wrote and published a pamphlet, entitled *Plain Truth,* in which I stated our defenseless situation in strong lights, with the necessity of union and discipline for our defense, and promised to propose in a few days an association to be generally signed for that purpose. The pamphlet had a sudden and surprising effect. I was called upon for the instrument of association, and having settled the draft of it with a few friends, I appointed a meeting of the citizens in the large building before mentioned. The house was pretty full; I had prepared a number of printed copies, and provided pens and ink dispersed all over the room. I harangued them a little on the subject, read the paper, and explained it, and then distributed the copies, which were eagerly signed, not the least objection being made.

When the company separated, and the papers were collected, we found above twelve hundred hands; and other copies being dispersed in the country, the subscribers amounted at length to upward of ten thousand. These all furnished themselves as soon as they could with arms, formed themselves into companies and regiments, chose their own officers, and met every week to be instructed in the manual exercise, and other parts of military discipline. The women, by subscriptions among themselves, provided silk colors, which they presented to the companies, painted with different devices and mottoes, which I supplied.

The officers of the companies composing the Philadelphia regiment being met, chose me for their colonel; but, conceiving myself unfit, I declined that station, and recommended Mr. Lawrence, a fine person, and man of influence, who was accordingly appointed. I then proposed a lottery to defray the expense of building a battery below the town, and furnishing it with cannon. It filled expeditiously, and the battery was soon erected, the merlons being framed of logs and filled with earth. We bought some old cannon from Boston, but, these not being sufficient, we wrote to England for more, soliciting, at the same time, our proprietaries for some assistance, though without much expectation of obtaining it.

Meanwhile, Colonel Lawrence, William Allen, Abram Taylor, Esq., and myself were sent to New York by the associators, commissioned to borrow some cannon of Governor Clinton. He at first refused us peremptorily; but at dinner with his council, where there was great drinking of Madeira wine, as the custom of that place then was, he softened by degrees, and said he would lend us six. After a few more bumpers he advanced to ten; and at length he very good-naturedly conceded eighteen. They were fine cannon, eighteen-pounders, with their carriages, which we soon transported and mounted on our battery, where the associators kept a nightly guard while the war lasted, and among the rest I regularly took my turn of duty there as a common soldier.

My activity in these operations was agreeable to the Governor and council; they took me into confidence, and I was consulted by them in every measure wherein their concurrence was thought useful to the association. Calling in the aid of religion, I proposed to them the proclaiming a fast to promote reformation and implore the blessing of Heaven on our undertaking. They embraced the motion, but, as it was the first fast ever thought of in the province, the secretary had no precedent from which to draw the proclamation. My education in New England, where a fast is proclaimed every year, was here of some advantage: I drew it in the accustomed style, it was translated into German, printed in both languages, and divulged through the province. This gave the clergy of the different sects an opportunity of influencing their congregations to join in the association, and it would probably have been general among all but Quakers if the peace had not soon intervened.

It was thought by some of my friends that, by my activity in these affairs, I should offend that sect, and thereby lose my interest in the Assembly of the province, where they formed a great majority. A young gentleman who had likewise some friends in the House, and wished to succeed me as their clerk, acquainted me that it was decided to displace me at the next election and he, therefore, in good will, advised me to resign, as more consistent with my honor than being turned out. My answer to him was, that I had read or heard of some public man who made it a rule never to ask for an office, and never to refuse one when offered to him. "I approve," says I, "of his rule, and will practice it with a small addition; I shall never *ask*, never *refuse*, nor ever *resign* an office. If they will have my office of clerk to dispose of to another, they shall take it from me. I will not, by giving it up, lose my right of some time or other making reprisals on my adversaries." I heard, however, no more of this; I was chosen again, unanimously as usual, at the next election. Possibly, as they disliked my late intimacy with the members of council, who had joined the governors in all the disputes about military preparations, with which the House had long been harassed, they might have been pleased if I would voluntarily have left them; but they did not care to displace me on account merely of my zeal for the association, and they could not well give another reason.

Indeed I had some cause to believe that the defense of the country was not disagreeable to any of them, provided they were not required to assist in it. And I found that a much greater number of them than I could have imagined, though against offensive war, were clearly for the defensive: Many pamphlets pro and con were published on the subject, and some by good Quakers, in favor of defense, which I believe convinced most of their younger people.

A transaction in our fire company gave me some insight into their prevailing sentiments. It had been proposed that we should encourage the scheme for building a battery by laying out the present stock, then about sixty pounds, in tickets of the lottery. By our rules, no money could be disposed of till the next meeting after the proposal. The company consisted of thirty members, of which twenty-two were Quakers, and eight only of other persuasions. We eight punctually attended the meeting; but, though we thought that some of the Quakers would join us, we were by no means sure of a majority. Only one Quaker, Mr. James Morris, appeared to oppose the measure. He expressed much sorrow that it had ever been proposed, as he said Friends were all against it, and it would create such discord as might break up the company. We told him that we saw no reason for that; we were the minority, and if Friends were against the measure, and outvoted us, we must and should, agreeably to the usage of all societies, submit. When the hour for business arrived it was moved to put the vote; he allowed we might then do it by the rules, but, as he could assure us that a number of members intended to be present for the purpose of opposing it, it would be but candid to allow a little time for their appearing.

While we were disputing this, a waiter came to tell me two gentlemen below desired to speak with me. I went down and found they were two of our Quaker members. They told me there were eight of them assembled at a tavern just by; that they were determined to come and vote with us if there should be occasion, which they hoped would not be the case, and desired we would not call for their assistance if we could do without it, as their voting for such a measure might embroil them with their elders and friends. Being thus secure of a majority. I went up, and after a little seeming hesitation, agreed to a delay of another hour. This Mr. Morris allowed to be extremely fair. Not one of his opposing friends appeared, at which he expressed great surprise; and, at the expiration of the hour, we carried the resolution eight to one; and as, of the twenty-two Quakers, eight were ready to vote with us, and thirteen, by their absence, manifested that they were not inclined to oppose the measure, I afterwards estimated the proportion of Quakers sincerely against defense as one to twenty-one only; for these were all regular members of that society, and in good reputation among them, and had due notice of what was proposed at that meeting.

The honorable and learned Mr. Logan, who had always been of that sect, was one who wrote an address to them, declaring his approbation of defensive war, and supporting his opinion by many strong arguments. He put into my hands sixty pounds to be laid out in lottery tickets for the battery, with direction, to apply what prizes might be drawn wholly to that service. He told me the following anecdote of his old master, William Penn, respecting defense. He came over from England, when a young man, with that proprietary, and as his secretary. It was wartime, and their ship was chased by an armed vessel, supposed to be an enemy. Their captain prepared for defense; but told William Penn, and his company of Quakers, that he did not expect their assistance, and they might retire into the cabin, which they did, except James Logan, who chose to stay upon deck, and was quartered to a gun. The supposed enemy proved a friend, so there was no fighting; but when the secretary went down to communicate the intelligence, William Penn rebuked him severely for staying upon deck, and undertaking to assist in defending the vessel, contrary to the principles of Friends, especially as it had not been required by the captain. This reproof, being before all the company, piqued the secretary who answered, "I being thy servant, why did thee not order me to come down? But thee was willing enough that I should stay and help to fight the ship when thee thought there was danger."

My being many years in the Assembly, the majority of which were constantly Quakers, gave me frequent opportunities of seeing the embarrassment given them by their principle against war, whenever application was made to them, by order of the Crown, to grant aids for military purposes. They were unwilling to offend government, on the one hand, by a direct refusal; and their friends, the body of the Quakers, on the other, by a compliance contrary to their principles; hence a variety of evasions to avoid complying, and modes of disguising the compliance when it became unavoidable. The common mode at last was, to grant money under the phrase of its being "for the King's use," and never to inquire how it was applied.

But, if the demand was not directly from the Crown, that phrase was found not so proper, and some other was to be invented. As, when powder was wanting (I think it was for the garrison at Louisburg), and the government of New England solicited a grant of some from Pennsylvania, which was much urged on the House by Governor Thomas, they could not grant money to buy powder, because that was an ingredient of war; but they voted an aid to New England of three thousand pounds, to be put into the hands of the Governor, and appropriated it for the purchasing of bread, flour wheat, or *other grain*. Some of the council, desirous of giving the House still further embarrassment, advised the Governor not to accept provision, as not being the thing he had demanded; but he replied, "I shall take the money, for I understand very well their meaning; other grain is gunpowder," which he accordingly bought, and they never objected to it.

It was in allusion to this fact that, when in our fire company we feared the success of our proposal in favor of the lottery, and I had said to my friend Mr. Syng, one of our members, "If we fail, let us move the purchase of a fire-engine with the money; the Quakers can have no objection to that; and then, if you nominate me and I you as a committee for that purpose, we will buy a great gun, which is certainly a *fire-engine*." "I see," says he, "you have improved by being so long in the Assembly; your equivocal project would be just a match for their wheat or *other grain*."

These embarrassments that the Quakers suffered from having established and published it as one of their principles that no kind of war was lawful, and which, being once published, they could not afterwards, however they might change their minds, easily get rid of, reminds me of what I think a more prudent conduct in another sect among us, that of the Dunkers. I was acquainted with one of its founders, Michael Welfare, soon after it appeared. He complained to me that they were grievously calumniated by the zealots of other persuasions, and charged with abominable principles and practices, to which they were utter strangers. I told him this had always been the case with new sects, and that, to put a stop to such abuse, I imagined it might be well to publish the articles of their belief, and the rules of their discipline. He said that it had been proposed among them, but not agreed to, for this reason: "When we were first drawn together as a society," says he, "it had pleased God to enlighten our minds so far as to see that some doctrines, which we once esteemed truths, were errors; and that others, which we had esteemed errors, were real truths. From time to time He has been pleased to afford us farther light, and our principles have been improving, and our errors diminishing. Now we are not sure that we are arrived at the end of this progression, and at the perfection of spiritual or theological knowledge; and we fear that, if we should once print our confession of faith, we should feel ourselves as if bound and confined by it, and perhaps be unwilling to receive farther improvement, and our successors still more so, as conceiving what we their elders and founders had done, to be something sacred, never to be departed from."

This modesty in a sect is perhaps a singular instance in the history of mankind, every other sect supposing itself in possession of all truth, and that those who differ are so far in the wrong; like a man

111

traveling in foggy weather, those at some distance before him on the road he sees wrapped up in the fog, as well as those behind him, and also the people in the fields on each side, but near him all appears clear, though in truth he is as much in the fog as any of them. To avoid this kind of embarrassment, the Quakers have of late years been gradually declining the public service in the Assembly and in the magistracy, choosing rather to quit their power than their principle.

In order of time, I should have mentioned before, that having, in 1742, invented an open stove for the better warming of rooms, and at the same time saving fuel, as the fresh air admitted was warmed on entering, I made a present of the model to Mr. Robert Grace, one of my early friends, who, having an iron-furnace, found the casting of the plates for these stoves a profitable thing, as they were growing in demand. To promote that demand, I wrote and published a pamphlet, entitled *An Account of the new-invented Pennsylvania Fireplaces; wherein their Construction and Manner of Operation is particularly explained; their Advantages above every other Method of warming Rooms demonstrated; and all Objections that have been raised against the Use of them answered and obviated,* etc. This pamphlet had a good effect. Governor Thomas was so pleased with the construction of this stove, as described in it, that he offered to give me a patent for the sole vending of them for a term of years; but I declined it from a principle which has ever weighed with me on such occasions, viz., That, as we enjoy great advantages from the inventions of others, we should be glad of an opportunity to serve others by any invention of ours; and this we should do freely and generously.

An ironmonger in London, however, assuming a good deal of my pamphlet, and working it up into his own, and making some small changes in the machine, which rather hurt its operation, got a patent for it there, and made, as I was told, a little fortune by it. And this is not the only instance of patents taken out for my inventions by others, though not always with the same success, which I never contested, as having no desire of profiting by patents myself, and hating disputes. The use of these fireplaces in very many houses, both of this and the neighboring colonies, has been, and is, a great saving of wood to the inhabitants.

Peace being concluded, and the association business therefore at an end, I turned my thoughts again to the affair of establishing an academy. The first step I took was to associate in the design a number of active friends, of whom the Junto furnished a good part; the next was to write and publish a pamphlet, entitled *Proposals Relating to the Education of Youth in Pennsylvania*. This I distributed among the principal inhabitants gratis; and as soon as I could suppose their minds a little prepared by the perusal of it, I set on foot a subscription for opening and supporting an academy; it was to be paid in quotas yearly for five years; by so dividing it, I judged the subscription might be larger, and I believe it was so, amounting to no less, if I remember right, than five thousand pounds.

In the introduction to these proposals, I stated their publication, not as an act of mine, but of some *public-spirited gentlemen*, avoiding as much as I could, according to my usual rule, the presenting myself to the public as the author of any scheme for their benefit.

The subscribers, to carry the project into immediate execution, chose out of their number twenty-four trustees, and appointed Mr. Francis, then attorney-general, and myself to draw up constitutions for the government of the academy; which being done and signed, a house was hired, masters engaged, and the schools opened, I think, in the same year, 1749.

The scholars increasing fast, the house was soon found too small, and we were looking out for a piece of ground, properly situated, with intention to build, when Providence threw into our way a large house ready built, which, with a few alterations, might well serve our purpose. This was the building before mentioned, erected by the hearers of Mr. Whitefield, and was obtained for us in the following manner.

It is to be noted that the contributions to this building being made by people of different sects, care was taken in the nomination of trustees, in whom the building and ground was to be vested, that a predominancy should not be given to any sect, lest in time that predominancy might be a means of appropriating the whole to the use of such sect, contrary to the original intention. It was therefore that one of each sect was appointed, viz., one Church-of-England man, one Presbyterian, one Baptist, one Moravian, etc.; those, in case of vacancy by death, were to fill it by election from among the contributors. The Moravian happened not to please his colleagues, and on his death they resolved to have no other of that sect. The difficulty then was, how to avoid having two of some other sect, by means of the new choice.

Several persons were named, and for that reason not agreed to. At length one mentioned me, with the observation that I was merely an honest man, and of no sect at all, which prevailed with them to choose me. The enthusiasm which existed when the house was built had long since abated, and its trustees had not been able to procure fresh contributions for paying the ground-rent and discharging some other debts the building had occasioned, which embarrassed them greatly. Being now a member of both sets of trustees, that for the building and that for the academy, I had a good opportunity of negotiating with both, and brought them finally to an agreement, by which the trustees for the building were to cede it to those of the academy, the latter undertaking to discharge the debt, to keep forever open in the building a large hall for occasional preachers, according to the original intention, and maintain a free school for the instruction of poor children. Writings were accordingly drawn, and on paying the debts the trustees of the academy were put in possession of the premises; and by dividing the great and lofty hall into stories, and different rooms above and below for the several schools, and purchasing some additional ground, the whole was soon made fit for our purpose, and the scholars removed into the building. The care and trouble of agreeing with the workmen, purchasing materials, and superintending the work, fell upon me; and I went through it the more cheerfully, as it did not then interfere with my private business, having the year before taken a very able, industrious, and honest partner, Mr. David Hall, with whose character I was well acquainted, as he had worked for me four years. He took off my hands all care of the printing-office, paying me punctually my share of the profits. This partnership continued eighteen years, successfully for us both.

The trustees of the academy, after a while, were incorporated by a charter from the governor; their funds were increased by contributions in Britain and grants of land from the prorietaries, to which the Assembly has since made considerable addition; and thus was established the present University of Philadelphia. I have been continued one of its trustees from the beginning, now near forty years, and have had the very great pleasure of seeing a number of the youth who have received their education in it distinguished by their improved abilities, serviceable in public stations, and ornaments to their country.

When I disengaged myself, as above mentioned, from private business, I flattered myself that, by the sufficient though moderate fortune I had acquired, I had secured leisure during the rest of my life for philosophical studies and amusements. I purchased all Dr. Spence's apparatus, who had come from England to lecture here, and I proceeded in my electrical experiments with great alacrity; but the public now considering me as a man of leisure laid hold of me for their purposes, every part of our civil government, and almost at the same time, imposing some duty upon me. The governor put me into the commission of the peace; the corporation of the city chose me of the common council, and soon after an alderman; and the citizens at large chose me a burgess to represent them in Assembly. This latter station was the more agreeable to me, as I was at length tired with sitting there to hear debates, in which, as clerk, I could take no part, and which were often so unentertaining that I was induced to amuse myself with making magic squares or circles or anything to avoid weariness; and I conceived my becoming a member would enlarge my power of doing good. I would not, however, insinuate that my ambition was not flattered by all these promotions; it certainly was; for, considering my low beginning, they were great things to me; and they were still more pleasing, as being so many spontaneous testimonies of the public good opinion, and by me entirely unsolicited.

The office of justice of the peace I tried a little, by attending a few courts, and sitting on the bench to hear causes; but finding that more knowledge of the common law than I possessed was necessary to act in that station with credit, I gradually withdrew from it, excusing myself by my being obliged to attend the higher duties of a legislator in the Assembly. My election to this trust was repeated every year for ten years, without my ever asking any elector for his vote, or signifiying, either directly or indirectly, any desire of being chosen. On taking my seat in the House, my son was appointed their clerk.

The year following, a treaty being to be held with the Indians at Carlisle, the Governor sent a message to the House, proposing that they should nominate some of their members, to be joined with some members of council, as commissioners for that purpose. The House named the speaker (Mr. Norris) and myself; and, being commissioned, we went to Carlisle, and met the Indians accordingly.

As those people are extremely apt to get drunk, and, when so, are very quarrelsome and disorderly, we strictly forbade the selling any liquor to them; and when they complained of this restriction, we told them that if they would continue sober during the treaty, we would give them plenty of rum when business was over. They promised this, and they kept their promise, because they could get no liquor, and the treaty was conducted very orderly, and concluded to mutual satisfaction. They then claimed and received the rum; this was in the afternoon: they were near one hundred men, women, and children, and were lodged in temporary cabins, built in the form of a square, just without the town. In the evening, hearing a great noise among them, the commissioners walked out to see what was the matter. We found they had made a great bonfire in the middle of the square; they were all drunk, men and women, quarreling and fighting. Their dark-colored bodies, half naked, seen only by the gloomy light of the bonfire, running after and beating one another with firebrands, accompanied by their horrid yellings, formed a scene the most resembling our ideas of hell that could well be imagined; there was no appeasing the tumult, and we retired to our lodging. At midnight a number of them came thundering at our door, demanding more rum, of which we took no notice.

The next day, sensible they had misbehaved in giving us that disturbance, they sent three of their old counselors to make their apology. The orator acknowledged the fault, but laid it upon the rum; and then endeavored to excuse the rum by saying, "The Great Spirit, who made all things, made everything for some use, and whatever use he designed any thing for, that use it should always be put to. Now, when he made rum, he said, 'Let this be for the Indians to get drunk with,' and it must be so." And, indeed, if it be the design of Providence to extirpate these savages in order to make room for cultivators of the earth, it seems not improbable that rum may be the appointed means. It has already annihilated all the tribes who formerly inhabited the sea-coast.

In 1751, Dr. Thomas Bond, a particular friend of mine, conceived the idea of establishing a hospital in Philadelphia (a very beneficent design, which has been ascribed to me, but was originally his), for the reception and cure of poor sick persons, whether inhabitants of the province or strangers. He was zealous and active in endeavoring to procure subscriptions for it, but the proposal being a novelty in America, and at first not well understood, he met with but small success.

At length he came to me with the compliment that he found there was no such thing as carrying a public-spirited project through without my being concerned in it. "For," says he, "I am often asked by those to whom I propose subscribing, Have you consulted Franklin upon this business? And what does he think of it? And when I tell them that I have not (supposing it rather out of your line), they do not subscribe, but say they will consider of it." I inquired into the nature and probable utility of his scheme, and receiving from him a very satisfactory explanation, I not only subscribed to it myself, but engaged heartily in the design of procuring subscriptions from others. Previously, however, to the solicitation, I endeavored to prepare the minds of the people by writing on the subject in the newspapers, which was my usual custom in such cases, but which he had omitted.

The subscriptions afterwards were more free and generous; but, beginning to flag, I saw they would be insufficient without some assistance from the Assembly, and therefore proposed to petition for it, which was done. The country members did not at first relish the project; they objected that it could only be serviceable to the city, and therefore the citizens alone should be at the expense of it; and they doubted whether the citizens themselves generally approved of it. My allegation on the contrary, that it met with such approbation as to leave no doubt of our being able to raise two thousand pounds by voluntary donations, they considered as a most extravagant supposition, and utterly impossible.

On this I formed my plan; and, asking leave to bring in a bill for incorporating the contributors according to the prayer of their petition, and granting them a blank sum of money, which leave was obtained chiefly on the consideration that the House could throw the bill out if they did not like it, I drew it so as to make the important clause a conditional one, viz., "And be it enacted, by the authority aforesaid, that when the said contributors shall have met and chosen their managers and treasurer, *and shall have raised by their contributions a capital stock of ——value* (the yearly interest of which is to be applied to the accommodating of the sick poor in the said hospital, free of charge for diet, attendance, advice, and medicines), *and shall make the same appear to the satisfaction of the speaker of the Assembly for the time being*, that *then* it shall and may be lawful for the said speaker, and he is hereby required, to sign an order on the provincial treasurer for the payment of two thousand pounds, in two yearly payments, to the treasurer of the said hospital, to be applied to the founding, building, and finishing of the same."

This condition carried the bill through; for the members, who had opposed the grant, and now conceived they might have the credit of being charitable without the expense, agreed to its passage; and then, in soliciting subscriptions among the people, we urged the conditional promise of the law as an additional motive to give, since every man's donation would be doubled; thus the clause worked both ways. The subscriptions accordingly soon exceeded the requisite sum, and we claimed and received the public gift, which enabled us to carry the design into execution. A convenient and handsome building was soon erected; the institution has by constant experience been found useful, and flourishes to this day; and I do not remember any of my political maneuvers the success of which gave me at the time more pleasure, or wherein, after thinking of it, I more easily excused myself for having made some use of cunning.

It was about this time that another projector, the Reverend Gilbert Tennent, came to me with a request that I would assist him in procuring a subscription for erecting a new meeting-house. It was to be for the use of a congregation he had gathered among the Presbyterians, who were originally disciples of Mr. Whitefield. Unwilling to make myself disagreeable to my fellow-citizens by too frequently soliciting their contributions, I absolutely refused. He then desired I would furnish him with a list of the names of persons I knew by experience to be generous and public-spirited. I thought it would be unbecoming in me, after their kind compliance with my solicitations, to mark them out to be worried by other beggars, and therefore refused also to give such a list. He then desired I would at least give him my advice. "That I will readily do," said I; "and, in the first place, I advise you to apply to all those whom you know will give something; next, to those whom you are uncertain whether they will give anything or not, and show them the list of those who have given; and, lastly, do not neglect those who you are sure will give nothing, for in some of them you may be mistaken." He laughed and thanked me, and said he would take my advice. He did so, for he asked of *everybody*, and he obtained a much larger sum than he expected, with which he erected the capacious and very elegant meeting-house that stands in Arch Street.

Our city, though laid out with a beautiful regularity, the streets large, straight, and crossing each other at right angles, had the disgrace of suffering those streets to remain long unpaved, and in wet weather the wheels of heavy carriages ploughed them into a quagmire, so that it was difficult to cross them; and in dry weather the dust was offensive. I had lived near what was called the Jersey Market, and saw with pain the inhabitants wading in mud while purchasing their provisions. A strip of ground down the middle of that market was at length paved with brick, so that, being once in the market, they had firm footing, but were often over shoes in dirt to get there. By talking and writing on the subject, I was at length instrumental in getting the street paved with stone between the market and the bricked foot-pavement, that was on each side next the houses. This, for some time, gave an easy access to the market dry-shod; but, the rest of the street not being paved, whenever a carriage came out of the mud upon this pavement, it shook off and left its dirt upon it, and it was soon covered with mire, which was not removed, the city as yet having no scavengers.

After some inquiry, I found a poor, industrious man, who was willing to undertake keeping the pavement clean, by sweeping it twice a week, carrying off the dirt from before all the neighbors' doors, for the sum of sixpence per month, to be paid by each house. I then wrote and printed a paper setting forth the advantages to the neighborhood that might be obtained by this small expense; the greater ease in keeping our houses clean, so much dirt not being brought in by people's feet; the benefit to the shops by more custom, etc., etc., as buyers could more easily get at them; and by not having, in windy weather, the dust blown in upon their goods, etc., etc. I sent one of these papers to each house, and in a day or two went round to see who would subscribe an agreement to pay these sixpences; it was unanimously signed, and for a time well executed. All the inhabitants of the city were delighted with the cleanliness of the pavement that surrounded the market, it being a convenience to all, and this raised a general desire to have all the streets paved, and made the people more willing to submit to a tax for that purpose.

After some time I drew a bill for paving the city, and brought it into the Assembly. It was just before I went to England, in 1757, and did not pass till I was gone, and then with an alteration in the mode of assessment, which I thought not for the better, but with an additional provision for lighting as well as paving the streets, which was a great improvement. It was by a private person, the late Mr. John Clifton, his giving a sample of the utility of lamps, by placing one at his door, that the people were first impressed with the idea of enlighting all the city. The honor of this public benefit has also been ascribed to me, but it belongs truly to that gentleman. I did but follow his example, and have only some merit to claim respecting the form of our lamps, as differing from the globe lamps we were at first supplied with from London. Those we found inconvenient in these respects: they admitted no air below; the smoke, therefore, did not readily go out above, but circulated in the globe, lodged on its inside, and soon obstructed the light they were intended to afford; giving, besides, the daily trouble of wiping them clean; and an accidental stroke on one of them would demolish it, and render it totally useless. I therefore suggested the composing them of four flat panes, with a long funnel above to draw up the smoke, and crevices admitting air below, to facilitate the ascent of the smoke; by this means they were kept clean, and did not grow dark in a few hours, as the London lamps do, but continued bright till morning, and an accidental stroke would generally break but a single pane, easily repaired.

I have sometimes wondered that the Londoners did not, from the effect holes in the bottom of the globe lamps used at Vauxhall have in keeping them clean, learn to have such holes in their street lamps. But, these holes being made for another purpose. viz., to communicate flame more suddenly to the wick by a little flax hanging down through them, the other use, of letting in air, seems not to have been thought of; and therefore, after the lamps have been lit a few hours, the streets of London are very poorly illuminated.

The mention of these improvements puts me in mind of one I proposed, when in London, to Dr. Fothergill, who was among the best men I have known, and a great promoter of useful projects. I had observed that the streets, when dry, were never swept, and the light dust carried away; but it was suffered to accumulate till wet weather reduced it to mud, and then, after lying some days so deep on the pavement that there was no crossing but in paths kept clean by poor people with brooms, it was with great labor raked together and thrown up into carts open above, the sides of which suffered some of the slush at every jolt on the pavement to shake out and fall, sometimes to the annoyance of foot-passengers. The reason given for not sweeping the dusty streets was, that the dust would fly into the windows of shops and houses.

An accidental occurrence had instructed me how much sweeping might be done in a little time. I found at my door in Craven Street, one morning, a poor woman sweeping my pavement with a birch broom; she appeared very pale and feeble, as just come out of a fit of sickness. I asked who employed her to sweep there; she said, "Nobody, but I am very poor and in distress, and I sweeps before gentlefolkses doors, and hopes they will give me something." I bid her sweep the whole street clean, and I would give her a shilling; this was at nine o'clock; at twelve she came for the shilling. From the slowness I saw at first in her working, I could scarce believe that the work was done so soon, and sent my servant to examine it, who reported that the whole street was swept perfectly clean, and all the dust placed in the gutter, which was in the middle; and the next rain washed it quite away, so that the pavement and even the kennel were perfectly clean.

I then judged that, if that feeble woman could sweep such a street in three hours, a strong active man might have done it in half the time. And here let me remark the convenience of having but one gutter in such a narrow street, running down its middle, instead of two, one on each side, near the footway; for where all the rain that falls on a street runs from the sides and meets in the middle, it forms there a current strong enough to wash away all the mud it meets with; but when divided into two channels, it is often too weak to cleanse either, and only makes the mud it finds more fluid, so that the wheels of carriages and feet of horses throw and dash it upon the foot-pavement, which is thereby rendered foul and slippery, and sometimes splash it upon those who are walking. My proposal, communicated to the good doctor, was as follows:

"For the more effectual cleaning and keeping clean the streets of London and Westminster, it is proposed that the several watchmen be contracted with to have the dust swept up in dry seasons, and the mud raked up at other times, each in the several streets and lanes of his round; that they be furnished with brooms and other proper instruments for these purposes, to be kept at their respective stands, ready to furnish the poor people they may employ in the service.

"That in the dry summer months the dust be all swept up into heaps at proper distances, before the shops and windows of houses are usually opened, when the scavengers, with close-covered carts, shall also carry it all away.

"That the mud, when raked up, be not left in heaps to be spread abroad again by the wheels of carriages and trampling of horses, but that the scavengers be provided with bodies of carts, not placed high upon wheels, but low upon sliders, with lattice bottoms, which, being covered with straw, will retain the mud thrown into them, and permit the water to drain from it, whereby it will become much lighter, water making the greatest part of its weight; these bodies of cars to be placed at convenient distances, and the mud brought to them in wheel-barrows; they remaining where placed till the mud is drained, and then horses brought to draw them away."

I have since had doubts of the practicability of the later part of this proposal, on account of the narrowness of some streets, and the difficulty of placing the draining-sleds so as not to encumber too much the passage; but I am still of opinion that the former, requiring the dust to be swept up and carried away before the shops are open, is very practicable in the summer, when the days are long; for, in walking through the Strand and Fleet Street one morning at seven o'clock, I observed there was not one shop open, though it had been daylight and the sun up above three hours; the inhabitants of London choosing voluntarily to live much by candle-light, and sleep by sunshine, and yet often complain, a little absurdly, of the duty on candles, and the high price of tallow.

Some may think these trifling matters not worth minding or relating; but when they consider that though dust blown into the eyes of a single person, or into a single shop on a windy day, is but of small importance, yet the great number of the instances in a populous city, and its frequent repetitions give it weight and consequence, perhaps they will not censure very severely those who bestow some attention to affairs of this seemingly low nature. Human felicity is produced not so much by great pieces of good fortune that seldom happen, as by little advantages that occur every day. Thus, if you teach a poor young man to shave himself, and keep his razor in order, you may contribute more to the happiness of his life than in giving him a thousand guineas. The money may be soon spent, the regret only remaining of having foolishly consumed it; but in the other case, he escapes the frequent vexation of waiting for barbers, and of their sometimes dirty fingers, offensive breaths, and dull razors; he shaves when most convenient to him, and enjoys daily the pleasure of its being done with a good instrument. With these senitiments I have hazarded the few preceding pages, hoping they may afford hints which some time or other may be useful to a city I love, having lived many years in it very happily, and perhaps to some of our towns in America.

Having been for some time employed by the postmaster-general of America as his comptroller in regulating several offices, and bringing the officers to account, I was, upon his death in 1753, appointed, jointly with Mr. William Hunter, to succeed him, by a commission from the postmaster-general in England. The American office never had hitherto paid anything to that of Britain. We were to have six hundred pounds a year between us, if we could make that sum out of the profits of the office. To do this, a variety of improvements were necessary; some of these were inevitably at first expensive, so that in the first four years the office became above nine hundred pounds in debt to us. But it soon after began to repay us; and before I was displaced by a freak of the ministers, of which I shall speak hereafter, we had brought it to yield *three times* as much clear revenue to the crown as the postoffice of Ireland. Since that imprudent transaction, they have received from it—not one farthing!

The business of the postoffice occasioned my taking a journey this year to New England, where the College of Cambridge, of their own motion, presented me with the degree of Master of Arts. Yale College, in Connecticut, had before made me a similar compliment. Thus, without studying in any college, I came to partake of their honors. They were conferred in consideration of my improvements and discoveries in the electric branch of natural philosophy.

In 1754, war with France being again apprehended, a congress of commissioners from the different colonies was, by order of the Lord of Trade, to be assembled at Albany, there to confer with the chiefs of the Six Nations concerning the means of defending both their country and ours. Governor Hamilton having received this order acquainted the House with it, requesting they would furnish proper presents for the Indians, to be given on this occasion; and naming the speaker (Mr. Norris) and myself to join Mr. Thomas Penn and Mr. Secretary Peters as commissioners to act for Pennsylvania. The House approved the nomination, and provided the goods for the present, and though they did not much like treating out of the provinces; and we met the other commissioners at Albany about the middle of June.

In our way thither, I projected and drew a plan for the union of all the colonies under one government, so far as might be necessary for defense, and other important general purposes. As we passed through New York, I had there shown my project to Mr. James Alexander and Mr. Kennedy, two gentlemen of great knowledge in public affairs, and, being fortified by their approbation, I ventured to lay it before the Congress. It then appeared that several of the commissioners had formed plans of the same kind. A previous question was first taken, whether a union should be established, which passed in the affirmative unanimously. A committee was then appointed, one member from each colony, to consider the several plans and report. Mine happened to be preferred, and, with a few amendments, was accordingly reported.

By this plan the general government was to be administered by a president-general, appointed and supported by the Crown, and a grand council was to be chosen by the representatives of the people of the several colonies, met in their respective assemblies. The debates upon it in Congress went on daily, hand in hand with the Indian business. Many objections and difficulties were started, but at length they were all overcome, and the plan was unanimously agreed to, and copies ordered to be transmitted to the Board of Trade and to the assemblies of the several provinces. Its fate was singular: the assemblies did not adopt it, as they all thought there was too much *prerogative* in it, and in England it was judged to have too much of the *democratic*. The Board of Trade therefore did not approve of it, nor recommend it for the approbation of His Majesty; but another scheme was formed, supposed to answer the same purpose better, whereby the governors of the provinces, with some members of their respective councils, were to meet and order the raising of troops, building of forts, etc., and to draw on the treasury of Great Britain for the expense, which was afterwards to be refunded by an act of Parliament laying a tax on America. My plan, with my reasons in support of it, is to be found among my political papers that are printed.

Being the winter following in Boston, I had much conversation with Governor Shirley upon both the plans. Part of what passed between us on the occasion may also be seen among those papers. The different and contrary reasons of dislike to my plan makes me suspect that it was really the true medium; and I am still of opinion it would have been happy for both sides the water if it had been adopted. The colonies, so united, would have been sufficiently strong to have defended themselves; there would then have been no need of troops from England; of course, the subsequent pretense for taxing America, and the bloody contest it occasioned, would have been avoided. But such mistakes are not new; history is full of the errors of states and princes.

> "Look around the habitable world, how few
>   Know their own good, or, knowing it, pursue!"

Those who govern, having much business on their hands, do not generally like to take the trouble of considering and carrying into execution new projects. The best public measures are therefore seldom adopted from previous wisdom, but forced by the occasion.

The Governor of Pennsylvania, in sending it down to the Assembly, expressed his approbation of the plan, "as appearing to him to be drawn up with great clearness and strength of judgment, and therefore recommended it as well worthy of their closest and most serious attention." The House, however, by the management of a certain member, took it up when I happened to be absent, which I thought not very fair, and reprobated it without paying any attention to it at all, to my no small mortification.

In my journey to Boston this year, I met at New York with our new governor, Mr. Morris, just arrived there from England, with whom I had been before intimately acquainted. He brought a commission to supersede Mr. Hamilton, who, tired with the disputes his proprietary instructions subjected him to, had resigned. Mr. Morris asked me if I thought he must expect as uncomfortable an administration. I said, "No; you may, on the contrary, have a very comfortable one, if you will only take care not to enter into any dispute with the Assembly." "My dear friend," says he, pleasantly, "how can you advise my avoiding disputes? You know I love disputing; it is one of my greatest pleasures; however, to show the regard I have for your counsel, I promise you I will, if possible, avoid them." He had some reason for loving to dispute, being eloquent, an acute sophister, and, therefore, generally successful in argumentative conversation. He had been brought up to it from a boy, his father, as I have heard, accustoming his children to dispute with one another for his diversion, while sitting at table after dinner; but I think the practice was not wise; for, in the course of my observation, these disputing, contradicting, and confuting people are generally unfortunate in their affairs. They get victory sometimes, but they never get good will, which would be of more use to them. We parted, he going to Philadelphia, and I to Boston.

In returning, I met at New York with the votes of the Assembly, by which it appeared that, notwithstanding his promise to me, he and the House were already in high contention; and it was a continual battle between them as long as he retained the government. I had my share of it; for, as soon as I got back to my seat in the Assembly, I was put on every committee for answering his speeches and messages, and by the committees always desired to make the drafts. Our answers, as well as his messages, were often tart, and sometimes indecently abusive; and, as he knew I wrote for the Assembly, one might have imagined that, when we met, we could hardly avoid cutting throats; but he was so good-natured a man that no personal difference between him and me was occasioned by the contest, and we often dined together.

One afternoon, in the height of this public quarrel, we met in the street. "Franklin," says he, "you must go home with me and spend the evening; I am to have some company that you will like"; and, taking me by the arm, he led me to his house. In gay conversation, over our wine, after supper, he told us, jokingly, that he much admired the idea of Sancho Panza, who, when it was proposed to give him a government, requested it might be a government of *blacks*, as then, if he could not agree with his people, he might sell them. One of his friends, who sat next to me, says, "Franklin, why do you continue to side with these damned Quakers? Had not you better sell them? The proprietor would give you a good price." "The Governor," says I, "has not yet *blacked* them enough." He, indeed, had labored hard to blacken the Assembly in all his messages, but they wiped off his coloring as fast as he laid it on, and placed it, in return, thick upon his own face; so that, finding he was likely to be negrofied himself, he, as well as Mr. Hamilton, grew tired of the contest, and quitted the government.

These public quarrels were all at bottom owing to the proprietaries, our hereditary governors, who, when any expense was to be incurred for the defense of their province, with incredible meanness instructed their deputies to pass no act for levying the necessary taxes, unless their vast estates were in the same act expressly excused; and they had even taken bonds of these deputies to observe such instructions. The Assemblies for three years held out against this injustice, though constrained to bend at last. At length Captain Denny, who was Governor Morris's successor, ventured to disobey those instructions; how that was brought about I shall show hereafter.

But I am got forward too fast with my story: there are still some transactions to be mentioned that happened during the administration of Governor Morris.

War being in a manner commenced with France, the government of Massachusetts Bay projected an attack upon Crown Point, and sent Mr. Quincy to Pennsylvania, and Mr. Pownall, afterward Governor Pownall, to New York, to solicit assistance. As I was in the Assembly, knew its temper, and was Mr. Quincy's countryman, he applied to me for my influence and assistance. I dictated his address to them, which was well received. They voted an aid of ten thousand pounds, to be laid out in provisions. But the Governor refusing his assent to their bill (which included this with other sums granted for the use of the Crown), unless a clause were inserted exempting the proprietary estate from bearing any part of the tax that would be necessary, the Assembly, though very desirous of making their grant to New England effectual, were at a loss how to accomplish it. Mr. Quincy labored hard with the Governor to obtain his assent, but he was obstinate.

I then suggested a method of doing the business without the Governor, by orders on the trustees of the Loan Office, which, by law, the Assembly had the right of drawing. There was, indeed, little or no money at that time in the office, and therefore I proposed that the orders should be payable in a year, and to bear an interest of five per cent. With these orders I supposed the provisions might easily be purchased. The Assembly, with very little hesitation, adopted the proposal. The orders were immediately printed, and I was one of the committee directed to sign and dispose of them. The fund for paying them was the interest of all the paper currency then extant in the province upon loan, together with the revenue arising from the excise, which being known to be more than sufficient, they obtained instant credit, and were not only received in payment for the provisions, but many monied people, who had cash lying by them, vested it in those orders, which they found advantageous, as they bore interest while upon hand, and might on any occasion be used as money; so that they were eagerly all bought up, and in a few weeks none of them were to be seen. Thus this important affair was by my means completed. Mr. Quincy returned thanks to the Assembly in a handsome memorial, went home highly pleased with the success of his embassy, and ever after bore for me the most cordial and affectionate friendship.

The British government, not choosing to permit the union of the colonies as proposed at Albany, and to trust that union with their defense, lest they should thereby grow too military and feel their own strength, suspicions and jealousies at this time being entertained of them, sent over General Braddock with two regiments of regular English troops for that purpose. He landed at Alexandria, in

Virginia, and thence marched to Fredericktown, in Maryland, where he halted for carriages. Our Assembly apprehending from some information that he had conceived violent prejudices against them, as averse to the service, wished me to wait upon him, not as from them, but as postmaster-general, under the guise of proposing to settle with him the mode of conducting with most celerity and certainty the dispatches between him and the governors of the several provinces, with whom he must necessarily have continual correspondence, and of which they proposed to pay the expense. My son accompanied me on this journey.

We found the General at Fredericktown, waiting impatiently for the return of those he had sent through the back parts of Maryland and Virginia to collect wagons. I stayed with him several days, dined with him daily, and had full opportunity of removing all his prejudices by the information of what the Assembly had before his arrival actually done, and were still willing to do, to facilitate his operations. When I was about to depart, the returns of wagons to be obtained were brought in, by which it appeared that they amounted only to twenty-five, and not all of those were in serviceable condition. The General and all the officers were surprised, declared the expedition was then at an end, being impossible, and exclaimed against the ministers for ignorantly landing them in a country destitute of the means of conveying their stores, baggage, etc., not less than one hundred and fifty wagons being necessary.

I happened to say I thought it was pity they had not been landed rather in Pennsylvania, as in that country almost every farmer had his wagon. The General eagerly laid hold of my words, and said, "Then you, sir, who are a man of interest there, can probably procure them for us; and I beg you will undertake it." I asked what terms were to be offered the owners of the wagons; and I was desired to put on paper the terms that appeared to me necessary. This I did, and they were agreed to, and a commission and instructions accordingly prepared immediately. What those terms were will appear in the advertisement I published as soon as I arrived at Lancaster, which being, from the great and sudden effect it produced, a piece of some curiosity, I shall insert it at length, as follows:

"ADVERTISEMENT.

"Lancaster, April 26, 1755.

"Whereas, one hundred and fifty waggons, with four horses to each waggon, and fifteen hundred saddle or pack horses, are wanted for the service of his majesty's forces now about to rendezvous at Will's Creek, and his excellency General Braddock having been pleased to empower me to contract for the hire of the same, I hereby give notice that I shall attend for that purpose at Lancaster from this day to next Wednesday evening, and at York from next Thursday morning till Friday evening, where I shall be ready to agree for waggons and teams, or single horses, on the following terms, viz.: 1. That there shall be paid for each waggon, with four good horses and a driver, fifteen shillings per diem; and for each able horse with a pack-saddle, or other saddle and furniture, two shillings per diem; and for each able horse without a saddle, eighteen pence per diem. 2. That the pay commence from the time of their joining the forces at Will's Creek, which must be on or before the 20th of May ensuing, and that a reasonable allowance be paid over and above for the time necessary for their travelling to Will's Creek and home again after their discharge. 3. Each waggon and team, and every saddle or pack horse, is to be valued by indifferent persons chosen between me and the owner; and in case of the loss of any waggon, team, or other horse in the service, the price according to such valuation is to be allowed and paid. 4. Seven days' pay is to be advanced and paid in hand by me to the owner of each waggon and team, or horse, at the time of contracting, if required, and the remainder to be paid by General Braddock, or by the paymaster of the army, at the time of their discharge, or from time to time, as it shall be demanded. 5. No drivers of waggons, or persons taking care of the hired horses, are on any account to be called upon to do the duty of soldiers, or be otherwise employed than in conducting or taking care of their carriages or horses. 6. All oats, Indian corn, or other forage that waggons or horses bring to the camp, more than is necessary for the subsistence of the horses, is to be taken for the use of the army, and a reasonable price paid for the same.

"Note.—My son, William Franklin, is empowered to enter into like contracts with any person in Cumberland county.

"B. Franklin."

"To the inhabitants of the Counties of Lancaster, York and Cumberland.

"Friends and Countrymen,

"Being occasionally at the camp of Frederic a few days since, I found the general and officers extremely exasperated on account of their not being supplied with horses and carriages, which had been expected from this province, as most able to furnish them; but, through the dissensions between our governor and Assembly, money had not been provided, nor any steps taken for that purpose.

"It was proposed to send an armed force immediately into these counties, to seize as many of the best carriages and horses as should be wanted, and compel as many persons into the service as would be necessary to drive and take care of them.

"I apprehended that the progress of British soldiers through these counties on such an occasion, especially considering the temper they are in, and their resentment against us, would be attended with many and great inconveniences to the inhabitants, and therefore more willingly took the trouble of trying first what might be done by fair and equitable means. The people of these back counties have lately complained to the Assembly that a sufficient currency was wanting; you have an opportunity of receiving and dividing among you a very considerable sum; for, if the service of this expedition should continue, as it is more than probable it will, for one hundred and twenty days, the hire of these waggons and horses will amount to upward of thirty thousand pounds, which will be paid you in silver and gold of the king's money.

"The service will be light and easy, for the army will scarce march above twelve miles per day, and the waggons and baggage-horses, as they carry those things that are absolutely necessary to the welfare of the army, must march with the army, and no faster; and are, for the army's sake, always placed where they can be most secure, whether in a march or in a camp.

"If you are really, as I believe you are, good and loyal subjects to his majesty, you may now do a most acceptable service, and make it easy to yourselves; for three or four of such as can not separately spare from the business of their plantations a waggon and four horses and a driver, may do it together, one furnishing the waggon, another one or two horses, and another the driver, and divide the pay proportionately between you; but if you do not this service to your king and country voluntarily, when such good pay and reasonable terms are offered to you, your loyalty will be strongly suspected. The king's business must be done; so many brave troops, come so far for your defense, must not stand idle through your backwardness to do what may be reasonably expected from you; waggons and horses must be had; violent measures will probably be used, and you will be left to seek for a recompense where you can find it, and your case, perhaps, be little pitied or regarded.

"I have no particular interest in this affair, as, except the satisfaction of endeavoring to do good, I shall have only my labour for my pains. If this method of obtaining the waggons and horses is not likely to succeed, I am obliged to send word to the general in fourteen days; and I suppose Sir John St. Clair, the hussar, with a body of soldiers, will immediately enter the province for the purpose, which I shall be sorry to hear, because I am very sincerely and truly you friend and well-wisher,

"B. FRANKLIN."

I received of the General about eight hundred pounds, to be disbursed in advance-money to the wagon owners, etc.; but that sum being insufficient, I advanced upward of two hundred pounds more, and in two weeks the one hundred and fifty wagons, with two hundred and fifty-nine carrying horses, were on their march for the camp. The advertisement promised payment according to the valuation, in case any wagon or horse should be lost. The owners, however, alleging they did not know General Braddock, or what dependence might be had on his promise, insisted on my bond for the performance, which I accordingly gave them.

While I was at the camp, supping one evening with the officers of Colonel Dunbar's regiment, he represented to me his concern for the subalterns, who, he said, were generally not in affluence and could ill afford, in this dear country, to lay in the stores that might be necessary in so long a march through a wilderness where nothing was to be purchased. I commiserated their case, and resolved to endeavor procuring them some relief. I said nothing, however, to him of my intention, but wrote the next morning to the committee of the Assembly, who had the disposition of some public money, warmly recommending the case of these officers to their consideration, and proposing that a present should be sent them of necessaries and refreshments. My son, who had some experience of a camp life and of its wants, drew up a list for me, which I enclosed in my letter. The committee approved, and used such diligence that, conducted by my son, the stores arrived at the camp as soon as the wagons. They consisted of twenty parcels, each containing

6 lbs. loaf sugar.	1 Gloucester cheese.
6 lbs. good Muscovado do.	1 keg containing 20 lbs. good butter.
1 lb. good green tea.	
1 lb. good bohea do.	2 doz. old Madeira wine.
6 lbs. good ground coffee.	2 gallons Jamaica spirits.
6 lbs. chocolate.	1 bottle flour of mustard.
½ cwt. best white biscuit.	2 well-cured hams.
½ lb. pepper.	½ dozen dried tongues.
1 quart best white wine vinegar.	6 lbs. rice.
	6 lbs. raisins.

These twenty parcels, well packed, were placed on as many horses, each parcel, with the horse, being intended as a present for one officer. They were very thankfully received, and the kindness acknowledged by letters to me from the colonels of both regiments, in the most grateful terms. The General, too, was highly satisfied with my conduct in procuring him the wagons, etc., and readily paid my account of disbursements, thanking me repeatedly, and requesting my farther assistance in sending provisions after him. I undertook this also, and was busily employed in it till we heard of his defeat, advancing for the service of my own money upwards of one thousand pounds sterling, of which I sent him an account. It came to his hands, luckily for me, a few days before the battle, and he returned me immediately an order on the paymaster for the round sum of one thousand pounds, leaving the remainder to the next account. I consider this payment as good luck, having never been able to obtain that remainder, of which more hereafter.

This General was, I think, a brave man, and might probably have made a figure as a good officer in some European war. But he had too much self-confidence, too high an opinion of the validity of regular troops, and too mean a one of both Americans and Indians. George Croghan, our Indian interpreter, joined him on his march with one hundred of those people, who might have been of great use to his army as guides, scouts, etc., if he had treated them kindly; but he slighted and neglected them, and they gradually left him.

In conversation with him one day, he was giving me some account of his intended progress. "After taking Fort Duquesne," says he, "I am to proceed to Niagara; and having taken that to Frontenac, if the season will allow time; and I suppose it will, for Duquesne can hardly detain me above three or four days; and then I see nothing that can obstruct my march to Niagara." Having before revolved in my mind the long line his army must make in their march by a very narrow road, to be cut for them through the woods and bushes, and also what I had read of a former defeat of fifteen hundred French who invaded the Iroquois country, I had conceived some doubts and some fears for the event of the campaign. But I ventured only to say, "To be sure, sir, if you arrive well before Duquesne, with these fine troops, so well provided with artillery, that place, not yet completely fortified, and as we hear with no very strong garrison, can probably make but a short resistance. The only danger I apprehend of obstruction to your march is from ambuscades of Indians, who, by constant practice, are dexterous in laying and executing them; and the slender line, near four miles long, which your army must make, may expose it to be attacked by surprise in its flanks, and to be cut like a thread into several pieces, which, from their distance, can not come up in time to support each other."

He smiled at my ignorance, and replied, "These savages may, indeed, be a formidable enemy to your raw American militia, but upon the king's regular and disciplined troops, sir, it is impossible they should make any impression." I was conscious of an impropriety in my disputing with a military man in matters of his profession, and said no more. The enemy, however, did not take the advantage of his army which I apprehended its long line of march exposed it to, but let it advance without interruption till within nine miles of the place; and then, when more in a body (for it had just passed a river, where the front had halted till all were come over), and in a more open part of the woods than any it had passed, attacked its advanced guard by a heavy fire from behind trees and bushes, which was the first intelligence the general had of an enemy's being near him. This guard being disordered, the general hurried the troops up to their assistance, which was done in great confusion, through wagons, baggage, and cattle; and presently the fire came upon their flank: the officers, being on horseback, were more easily distinguished, picked out as marks, and fell very fast; and the soldiers were crowded together in a huddle, having or hearing no orders, and standing to be shot at till two-thirds of them were killed; and then, being seized with a panic, the whole fled with precipitation.

The wagoners took each a horse out of his team and scampered; their example was immediately followed by others; so that all the wagons, provisions, artillery, and stores were left to the enemy. The General, being wounded, was brought off with difficulty; his secretary, Mr. Shirley, was killed by his side; and out of eighty-six officers, sixty-three were killed or wounded, and seven hundred and fourteen men killed out of eleven hundred. These eleven hundred had been picked men from the whole army; the rest had been left behind with Colonel Dunbar, who was to follow with the heavier part of the stores, provisions, and baggage. The flyers, not being pursued, arrived at Dunbar's camp, and the panic they brought with them instantly seized him and all his people; and, though he had now above one thousand men, and the enemy who had beaten Braddock did not at most exceed four hundred Indians and French together, instead of proceeding and endeavoring to recover some of the lost honor, he ordered all the stores, ammunition, etc., to be destroyed, that he might have more horses to assist his flight towards the settlements, and less lumber to remove. He was there met with requests from the governors of Virginia, Maryland, and Pennsylvania, that he would post his troops on the frontier, so as to afford some protection to the inhabitants; but he continued his hasty march through all the country, not thinking himself safe till he arrived at Philadelphia, where the inhabitants could protect him. This whole transaction gave us Americans the first suspicion that our exalted ideas of the prowess of British regulars had not been well founded.

In their first march, too, from their landing till they got beyond the settlements they had plundered and stripped the inhabitants, totally ruining some poor families, besides insulting, abusing, and confining the people if they remonstrated. This was enough to put us out of conceit of such defenders, if we had really wanted any. How different was the conduct of our French friends in 1781, who, during a march through the most inhabited part of our country from Rhode Island to Virginia, near seven hundred miles, occasioned not the smallest complaint for the loss of a pig, a chicken, or even an apple.

Captain Orme, who was one of the General's *aides-de-camp*, and, being grievously wounded, was brought off with him, and continued with him to his death, which happened in a few days, told me that he was totally silent all the first day, and at night only said, "Who would have thought it?" That he was silent again the following day, saying only at last, "We shall better know how to deal with them another time"; and died in a few minutes after.

The secretary's papers, with all the General's orders, instructions, and correspondence, falling into the enemy's hands, they selected and translated into French a number of the articles, which they printed to prove the hostile intentions of the British court before the declaration of war. Among these I saw some letters of the General to the ministry, speaking highly of the great service I had rendered the army, and recommending me to their notice. David Hume, too, who was some years after secretary to Lord Hertford, when minister in France, and afterward to General Conway, when Secretary of State, told me he had seen among the papers in that office, letters from Braddock highly recommending me. But the expedition having been unfortunate my service, it seems, was not thought of much value, for those recommendations were never of any use to me.

As to rewards from himself, I asked only one, which was, that he would give orders to his officers not to enlist any more of our bought servants, and that he would discharge such as had been already enlisted. This he readily granted, and several were accordingly returned to their masters, on my application. Dunbar, when the command devolved on him, was not so generous. He being at Philadelphia on his retreat, or rather flight, I applied to him for the discharge of the servants of three poor farmers of Lancaster County that he had enlisted, reminding him of the late General's orders on that head. He promised me that, if the masters would come to him at Trenton, where he should be in a few days on his march to New York, he would there deliver their men to them. They accordingly were at the expense and trouble of going to Trenton, and there he refused to perform his promise, to their great loss and disappointment.

As soon as the loss of the wagons and horses was generally known, all the owners came upon me for the valuation which I had given bond to pay. Their demands gave me a great deal of trouble, my acquainting them that the money was ready in the paymaster's hands, but that orders for paying it must first be obtained from General Shirley, and my assuring them that I had applied to that General by letter, but he being at a distance, an answer could not soon be received, and they must have patience, all this was not sufficient to satisfy, and some began to sue me. General Shirley at length relieved me from this terrible situation by appointing commissioners to examine the claims, and ordering payment. They amounted to near twenty thousand pound, which to pay would have ruined me.

Before we had the news of this defeat, the two Doctors Bond came to me with a subscription paper for raising money to defray the expense of a grand firework, which it was intended to exhibit at a rejoicing on receipt of the news of our taking Fort Duquesne. I looked grave, and said it would, I thought, be time enough to prepare for the rejoicing when we knew we should have occasion to rejoice. They seemed surprised that I did not immediately comply with their proposal. "Why the d—l!" says one of them, "you surely don't suppose that the fort will not be taken?" "I don't know that it will not be taken, but I know that the events of war are subject to great uncertainty." I gave them the reasons of my doubting; the subscription was dropped, and the projectors thereby missed the mortification they would have undergone if the firework had been prepared. Dr. Bond, on some other occasion afterward said that he did not like Franklin's forebodings.

Governor Morris, who had continually worried the Assembly with message after message before the defeat of Braddock, to beat them into the making of acts to raise money for the defense of the province without taxing, among others, the proprietary estates, and had rejected all their bills for not having such an exempting clause, now redoubled his attacks with more hope of success, the danger and necessity being greater. The Assembly, however, continued firm, believing they had justice on their side, and that it would be giving up an essential right if they suffered the Governor to amend their money-bills. In one of the last, indeed, which was for granting fifty thousand pounds, his proposed amendment was only of a single word. The bill expressed "that all estates, real and personal, were to be taxed, those of the proprietaries *not* excepted." His amendment was, for *not* read *only*: a small, but very material alteration. However, when the news of this disaster reached England, our friends there, whom we had taken care to furnish with all the Assembly's answers to the Governor's messages, raised a clamor against the proprietaries for their meanness and injustice in giving their Governor such instructions; some going so far as to say that by obstructing the defense of their province, they forfeited their right to it. They were intimidated by this, and sent orders to their receiver-general to add five thousand pounds of their money to whatever sum might be given by the Assembly for such purpose.

This being notified to the House was accepted in lieu of their share of a general tax, and a new bill was formed, with an exempting clause, which passed accordingly. By this act I was appointed one of the commissioners for disposing of the money, sixty thousand pounds. I had been active in modeling the bill and procuring its passage, and had, at the same time, drawn a bill for establishing and disciplining a voluntary militia, which I carried through the House without much difficulty, as care was taken in it to leave the Quakers at their liberty. To promote the association necessary to form the militia, I wrote a dialogue* stating and answering all the objections I could think of to such a militia, which was printed, and had, as I thought, great effect.

While the several companies in the city and country were forming, and learning their exercise, the governor prevailed with me to take charge of our northwestern frontier, which was infested by the enemy, and provide for the defense of the inhabitants by raising troops and building a line of forts. I undertook this military business, though I did not conceive myself well qualified for it. He gave me a commission with full powers, and a parcel of blank commissions for officers, to be given to whom I thought fit. I had but little difficulty in raising men, having soon five hundred and sixty under my command. My son, who had in the preceding war been an officer in the army raised against Canada, was my *aide-de-camp*, and of great use to me. The Indians had burned Gnadenhut, a village settled by the Moravians, and massacred the inhabitants; but the place was thought a good situation for one of the forts.

In order to march thither, I assembled the companies at Bethlehem, the chief establishment of those people. I was surprised to find it in so good a posture of defense; the destruction of Gnadenhut had made them apprehend danger. The principal buildings were defended by a stockade; they had purchased a quantity of arms and ammunition from New York, and had even placed quantities of small paving stones between the windows of their high stone houses, for their women to throw down upon the heads of any Indians that

* This dialogue and the militia act in the *Gentleman's Magazine*, February and March, 1756. [FRANKLIN'S NOTE.]

should attempt to force into them. The armed brethren, too, kept watch, and relieved as methodically as in any garrison town. In conversation with the bishop, Spangenberg, I mentioned this my surprise; for, knowing they had obtained an act of Parliament exempting them from military duties in the colonies, I had supposed they were conscientiously scrupulous of bearing arms. He answered me that it was not one of their established principles, but that, at the time of their obtaining that act, it was thought to be a principle with many of their people. On this occasion, however, they, to their surprise, found it adopted by but a few. It seems they were either deceived in themselves, or deceived the Parliament; but common sense, aided by present danger, will sometimes be too strong for whimsical opinions.

It was the beginning of January when we set out upon this business of building forts. I sent one detachment toward the Minisink, with instructions to erect one for the security of that upper part of the country, and another to the lower part, with similar instructions; and I concluded to go myself with the rest of my force to Gnadenhut, where a fort was thought more immediately necessary. The Moravians procured me five wagons for our tools, stores, baggage, etc.

Just before we left Bethlehem, eleven farmers, who had been driven from their plantations by the Indians, came to me requesting a supply of firearms, that they might go back and fetch off their cattle. I gave them each a gun with suitable ammunition. We had not marched many miles before it began to rain, and it continued raining all day; there were no habitations on the road to shelter us, till we arrived near night at the house of a German, where, and in his barn, we were all huddled together, as wet as water could make us. It was well we were not attacked in our march, for our arms were of the most ordinary sort, and our men could not keep their gunlocks dry. The Indians are dexterous in contrivances for that purpose, which we had not. They met that day the eleven poor farmers above mentioned, and killed ten of them. The one who escaped informed that his and his companions' guns would not go off, the priming being wet with the rain.

The next day being fair, we continued our march, and arrived at the desolated Gnadenhut. There was a sawmill near, round which were left several piles of boards, with which we soon hutted ourselves; an operation the more necessary at that inclement season as we had no tents. Our first work was to bury more effectually the dead we found there, who had been half interred by the country people.

The next morning our fort was planned and marked out, the circumference measuring four hundred and fifty-five feet, which would require as many palisades to be made of trees, one with another, of a foot diameter each. Our axes, of which we had seventy, were immediately set to work to cut down trees, and our men being dexterous in the use of them, great dispatch was made. Seeing the trees fall so fast, I had the curiosity to look at my watch when two men began to cut at a pine; in six minutes they had it upon the ground, and I found it of fourteen inches diameter. Each pine made three palisades of eighteen feet long, pointed at one end. While these were preparing, our other men dug a trench all round, of three feet deep, in which the palisades were to be planted; and our wagons, the bodies being taken off, and the fore and hind wheels separated by taking out the pin which united the two parts of the perch, we had ten carriages, with two horses each, to bring the palisades from the woods to the spot. When they were set up, our carpenters built a stage of boards all round within, about six feet high, for the men to stand on when to fire through loopholes. We had one swivel gun, which we mounted on one of the angles, and fired it as soon as fixed, to let the Indians know, if any were within hearing, that we had such pieces; and thus our fort, if such a magnificent name may be given to so miserable a stockade, was finished in a week, though it rained so hard every other day that the men could not work.

This gave me occasion to observe that when men are employed they are best contented; for on the days they worked they were good-natured and cheerful, and, with the consciousness of having done a good day's work, they spent the evening jollily; but on our idle days they were mutinous and quarrelsome, finding fault with their pork, the bread, etc., and in continual ill-humor, which put me in mind of a sea-captain, whose rule it was to keep his men constantly

142

at work; and, when his mate once told him that they had done everything, and there was nothing further to employ them about, "Oh," says he, "make them scour the anchor."

This kind of fort, however contemptible, is a sufficient defense against Indians who have no cannon. Finding ourselves now posted securely, and having a place to retreat to on occasion, we ventured out in parties to scour the adjacent country. We met with no Indians, but we found the places on the neighboring hills where they had lain to watch our proceedings. There was an art in their contrivance of those places that seems worth mention. It being winter, a fire was necessary for them; but a common fire on the surface of the ground would by its light have discovered their position at a distance. They had therefore dug holes in the ground about three feet diameter, and somewhat deeper; we saw where they had with their hatchets cut off the charcoal from the sides of burnt logs lying in the woods. With these coals they had made small fires in the bottom of the holes, and we observed among the weeds and grass the prints of their bodies, made by their laying all round, with the legs hanging down in the holes to keep their feet warm, which, with them, is an essential point. This kind of fire, so managed, could not discover them, either by its light, flame, sparks, or even smoke; it appeared that their number was not great, and it seems they saw we were too many to be attacked by them with prospect of advantage.

We had for our chaplain a zealous Presbyterian minister, Mr. Beatty, who complained to me that the men did not generally attend his prayers and exhortations. When they enlisted, they were promised, besides pay and provisions, a gill of rum a day, which was punctually served out to them, half in the morning, and the other half in the evening; and I observed they were as punctual in attending to receive it; upon which I said to Mr. Beatty, "It is, perhaps, below the dignity of your profession to act as steward of the rum, but if you were to deal it out and only just after prayers, you would have them all about you." He liked the thought, undertook the office, and with the help of a few hands to measure out the liquor, executed it to satisfaction, and never were prayers more generally and more punctually attended; so that I thought this method preferable to the punishment inflicted by some military laws for nonattendance on divine service.

I had hardly finished this business, and got my fort well stored with provisions, when I received a letter from the Governor, acquainting me that he had called the Assembly, and wished my attendance there, if the posture of affairs on the frontiers was such that my remaining there was no longer necessary. My friends, too, of the Assembly, pressing me by their letters to be, if possible, at the meeting, and my three intended forts being now completed, and the inhabitants contented to remain on their farms under that protection, I resolved to return; the more willingly, as a New England officer, Colonel Clapham, experienced in Indian war, being on a visit to our establishment, consented to accept the command. I gave him a commission, and parading the garrison, had it read before them, and introduced him to them as an officer who, from his skill in military affairs, was much more fit to command them than myself; and giving them a little exhortation, took my leave. I was escorted as far as Bethlehem, where I rested a few days to recover from the fatigue I had undergone. The first night, being in a good bed, I could hardly sleep, it was so different from my hard lodging on the floor of our hut at Gnaden wrapped only in a blanket or two.

While at Bethlehem, I inquired a little into the practice of the Moravians: some of them had accompanied me, and all were very kind to me. I found they worked for a common stock, eat at common tables, and slept in common dormitories, great numbers together. In the dormitories I observed loopholes, at certain distances all along just under the ceiling, which I thought judiciously placed for change of air. I was at their church, where I was entertained with good music, the organ being accompanied with violins, hautboys, flutes, clarinets, etc. I understood that their sermons were not usually preached to mixed congregations of men, women, and children, as is our common practice, but that they assembled sometimes the married men, at other times their wives, then the young men, the young women, and the little children, each division by itself. The sermon I heard was to the latter, who came in and were placed in rows on benches; the boys under the conduct of a young man, their tutor, and the girls conducted by a young woman. The discourse seemed well adapted to their capacities, and was delivered in a pleasing, familiar manner, coaxing them, as it were, to be good. They behaved very orderly, but looked pale and unhealthy, which made me suspect they were kept too much within doors, or not allowed sufficient exercise.

I inquired concerning the Moravian marriages, whether the report was true that they were by lot. I was told that lots were used only in particular cases; that generally, when a young man found himself disposed to marry, he informed the elders of his class, who consulted the elder ladies that governed the young women. As these elders of the different sexes were well acquainted with the tempers and dispositions of their respective pupils, they could best judge what matches were suitable, and their judgments were generally acquiesced in; but if, for example, it should happen that two or three young women were found to be equally proper for the young man, the lot was then recurred to. I objected, if the matches are not made by the mutual choice of the parties, some of them may chance to be very unhappy. "And so they may," answered my informer, "if you let the parties choose for themselves"; which, indeed, I could not deny.

Being returned to Philadelphia, I found the association went on swimmingly, the inhabitants that were not Quakers having pretty generally come into it, formed themselves into companies, and chose their captains, lieutenants, and ensigns, according to the new law. Dr. B. visited me, and gave me an account of the pains he had taken to spread a general good liking to the law, and ascribed much to those endeavors. I had had the vanity to ascribe all to my *Dialogue*; however, not knowing but that he might be in the right, I let him enjoy his opinion, which I take to be generally the best way in such cases. The officers, meeting, chose me to be colonel of the regiment, which I this time accepted. I forget how many companies we had, but we paraded about twelve hundred well-looking men, with a company of artillery, who had been furnished with six brass field-pieces, which they had become so expert in the use of as to fire twelve times in a minute. The first time I reviewed my regiment they accompanied me to my house, and would salute me with some rounds fired before my door, which shook down and broke several glasses of my electrical apparatus. And my new honor proved not much less brittle; for all our commissions were soon after broken by a repeal of the law in England.

During this short time of my colonelship, being about to set out on a journey to Virginia, the officers of my regiment took it into their heads that it would be proper for them to escort me out of town, as far as the Lower Ferry. Just as I was getting on horseback they came to my door, between thirty and forty, mounted, and all in their uniforms. I had not been previously acquainted with the project, or I should have prevented it, being naturally averse to the assuming of state on any occasion; and I was a good deal chagrined at their appearance, as I could not avoid their accompanying me. What made it worse was that as soon as we began to move they drew their swords and rode with them naked all the way. Somebody wrote an account of this to the proprietor, and it gave him great offense. No such honor had been paid him when in the province, nor to any of his governors; and he said it was only proper to princes of the blood royal, which may be true for aught I know, who was, and still am, ignorant of the etiquette in such cases.

This silly affair, however, greatly increased his rancor against me, which was before not a little, on account of my conduct in the Assembly respecting the exemption of his estate from taxation, which I had always opposed very warmly, and not without severe reflections on his meanness and injustice of contending for it. He accused me to the ministry as being the great obstacle to the king's service, preventing, by my influence in the House, the proper form of the bills for raising money, and he instanced this parade with my officers as a proof of my having an intention to take the government of the province out of his hands by force. He also applied to Sir Everard Fawkener, the postmaster-general, to deprive me of my office; but it had no other effect than to procure from Sir Everard a gentle admonition.

Notwithstanding the continual wrangle between the Governor and the House, in which I, as a member, had so large a share, there

146

still subsisted a civil intercourse between that gentleman and myself, and we never had any personal difference. I have sometimes since thought that his little or no resentment against me, for the answers it was known I drew up to his messages, might be the effect of professional habit, and that, being bred a lawyer, he might consider us both as merely advocates for contending clients in a suit, he for the proprietaries and I for the Assembly. He would, therefore, sometimes call in a friendly way to advise with me on difficult points, and sometimes, though not often, take my advice.

We acted in concert to supply Braddock's army with provisions; and when the shocking news arrived of his defeat the Governor sent in haste for me to consult with him on measures for preventing the desertion of the back counties. I forget now the advice I gave; but I think it was that Dunbar should be written to, and prevailed with, if possible, to post his troops on the frontiers for their protection, till, by re-enforcements from the colonies, he might be able to proceed on the expedition. And after my return from the frontier, he would have had me undertake the conduct of such an expedition with provincial troops, for the reduction of Fort Duquesne, Dunbar and his men being otherwise employed; and he proposed to commission me as general. I had not so good an opinion of my military abilities as he professed to have, and I believe his professions must have exceeded his real sentiments; but probably he might think that my popularity would facilitate the raising of the men, and my influence in Assembly, the grant of money to pay them, and that, perhaps, without taxing the proprietary estate. Finding me not so forward to engage as he expected, the project was dropped, and he soon after left the government, being superseded by Captain Denny.

Before I proceed in relating the part I had in public affairs under this new governor's administration, it may not be amiss here to give some account of the rise and progress of my philosophical reputation.

In 1746, being at Boston, I met there with a Dr. Spence, who was lately arrived from Scotland and showed me some electric experiments. They were imperfectly performed, as he was not very expert; but, being on a subject quite new to me, they equally surprised and pleased me. Soon after my return to Philadelphia, our library company received from Mr. P. Collinson, Fellow of the Royal Society of London, a present of a glass tube, with some account of the use of it in making such experiments. I eagerly seized the opportunity of repeating what I had seen at Boston; and by much practice, acquired great readiness in performing those, also, which we had an account of from England, adding a number of new ones. I say much practice for my house was continually full for some time with people who came to see these new wonders.

To divide a little this incumbrance among my friends, I caused a number of similar tubes to be blown at our glass-house, with which they furnished themselves, so that we had at length several performers. Among these, the principal was Mr. Kinnersley, an ingenious neighbor, who, being out of business, I encouraged to undertake showing the experiments for money, and drew up for him two lectures, in which the experiments were ranged in such order, and accompanied with such explanations in such method, as that the foregoing should assist in comprehending the following. He procured an elegant apparatus for the purpose, in which all the little machines that I had roughly made for myself were nicely formed by instrument-makers. His lectures were well attended, and gave great satisfaction; and after some time he went through the colonies, exhibiting them in every capital town, and picked up some money. In the West India islands, indeed, it was with difficulty the experiments could be made, from the general moisture of the air.

Obliged as we were to Mr. Collinson for his present of the tube, etc., I thought it right he should be informed of our success in using it, and wrote him several letters containing accounts of our experiments. He got them read in the Royal Society, where they were not at first thought worth so much notice as to be printed in their *Transactions*. One paper, which I wrote for Mr. Kinnersley on the sameness of lightning with electricity, I sent to Dr. Mitchel, an acquaintance of mine, and one of the members also of that society, who wrote me word that it had been read, but was laughed at by the connoisseurs. The papers, however, being shown to Dr. Fothergill, he thought them of too much value to be stifled, and advised the printing of them. Mr. Collinson then gave them to Cave for publication in his *Gentleman's Magazine;* but he chose to print them separately in a pamphlet, and Dr. Fothergill wrote the preface. Cave, it seems, judged rightly for his profit, for by the additions that arrived afterward they swelled to a quarto volume, which has had five editions, and cost him nothing for copy-money.

It was, however, some time before those papers were much taken notice of in England. A copy of them happening to fall into the hands of the Count de Buffon, a philosopher deservedly of great reputation in France, and, indeed, all over Europe, he prevailed with M. Dalibard to translate them into French, and they were printed at Paris. The publication offended the Abbé Nollet, preceptor in natural philosophy to the royal family, and an able experimenter, who had formed and published a theory of electricity, which then had the general vogue. He could not at first believe that such a work came from America, and said it must have been fabricated by his enemies at Paris to decry his system. Afterwards, having been assured that there really existed such a person as Franklin at Philadelphia, which he had doubted, he wrote and published a volume of letters, chiefly addressed to me, defending his theory, and denying the verity of my experiments, and of the positions deduced from them.

I once purposed answering the Abbé, and actually began the answer; but, on consideration that my writings contained a description of experiments which any one might repeat and verify, and if not to be verified, could not be defended; or of observations offered as conjectures, and not delivered dogmatically, therefore not laying me under any obligation to defend them; and reflecting that a dispute between two persons, writing in different languages, might be lengthened greatly by mistranslations, and thence misconceptions of one another's meaning, much of one of the Abbé's letters being founded on an error in the translation, I concluded to let my papers shift for themselves, believing it was better to spend what time I could spare from public business in making new experiments than in disputing about those already made. I therefore never answered M. Nollet, and the event gave me no cause to repent my silence; for my friend M. le Roy, of the Royal Academy of Sciences, took up my cause and refuted him; my book was translated into the Italian, German, and Latin languages; and the doctrine it contained was by degrees universally adopted by the philosophers of Europe, in preference to that of the Abbé; so that he lived to see himself the last of his sect, except Monsieur B——, of Paris, his *élève* and immediate disciple.

What gave my book the more sudden and general celebrity was the success of one of its proposed experiments, made by Messrs. Dalibard and De Lor at Marly, for drawing lightning from the clouds. This engaged the public attention everywhere. M. de Lor, who had an apparatus for experimental philosophy, and lectured in that branch of science, undertook to repeat what he called the Philadelphia Experiments, and after they were performed before the king and court, all the curious of Paris flocked to see them. I will not swell this narrative with an account of that capital experiment, nor of the infinite pleasure I received in the success of a similar one I made soon after with a kite at Philadelphia, as both are to be found in the histories of electricity.

Dr. Wright, an English physician, when at Paris wrote to a friend who was of the Royal Society an account of the high esteem my experiments were in among the learned abroad, and of their wonder that my writings had been so little noticed in England. The society, on this, resumed the consideration of the letters that had been read to them; and the celebrated Dr. Watson drew up a summary account of them, and of all I had afterwards sent to England on the subject, which he accompanied with some praise of the writer. This summary was then printed in their *Transactions;* and some members of the society in London, particularly the very ingenious Mr. Canton, having verified the experiment of procuring lightning from the clouds by a pointed rod, and acquainting them with the success, they soon made me more than amends for the slight with which they had before treated me. Without my having made any application for that honor, they chose me a member, and voted that I should be excused the customary payments, which would have amounted to twenty-five guineas; and ever since have given me their *Transactions* gratis. They also presented me with the gold medal of Sir Godfrey Copley for the year 1753, the delivery of which was accompanied by a very handsome speech of the president, Lord Macclesfield, wherein I was highly honored.

Our new governor, Captain Denny, brought over for me the before-mentioned medal from the Royal Society, which he presented to me at an entertainment given him by the city. He accompanied it with very polite expressions of his esteem for me, having, as he said, been long acquainted with my character. After dinner, when the company, as was customary at that time, were engaged in drinking, he took me aside into another room, and acquainted me that he had been advised by his friends in England to cultivate a friendship with me, as one who was capable of giving him the best advice, and of contributing most effectually to the making his administration easy; that he therefore desired of all things to have a good understanding with me, and he begged me to be assured of his readiness on all occasions to render me every service that might be in his power. He said much to me, also, of the proprietor's good disposition towards the province, and of the advantage it might be to us all, and to me in particular, if the opposition that had been so long continued to his measures was dropped, and harmony restored between him and the people; in effecting which, it was thought no one could be more serviceable than myself; and I might depend on adequate acknowledgments and recompenses, etc., etc. The drinkers, finding we did not return immediately to the table, sent us a decanter of Madeira, which the Governor made liberal use of, and in proportion became more profuse of his solicitations and promises.

My answers were to this purpose: that my circumstances, thanks to God, were such as to make proprietary favors unnecessary to me; and that, being a member of the Assembly, I could not possibly accept of any; that, however, I had no personal enmity to the proprietary, and that, whenever the public measures he proposed should appear to be for the good of the people, no one should espouse and forward them more zealously than myself; my past opposition having been founded on this, that the measures which

151

had been urged were evidently intended to serve the proprietary interest, with great prejudice to that of the people; that I was much obliged to him (the Governor) for his professions of regard to me, and that he might rely on everything in my power to make his administration as easy as possible, hoping at the same time that he had not brought with him the same unfortunate instruction his predecessor had been hampered with.

On this he did not then explain himself; but when he afterwards came to do business with the Assembly, they appeared again, the disputes were renewed, and I was as active as ever in the opposition, being the penman, first, of the request to have a communication of the instructions, and then of the remarks upon them, which may be found in the votes of the time, and in the historical review I afterward published. But between us personally no enmity arose; we were often together; he was a man of letters, had seen much of the world, and was very entertaining and pleasing in conversation. He gave me the first information that my old friend James Ralph was still alive; that he was esteemed one of the best political writers in England; had been employed in the dispute between Prince Frederic and the King, and had obtained a pension of three hundred a year; that his reputation was indeed small as a poet, Pope having damned his poetry in the *Dunciad;* but his prose was thought as good as any man's.

*The Assembly, finally finding the proprietary obstinately persisted in manacling their deputies with instructions inconsistent, not only with the privileges of the people, but with the service of the Crown, resolved to petition the King against them, and appointed me their agent to go over to England to present and support the petition. The House had sent up a bill to the Governor, granting a sum of sixty thousand pounds for the king's use (ten thousand pounds of which was subjected to the orders of the then general, Lord Loudoun), which the Governor absolutely refused to pass, in compliance with instructions.

I had agreed with Captain Morris, of the paquet at New York,

* The many unanimous resolves of the Assembly—what date ?—[FRANKLIN'S QUERY IN MARGIN.]

for my passage, and my stores were put on board, when Lord Loudoun arrived at Philadelphia, expressly, as he told me, to endeavor an accommodation between the Governor and Assembly, that His Majesty's service might not be obstructed by their dissensions. Accordingly, he desired the Governor and myself to meet him, that he might hear what was to be said on both sides. We met and discussed the business. In behalf of the Assembly, I urged all the various arguments that may be found in the public papers of that time, which were of my writing, and are printed with the minutes of the Assembly; and the Governor pleaded his instructions; the bond he had given to observe them, and his ruin if he disobeyed, yet seemed not unwilling to hazard himself if Lord Loudoun would advise it. This his lordship did not choose to do, though I once thought I had nearly prevailed with him to do it; but finally he rather chose to urge the compliance of the Assembly; and he entreated me to use my endeavors with them for that purpose, declaring that he would spare none of the king's troops for the defense of our frontiers, and that, if we did not continue to provide for that defense ourselves, they must remain exposed to the enemy.

I acquainted the House with what had passed, and, presenting them with a set of resolutions I had drawn up declaring our rights and that we did not relinquish our claim to those rights but only suspended the exercise of them on this occasion through *force*, against which we protested, they at length agreed to drop that bill, and frame another conformable to the proprietary instructions. This of course the Governor passed, and I was then at liberty to proceed on my voyage. But in the meantime the paquet had sailed with my sea-stores, which was some loss to me, and my only recompense was his lordship's thanks for my service, all the credit of obtaining the accommodation falling to his share.

He set out for New York before me; and, as the time for dispatching the paquet-boats was at his disposition, and there were two then remaining there, one of which, he said, was to sail very soon, I requested to know the precise time, that I might not miss her by any delay of mine. His answer was, "I have given out that she is to sail on Saturday next; but I may let you know, *entre nous,* that if you are there by Monday morning, you will be in time, but do not delay longer." By some accidental hindrance at a ferry, it was Monday noon before I arrived, and I was much afraid she might have sailed, as the wind was fair; but I was soon made easy by the information that she was still in the harbor, and would not move till the next day. One would imagine that I was now on the very point of departing for Europe. I thought so; but I was not then so well acquainted with his lordship's character, of which *indecision* was one of the strongest features. I shall give some instances. It was about the beginning of April that I came to New York, and I think it was near the end of June before we sailed. There were then two of the paquet-boats, which had been long in port, but were detained for the General's letters, which were always to be ready tomorrow. Another paquet arrived; she too was detained; and, before we sailed, a fourth was expected. Ours was the first to be dispatched, as having been there longest. Passengers were engaged in all, and some extremely impatient to be gone, and the merchants uneasy about their letters, and the orders they had given for insurance (it being war time) for fall goods; but their anxiety availed nothing; his lordship's letters were not ready; and yet whoever waited on him found him always at his desk, pen in hand, and concluded he must needs write abundantly.

Going myself one morning to pay my respects, I found in his antechamber one Innis, a messenger of Philadelphia, who had come from thence express with a paquet from Governor Denny for the General. He delivered to me some letters from my friends there, which occasioned my inquiring when he was to return, and where he lodged, that I might send some letters by him. He told me he was ordered to call tomorrow at nine for the General's answer to the Governor, and should set off immediately. I put my letters into his hands the same day. A fortnight after I met him again in the same place. "So, you are soon returned, Innis?" "*Returned!* no, I am not *gone* yet." "How so?" "I have called here by order every morning these two weeks past for his lordship's letter, and it is not yet ready." "Is it possible, when he is so great a writer? for I see him constantly at his escritoire." "Yes," says Innis, "but he is like St. George on the signs, *always on horseback, and never rides on.*" This observation of the messenger was, it seems, well founded; for, when in England, I understood that Mr. Pitt gave it as one reason for removing this General, and sending generals Amherst and Wolfe, *that the minister never heard from him, and could not know what he was doing.*

This daily expectation of sailing, and all the three paquets going down to Sandy Hook, to join the fleet there, the passengers thought it best to be on board, lest by a sudden order the ships should sail, and they be left behind. There, if I remember right, we were about six weeks, consuming our sea-stores, and obliged to procure more. At length the fleet sailed, the General and all his army on board, bound to Louisburg, with intent to besiege and take that fortress; all the paquet-boats in company ordered to attend the General's ship, ready to receive his dispatches when they should be ready. We were out five days before we got a letter with leave to part, and then our ship quitted the fleet and steered for England. The other two paquets he still detained, carried them with him to Halifax, where he stayed some time to exercise the men in sham attacks upon sham forts, then altered his mind as to besieging Louisburg, and returned to New York, with all his troops, together with the two paquets above mentioned, and all their passengers! During his absence the French and savages had taken Fort George, on the frontier of that province, and the savages had massacred many of the garrison after capitulation.

I saw afterwards in London Captain Bonnell, who commanded one of these paquets. He told me that when he had been detained a month, he acquainted his lordship that his ship was grown foul, to a degree that must necessarily hinder her fast sailing, a point of consequence for a paquet-boat, and requested an allowance of time to heave her down and clean her bottom. He was asked how long time that would require. He answered, three days. The General replied, "If you can do it in one day, I give leave; otherwise not; for you must certainly sail the day after tomorrow." So he never obtained leave, though detained afterwards from day to day during full three months.

I saw also in London one of Bonnell's passengers, who was so enraged against his lordship for deceiving and detaining him so long at New York, and then carrying him to Halifax and back again, that he swore he would sue him for damages. Whether he did or not, I never heard; but, as he represented the injury to his affairs, it was very considerable.

On the whole, I wondered much how such a man came to be intrusted with so important a business as the conduct of a great army; but, having since seen more of the great world, and the means of obtaining, and motives for giving places, my wonder is diminished. General Shirley, on whom the command of the army devolved upon the death of Braddock, would, in my opinion, if continued in place, have made a much better campaign than that of Loudoun in 1757, which was frivolous, expensive, and disgraceful to our nation beyond conception; for, though Shirley was not a bred soldier, he was sensible and sagacious in himself, and attentive to good advice from others, capable of forming judicious plans, and quick and active in carrying them into execution. Loudoun, instead of defending the colonies with his great army, left them totally exposed while he paraded idly at Halifax, by which means Fort George was lost; besides, he deranged all our mercantile operations, and distressed our trade, by a long embargo on the exportation of provisions, on pretense of keeping supplies from being obtained by the enemy, but in reality for beating down their price in favor of the contractors in whose profits, it was said (perhaps from suspicion only), he had a share. And when at length the embargo was taken off, by neglecting to send notice of it to Charlestown, the Carolina fleet was detained near three months longer, whereby their bottoms were so much damaged by the worm that a great part of them foundered in their passage home.

Shirley was, I believe, sincerely glad of being relieved from so burdensome a charge as the conduct of an army must be to a man unacquainted with military business. I was at the entertainment given by the city of New York to Lord Loudoun, on his taking upon him the command. Shirley, though thereby superseded, was present also. There was a great company of officers, citizens, and strangers, and, some chairs having been borrowed in the neighborhood, there was one among them very low, which fell to the lot of Mr. Shirley. Perceiving it as I sat by him, I said, "They have given you, sir, too low a seat." "No matter," says he, "Mr. Franklin, I find *a low seat* the easiest."

While I was, as aforementioned, detained at New York, I received all the accounts of the provisions, etc., that I had furnished to Braddock, some of which accounts could not sooner be obtained from the different persons I had employed to assist in the business. I presented them to Lord Loudoun, desiring to be paid the balance. He caused them to be regularly examined by the proper officer, who, after comparing every article with its voucher, certified them to be right and the balance due, for which his lordship promised to give me an order on the paymaster. This was, however, put off from time to time; and though I called often for it by appointment, I did not get it. At length, just before my departure, he told me he had, on better consideration, concluded not to mix his accounts with those of his predecessors. "And you," says he, "when in England, have only to exhibit your accounts at the treasury, and you will be paid immediately."

I mentioned, but without effect, the great and unexpected expense I had been put to by being detained so long at New York, as a reason for my desiring to be presently paid; and on my observing that it was not right I should be put to any further trouble or delay in obtaining the money I had advanced, as I charged no commission for my service, "O, sir," says he, "you must not think of persuading us that you are no gainer; we understand better those affairs, and know that everyone concerned in supplying the army finds means, in the doing it, to fill his own pockets." I assured him that was not my case, and that I had not pocketed a farthing; but he appeared clearly not to believe me; and indeed, I have since learned that immense fortunes are often made in such employments. As to my balance, I am not paid it to this day, of which more hereafter.

Our captain of the paquet had boasted much, before we sailed, of the swiftness of his ship; unfortunately, when we came to sea, she proved the dullest of ninety-six sail, to his no small mortification. After many conjectures respecting the cause, when we were near another ship almost as dull as ours, which, however, gained upon us, the captain ordered all hands to come aft, and stand as near the ensign staff as possible. We were, passengers included, about forty persons. While we stood there, the ship mended her pace, and soon left her neighbor far behind, which proved clearly what our captain suspected, that she was loaded too much by the head. The casks of water, it seems, had been all placed forward; these he therefore ordered to be moved further aft, on which the ship recovered her character, and proved the best sailer in the fleet.

The captain said she had once gone at the rate of thirteen knots, which is accounted thirteen miles per hour. We had on board, as a passenger, Captain Kennedy, of the Navy, who contended that it was impossible, and that no ship ever sailed so fast, and that there must have been some error in the division of the log-line, or some mistake in heaving the log. A wager ensued between the two captains, to be decided when there should be sufficient wind. Kennedy thereupon examined rigorously the log-line and being satisfied with that, he determined to throw the log himself. Accordingly some days after, when the wind blew very fair and fresh, and the captain of the paquet, Lutwidge, said he believed she then went at the rate of thirteen knots, Kennedy made the experiment, and owned his wager lost.

The above fact I give for the sake of the following observation. It has been remarked, as an imperfection in the art of shipbuilding, that it can never be known, till she is tried, whether a new ship will or will not be a good sailer; for that the model of a good-sailing ship has been exactly followed in a new one, which has proved, on the contrary, remarkably dull. I apprehend that this may partly be occasioned by the different opinions of seamen respecting the modes of lading, rigging, and sailing of a ship; each has his system; and the same vessel, laden by the judgment and orders of one captain, shall sail better or worse than when by the orders of another. Besides, it scarce ever happens that a ship is formed, fitted for the sea, and sailed by the same person. One man builds the hull, another rigs her, a third lades and sails her. No one of these has the advantage of knowing all the ideas and experience of the others, and therefore cannot draw just conclusions from a combination of the whole.

Even in the simple operation of sailing when at sea, I have often observed different judgments in the officers who commanded the successive watches, the wind being the same. One would have the sails trimmed sharper or flatter than another, so that they seemed to have no certain rule to govern by. Yet I think a set of experiments might be instituted, first, to determine the most proper form of the hull for swift sailing; next, the best dimensions and properest place for the masts; then the form and quantity of sails, and their position, as the wind may be; and, lastly, the disposition of the lading. This is an age of experiments, and I think a set accurately made and combined would be of great use. I am persuaded, therefore, that ere long some ingenious philosopher will undertake it, to whom I wish success.

We were several times chased in our passage, but outsailed everything, and in thirty days had soundings. We had a good observation, and the captain judged himself so near our port, Falmouth, that if we made a good run in the night, we might be off the mouth of that harbor in the morning, and by running in the night might escape the notice of the enemy's privateers, who often cruised near the entrance of the channel. Accordingly, all the sail was set that we could possibly make, and the wind being very fresh and fair, we went right before it and made great way. The captain, after his observation, shaped his course, as he thought, so as to pass wide of the Scilly Isles; but it seems there is sometimes a strong indraught setting up St. George's Channel, which deceives seamen and caused the loss of Sir Cloudesley Shovel's squadron. This indraught was probably the cause of what happened to us.

We had a watchman placed in the bow, to whom they often called, *"Look well out before there,"* and he as often answered, *"Aye, aye"*; but perhaps had his eyes shut, and was half asleep at the time; they sometimes answering, as is said, mechanically; for he did not see a light just before us, which had been hid by the studding-sails from the man at the helm, and from the rest of the watch, but by an accidental yaw of the ship was discovered and occasioned a great alarm, we being very near it, the light appearing to me as big as a cart-wheel. It was midnight, and our captain fast asleep; but Captain Kennedy, jumping upon deck and seeing the danger, ordered the ship to wear round, all sails standing; an operation dangerous to the masts, but it carried us clear, and we escaped shipwreck, for we were runnning right upon the rocks on which the light-house was erected. This deliverance impressed me strongly with the utility of light-houses, and made me resolve to encourage the building more of them in America, if I should live to return there.

In the morning it was found by the soundings, etc., that we were near our port, but a thick fog hid the land from our sight. About nine o'clock the fog began to rise, and seemed to be lifted up from the water like the curtain at a play-house, discovering underneath the town of Falmouth, the vessels in its harbor, and the fields that surrounded it. This was a most pleasing spectacle to those who had been so long without any other prospects than the uniform view of a vacant ocean, and it gave us the more pleasure as we were now free from the anxieties which the state of war occasioned.

I set out immediately, with my son, for London, and we only stopped a little by the way to view Stonehenge on Salisbury Plain and Lord Pembroke's house and gardens, with his very curious antiquities at Wilton. We arrived in London the 27th of July 1757.

As soon as I was settled in a lodging Mr. Charles had provided for me, I went to visit Dr. Fothergill, to whom I was strongly recommended, and whose counsel respecting my proceedings I was advised to obtain. He was against an immediate complaint to government, and thought the proprietaries should first be personally applied to, who might possibly be induced by the interposition and persuasion of some private friends, to accommodate matters amicably. I then waited on my old friend and correspondent, Mr. Peter Collinson, who told me that John Hanbury, the great Virginia merchant, had requested to be informed when I should arrive, that he might carry me to Lord Granville's, who was then President of the Council and wished to see me as soon as possible. I agreed to go with him the next morning. Accordingly Mr. Hanbury alled for me and took me in his carriage to that nobleman's, who received me with great civility; and after some questions respecting the present state of affairs in America and discourse thereupon, he said to me: "You Americans have wrong ideas of the nature of your constitution; you contend that the king's instructions to his governors are not laws, and think yourselves at liberty to regard or disregard them at your own discretion. But those instructions are not like the pocket instructions given to a minister going abroad, for regulating his conduct in some trifling point of ceremony. They are first drawn up by judges learned in the laws; they are then considered, debated, and perhaps amended in Council, after which they are signed by the king. They are then, as far as they relate to you, the *law of the land,* for the king is the 'Legislator of the Colonies.' " I told his lordship this was new doctrine to me. I had always understood from our charters that our laws were to be made by our assemblies, to be presented indeed to the king for his royal assent, but that, being once given, the king could not repeal or alter them. And as the assemblies could not make permanent laws without his assent, so neither could he make a law for them without theirs. He assured me I was totally mistaken. I did not think so, however, and his lordship's conversation having a little alarmed me as to what might be the sentiments of the court concerning us, I wrote it down as soon as I returned to my lodgings. I recollected that about twenty years before, a clause in a bill brought into Parliament by the ministry had proposed to make the king's instructions laws in the colonies, but the clause was thrown out by the Commons, for which we adored them as our friends and friends of liberty, till by their conduct towards us in 1765 it seemed that they had refused that point of sovereignty to the king only that they might reserve it for themselves.

After some days, Dr. Fothergill having spoken to the proprietaries, they agreed to a meeting with me at Mr. T. Penn's house in Spring Garden. The conversation at first consisted of mutual declarations of disposition to reasonable accommodations, but I suppose each party had its own ideas of what should be meant by *reasonable.* We then went into consideration of our several points of complaint, which I enumerated. The proprietaries justified their conduct as well as they could, and I the Assembly's. We now appeared very wide, and so far from each other in our opinions as to discourage all hope of agreement. However, it was concluded that I should give them the heads of our complaints in writing, and they promised then to consider them. I did so soon after, but they put the paper into the hands of their solicitor, Ferdinand John Paris, who managed for them all their law business in their great suit with the neighboring proprietary of Maryland, Lord Baltimore, which had subsisted seventy years, and wrote for them all their papers and messages in their dispute with the Assembly. He was a proud, angry man, and as I had occasionally in the answers of the Assembly treated his papers with some severity, they being really weak in point of argument and haughty in expression, he had conceived a mortal enmity to me, which discovering itself whenever we met, I declined the proprietary's proposal that he and I should discuss the heads of complaint between our two selves and refused treating with any one but them. They then, by his advice, put the paper into the hands of the Attorney and Solicitor-General for their opinion and counsel upon it, where it lay unanswered a year wanting eight days, during which time I made frequent demands of an answer from the proprietaries, but without obtaining any other than that they had not yet received the opinion of the Attorney and Solicitor-General. What it was when they did receive it I never learned, for they did not communicate it to me, but sent a long message to the Assembly, drawn and signed by Paris, reciting my paper, complaining of its want of formality as a rudeness on my part, and giving a flimsy justification of their conduct, adding that they should be willing to accommodate matters if the Assembly would send out *some person of candor* to treat with them for that purpose, intimating thereby that I was not such.

The want of formality, or rudeness, was probably my not having addressed the paper to them with their assumed titles of True and Absolute Proprietaries of the Province of Pennsylvania, which I omitted as not thinking it necessary in a paper, the intention of which was only to reduce to a certainty by writing, what in conversation I had delivered *viva voce*.

But during this delay, the Assembly having prevailed with Governor Denny to pass an act taxing the proprietary estate in common with the estates of the people, which was the grand point in dispute, they omitted answering the message.

When this act, however, came over, the proprietaries, counseled by Paris, determined to oppose its receiving the royal assent. Accordingly they petitioned the king in Council, and a hearing was appointed in which two lawyers were employed by them against the act, and two by me in support of it. They alleged that the act was intended to load the proprietary estate in order to spare those of the people, and that if it were suffered to continue in force and the proprietaries, who were in odium with the people, left to their mercy in proportioning the taxes, they would inevitably be ruined. We replied that the act had no such intention, and would have no such effect. That the assessors were honest and discreet men under an oath to assess fairly and equitably, and that any advantage each of them might expect in lessening his own tax by augmenting that of the proprietaries was too trifling to induce them to perjure themselves. This is the purport of what I remember as urged by both sides, except that we insisted strongly on the mischievous consequences that must attend a repeal, for that the money, £100,000, being printed and given to the king's use, expended in his service, and now spread among the people, the repeal would strike it dead in their hands, to the ruin of many and the total discouragement of future grants; and the selfishness of the proprietors in soliciting such a general catastrophe, merely from a groundless fear of their estate being taxed too highly, was insisted on in the strongest terms. On this, Lord Mansfield, one of the Council, rose and, beckoning me, took me into the clerk's chamber, while the lawyers were pleading, and asked me if I was really of opinion that no injury would be done the proprietary estate in the execution of the act. I said certainly, "Then," says he, "you can have little objection to enter into an engagement to assure that point." I answered, "None at all." He then called in Paris, and after some discourse, his lordship's proposition was accepted on both sides; a paper to the purpose was drawn up by the Clerk of the Council, which I signed with Mr. Charles, who was also an Agent of the Province for their ordinary affairs, when Lord Mansfield returned to the Council Chamber, where finally the law was allowed to pass. Some changes were, however, recommended, and we also engaged they should be made by a subsequent law, but the Assembly did not think them necessary; for, one year's tax having been levied by the act before the order of Council arrived, they appointed a committee to examine the proceedings of the assessors, and on this committee they put several particular friends of the proprietaries. After a full inquiry, they unanimously signed a report that they found the tax had been assessed with perfect equity.

The Assembly looked into my entering into the first part of the engagement as an essential service to the Province, since it secured the credit of the paper money then spread over all the country. They gave me their thanks in form when I returned. But the proprietaries were enraged at Governor Denny for having passed the act, and turned him out with threats of suing him for breach of instructions which he had given bond to observe. He, however, having done it at the instance of the General, and for His Majesty's service, and having some powerful interest at court, despised the threats and they were never put in execution.

SELECTED WRITINGS
THE DOGOOD PAPERS*

THE NEW-ENGLAND COURANT.

From Monday March 26. to Monday April 2. 1722.

To the Author of the *New-England Courant*.

SIR,   No. I

It may not be improper in the first Place to inform your Readers, that I intend once a Fortnight to present them, by the Help of this Paper, with a short Epistle, which I presume will add somewhat to their Entertainment.

And since it is observed, that the Generality of People, now a days, are unwilling either to commend or dispraise what they read, until they are in some measure informed who or what the Author

---

* Franklin describes the circumstances surrounding his composition of these papers in the *Autobiography,* pages 17-18. He was indebted to Addison's *Spectator* for some of his subject matter as well as for his style, a style which Dr. Johnson, speaking of Addison, characterized as "on grave subjects not formal, on light occasions not groveling."

of it is, whether he be *poor* or *rich, old* or *young,* a *Scollar* or a *Leather Apron Man,* &c. and give their Opinion of the Performance, according to the Knowledge which they have of the Author's Circumstances, it may not be amiss to begin with a short Account of my past Life and present Condition, that the Reader may not be at a Loss to judge whether or no my Lucubrations are worth his reading.

At the time of my Birth, my Parents were on Ship-board in their Way from *London* to *N. England.* My Entrance into this troublesome World was attended with the Death of my Father, a Misfortune, which tho' I was not then capable of knowing, I shall never be able to forget; for as he, poor Man, stood upon the Deck rejoycing at my Birth, a merciless Wave entred the Ship, and in one Moment carry'd him beyond Reprieve. Thus was the *first* Day which I saw, the *last* that was seen by my Father; and thus was my disconsolate Mother at once made both a *Parent* and a *Widow.*

When we arrived at *Boston* (which was not long after) I was put to Nurse in a Country Place, at a small Distance from the Town, where I went to School, and past my Infancy and Childhood in Vanity and Idleness, until I was bound out Apprentice, that I might no longer be a Charge to my Indigent Mother, who was put to hard Shifts for a Living.

My Master was a Country Minister, a pious good-natur'd young Man, & a Batchelor: He labour'd with all his Might to instil vertuous and godly Principles into my tender Soul, well knowing that it was the most suitable Time to make deep and lasting Impressions on the Mind, while it was yet untainted with Vice, free and unbiass'd. He endeavour'd that I might be instructed in all that Knowledge and Learning which is necessary for our Sex, and deny'd me no Accomplishment that could possibly be attained in a Country Place, such as all Sorts of Needle-Work, Writing, Arithmetick, &c. and observing that I took a more than ordinary Delight in reading ingenious Books, he gave me the free Use of his Library, which tho' it was but small, yet it was well chose, to inform the Understanding rightly and enable the Mind to frame great and noble Ideas.

Before I had liv'd quite two Years with this Reverend Gentleman, my indulgent Mother departed this Life, leaving me as it were by my self, having no Relation on Earth within my Knowledge.

I will not abuse your Patience with a tedious Recital of all the frivolous Accidents of my Life, that happened from this Time until I arrived to Years of Discretion, only inform you that I liv'd a chearful Country Life, spending my leisure Time either in some innocent Diversion with the neighbouring Females, or in some shady Retirement, with the best of Company, *Books*. Thus I past away the Time with a Mixture of Profit and Pleasure, having no Affliction but what was imaginary, and created in my own Fancy; as nothing is more common with us Women, than to be grieving for nothing, when we have nothing else to grieve for.

As I would not engross too much of your Paper at once, I will defer the Remainder of my Story until my next Letter; in the mean time desiring your Readers to exercise their Patience, and bear with my Humours now and then, because I shall trouble them but seldom. I am not insensible of the Impossibility of pleasing all, but I would not willingly displease any; and for those who will take Offence where none is intended, they are beneath the Notice of

Your Humble Servant,
SILENCE DOGOOD.

THE NEW-ENGLAND COURANT.

From Monday April 9. to Monday April 16.
1722.

To the Author of the *New-England Courant*.

SIR,   **No. II**

Histories of Lives are seldom entertaining unless they contain something either admirable or exemplar: And since there is little or nothing of this Nature in my own Adventures, I will not tire your Readers with tedious Particulars of no Consequence, but will briefly, and in as few Words as possible relate, the most material Occurrences of my Life, and according to my Promise, confine all to this Letter.

MY Reverend Master who had hitherto remained a Batchelor, (after much Meditation on the Eighteenth verse of the second Chapter of *Genesis*,) took up a Resolution to marry; and having made several unsuccessful fruitless Attempts on the more topping Sort of our Sex, and being tir'd with making troublesome Journeys and Visits to no Purpose, he began unexpectedly to cast a loving Eye upon Me, whom he had brought up cleverly to his Hand.

THERE is certainly scarce any Part of a Man's Life in which he appears more silly and ridiculous, than when he makes his first Onset in Courtship. The aukward Manner in which my Master first discover'd his Intentions, made me, in spite of my Reverence to his Person, burst out into an unmannerly Laughter: However, having ask'd his Pardon, and with much ado compos'd my Countenance, I promis'd him I would take his Proposal into serious Consideration, and speedily give him an Answer.

AS he had been a great Benefactor (and in a Manner a Father to me) I could not well deny his Request, when I once perceived he was in earnest. Whether it was Love, or Gratitude, or Pride, or all Three that made me consent, I know not; but it is certain, he found it no hard Matter, by the Help of his Rhetorick to conquer my Heart, and perswade me to marry him.

THIS unexpected Match was very astonishing to all the Country round about and served to furnish them with Discourse for a long Time after; some approving it, others disliking it, as they were led by their various Fancies and Inclinations.

WE lived happily together in the Heighth of conjugal Love and mutual Endearments, for near Seven Years in which Time we added Two likely Girls and a Boy to the Family of the *Dogoods*: But alas! When my Sun was in its meridian Altitude, inexorable unrelenting Death, as if he had envy'd my Happiness and Tranquility, and resolv'd to make me entirely miserable by the Loss of so good an Husband, hastened his Flight to the Heavenly World, by a sudden unexpected Departure from this.

I HAVE now remained in a State of Widowhood for several Years, but it is a State I never much admir'd, and I am apt to fancy that I could be easily perswaded to marry again, provided I was sure of a good-humour'd, sober, agreeable Companion: But one, even with these few good Qualities, being hard to find, I have lately relinquished all Thoughts of that Nature.

AT present I pass away my leisure Hours in Conversation, either with my honest Neighbour *Rusticus* and his Family, or with the ingenious Minister of our Town, who now lodges at my House, and by whose Assistance I intend now and then to beautify my Writings with a Sentence of two in the learned Languages, which will not only be fashionable, and pleasing to those who do not understand it, but will likewise be very ornamental.

I SHALL conclude this with my own Character, which (one would think) I should be best able to give. *Know then,* that I am an Enemy to Vice, and a Friend to Vertue. I am one of an extensive Charity, and a great Forgiver of *private* Injuries: A hearty Lover of the Clergy and all good Men, and a mortal Enemy to arbitrary Government & unlimited Power. I am naturally very jealous for the Rights and Liberties of my Country: & the least appearance of an Incroachment on those invaluable Priviledges, is apt to make my Blood boil exceedingly. I have likewise a natural Inclination to observe and reprove the Faults of others, at which I have an excellent Faculty. I speak this by Way of Warning to all such whose offences shall come under my Cognizance, for I never intend to wrap my Talent in a Napkin. To be brief; I am courteous and affable, good-humour'd (unless I am first provok'd,) and handsome, and sometimes witty, but always,

SIR, *Your Friend, and*
Humble Servant,
SILENCE DOGOOD.

THE NEW-ENGLAND COURANT.

From Monday May 7. to Monday May 14. 1722.

An sum etiam nunc vel Græcè loqui vel Latinè docendus?*
                                                    CICERO.

To the Author of the *New-England Courant.*

SIR,   **No. IV**

DISCOURSING the other Day at Dinner with my Reverend Boarder, formerly mention'd, (whom for Distinction sake we will call by the Name of *Clericus,*) concerning the Education of Children, I ask'd his Advice about my young Son *William*, whether or no I had best bestow upon him Academical Learning, or (as our Phrase is) *bring him up at our College:* He perswaded me to do it by all Means, using many weighty Arguments with me, and answering all the Objections that I could form against it; telling me withal, that he did not doubt but that the Lad would take his Learning very well, and not idle away his Time as too many there now-a-days do. These words of *Clericus* gave me a Curiosity to inquire a little more strictly into the present Circumstances of that famous Seminary of Learning; but the Information which he gave me, was neither pleasant, nor such as I expected.

AS soon as Dinner was over, I took a solitary Walk into my Orchard, still ruminating on *Clericus's* Discourse with much Consideration, until I came to my usual Place of Retirement under the *Great Apple-Tree;* where having seated my self, and carelesly laid my Head on a verdant Bank, I fell by Degrees into a soft and undisturbed Slumber. My waking Thoughts remained with me in my

---

* "And furthermore whether I am to be taught to speak in Greek or in Latin?"

Sleep, and before I awak'd again, I dreamt the following DREAM.

I FANCY'D I was travelling over pleasant and delightful Fields and Meadows, and thro' many small Country Towns and Villages; and as I pass'd along, all Places resounded with the Fame of the Temple of LEARNING: Every Peasant, who had where-withal, was preparing to send one of his Children at least to this famous Place; and in this Case most of them consulted their own Purses instead of their Childrens Capacities: So that I observed, a great many, yea, the most part of those who were travelling thither, were little better than Dunces and Blockheads. Alas! Alas!

AT length I entred upon a spacious Plain, in the Midst of which was erected a large and stately Edifice: It was to this that a great Company of Youths from all Parts of the Country were going; so stepping in among the Crowd, I passed on with them, and presently arrived at the Gate.

THE Passage was Kept by two sturdy Porters named *Riches* and *Poverty,* and the latter obstinately refused to give Entrance to any who had not first gain'd the Favour of the former; so that I observed, many who came even to the very Gate, were obliged to travel back again as ignorant as they came, for want of this necessary Qualification. However, as a Spectator I gain'd Admittance, and with the rest entred directly into the Temple.

IN the Middle of the great Hall stood a stately and magnificent Throne, which was ascending to by two high and difficult Steps. On the Top of it sat LEARNING in awful State; she was apparelled wholly in Black, and surrounded almost on every Side with innumerable Volumes in all Languages. She seem'd very busily employ'd in writing something on half a Sheet of Paper, and upon Enquiry, I understood she was preparing a Paper, call'd, *The New-England Courant.* On her Right Hand sat *English,* with a pleasant smiling Countenance, and handsomely attir'd; and on her left were seated several *Antique Figures* with their Faces vail'd. I was considerably puzzl'd to guess who they were, until one informed me, (who stood beside me,) that those Figures on her left Hand were *Latin, Greek, Hebrew,* &c. and that they were very much reserv'd, and seldom or never unvail'd their Faces here, and then to few or none, tho' most of those who have in this Place acquir'd so much Learning as to distinguish them from *English,* pretended to an intimate Acquaintance with them. I then enquir'd of him, what could be the Reason why they continued vail'd, in this Place especially: He pointed to the Foot of the Throne, where I saw *Idleness,* attended with *Ignorance,* and these (he informed me) were they, who first vail'd them, and still kept them so.

NOW I observed, that the whole Tribe who entred into the Temple with me, began to climb the Throne; but the Work proving troublesome and difficult to most of them, they withdrew their Hands from the Plow, and contented themselves to sit at the Foot, with Madam *Idleness* and her Maid *Ignorance,* until those who were assisted by Diligence and a docible Temper, had well nigh got up the first Step: But the Time drawing nigh in which they could no way avoid ascending, they were fain to crave the Assistance of those who had got up before them, and who, for the Reward perhaps of a *Pint of Milk,* or a *Piece of Plumb-Cake,* lent the Lubbers a helping Hand, and sat them in the Eye of the World, upon a Level with themselves.

THE other Step being in the same Manner ascended, and the usual Ceremonies at an End, every Beetle-Scull seem'd well satisfy'd with his own Portion of Learning, tho' perhaps he was *e'en just* as ignorant as ever. And now the Time of their Departure being come, they march'd out of Doors to make Room for another Company, who waited for Entrance: And I, having seen all that was to be seen, quitted the Hall likewise, and went to make my Observations on those who were just gone out before me.

SOME I perceiv'd took to Merchandizing, others to Travelling, some to one Thing, some to another, and some to Nothing; and many of them from henceforth, for want of Patrimony, liv'd as poor as church Mice, being unable to dig, and asham'd to beg, and to live by their Wits it was impossible. But the most Part of the Crowd went along a large beaten Path, which led to a Temple at the further End of the Plain, call'd, *The Temple of Theology.* The Business of those who were employ'd in this Temple being laborious and painful, I wonder'd exceedingly to see so many go towards it; but while

I was pondering this Matter in my Mind, I spy'd *Pecunia* behind a Curtain, beckoning to them with her Hand, which Sight immediately satisfy'd me for whose Sake it was, that a great Part of them (I will not say all) travel'd that Road. In this Temple I saw nothing worth mentioning, except the ambitious and fraudulent Contrivances of *Plagius,* who (notwithstanding he had been severely reprehended for such Practices before) was diligently transcribing some eloquent Paragraphs out of *Tillotson's* Works, &c. to embellish his own.

NOW I bethought my self in my Sleep, that it was Time to be at Home, and as I fancy'd I was travelling back thither, I reflected in my Mind on the extream Folly of those Parents, who, blind to their Childrens Dulness, and insensible of the Solidity of their Skulls, because they think their Purses can afford it, will needs send them to the Temple of Learning, where, for want of a suitable Genius, they learn little more than how to carry themselves handsomely, and enter a Room genteely, (which might as well be acquir'd at a Dancing-School,) and from whence they return, after Abundance of Trouble and Charge, as great Blockheads as ever, only more proud and selfconceited.

WHILE I was in the midst of these unpleasant Reflections, *Clericus* (who with a Book in his Hand was walking under the Trees) accidentally awak'd me; to him I related my Dream with all its Particulars, and he, without much Study, presently interpreted it, assuring me, *That it was a lively Representation of* HARVARD COLLEGE, *Etcetera.*

> *I remain, Sir,*
> *Your Humble Servant,*
> SILENCE DOGOOD.

THE NEW-ENGLAND COURANT.

June 18. to Monday June 25. 1722.

Give me the Muse, whose generous Force,
*   Impatient of the Reins,*
Pursues an unattempted Course,
*   Breaks all the Criticks Iron Chains.*

WATTS.

To the Author of the *New-England Courant*.

SIR,   No. VII

It has been the Complaint of many Ingenious Foreigners, who
have travell'd amongst us, *That good Poetry is not to be expected in*
New-England. I am apt to Fancy, the Reason is, not because our
Countrymen are altogether void of a Poetical Genius, nor yet
because we have not those Advantages of Education which other
Countries have, but purely because we do not afford that Praise
and Encouragement which is merited, when any thing extraordinary of this Kind is produc'd among us: Upon which Consideration I have determined, when I meet with a Good Piece of
New-England Poetry, to give it a suitable Encomium, and thereby
endeavour to discover to the World some of its Beautys, in order
to encourage the Author to go on, and bless the World with more,
and more Excellent Productions.

THERE has lately appear'd among us a most Excellent Piece
of Poetry, entituled, *An Elegy upon the much Lamented Death of Mrs.*
Mehitebell Kitel, *Wife of Mr.* John Kitel *of* Salem, *Etc.* It may
justly be said in its Praise, without Flattery to the Author, that it is
the most *Extraordinary* Piece that was ever wrote in *New-England.*
The Language is so soft and Easy, the Expression so moving and
pathetick, but above all, the Verse and Numbers so Charming and
Natural, that it is almost beyond Comparison.

The Muse *disdains*
Those Links and Chains,
Measures and Rules of Vulgar Strains,
And o'er the Laws of Harmony a Sovereign Queen she reigns.*

I FIND no English Author, Ancient or Modern, whose Elegies
may be compar'd with this, in respect to the Elegance of Stile, or
Smoothness of Rhime; and for the affecting Part, I will leave your
Readers to judge, if ever they read any Lines, that would sooner
make them *draw their Breath* and Sigh, if not shed Tears, than these
following.

Come let us mourn, for we have lost a
    Wife, a Daughter, and a Sister,
Who has lately taken Flight, and
    Greatly we have mist her.

In another place,

Some little Time before she yielded up her Breath,
She said, I ne'er shall hear one Sermon more on Earth.
She kist her Husband some little Time before she expir'd,
Then lean'd her Head the Pillow on, just out of Breath and tir'd.

BUT the Threefold Appellation in the first Line

—a Wife, a Daughter, and a Sister,

must not pass unobserved. That Line in the celebrated *Watts,*

GUNSTON *the Just, the Generous, and the Young,*

is nothing Comparable to it. The latter only mentions three Qualifi-
cations of *one* Person who was deceased, which therefore could

* An adaptation of Isaac Watts's "Two Happy Rivals."

raise Grief and Compassion but for *One*. Whereas the former, (*our most excellent Poet*) gives his Reader a Sort of an Idea of the Death of *Three Persons,* viz.

—*a Wife, a Daughter, and a Sister,*

which is *Three Times* as great a Loss as the Death of *One,* and consequently must raise *Three Times* as much Grief and Compassion in the Reader.

I SHOULD be very much straitened for Room, if I should attempt to discover even half the Excellencies of this Elegy which are obvious to me. Yet I cannot omit one Observation, which is, that the Author has (to his Honour) invented a new Species of Poetry, which wants a Name, and was never before known. His muse scorns to be confin'd to the old Measures and Limits, or to observe the dull Rules of Criticks;

Nor Rapin *gives her Rules to fly, nor* Purcell *Notes to Sing.*
                                                        Watts.

NOW 'tis Pity that such an Excellent Piece should not be dignify'd with a particular Name; and seeing it cannot justly be called, either *Epic, Sapphic, Lyric,* or *Pindaric,* nor any other Name yet invented, I presume it may, (in Honour and Remembrance of the Dead) be called the KITELIC. Thus much in the Praise of *Kitelic Poetry.*

IT is certain, that those Elegies which are of our own Growth, (and our Soil seldom produces any other sort of Poetry) are by far the greatest part, wretchedly Dull and Ridiculous. Now since it is imagin'd by many, that our Poets are honest, well-meaning Fellows, who do their best, and that if they had but some Instructions how to govern Fancy with Judgment, they would make indifferent good Elegies; I shall here subjoin a Receipt for that purpose, which was left me as a Legacy, (among other valuable Rarities) by my Reverend Husband. It is as follows,

A RECEIPT *to make a* New England
Funeral ELEGY.

For the Title of your Elegy. *Of these you may have enough ready made to your Hands; but if you should chuse to make it your self, you must be sure not to omit the words* Ætatis Suæ, *which will Beautify it exceedingly.*

For the Subject of your Elegy. *Take one of your Neighbours who has lately departed this Life; it is no great matter at what Age the Party dy'd, but it will be best if he went away suddenly, being* Kill'd, Drown'd, *or* Frose to Death.

Having chose the Person, take all his Virtues, Excellencies, &c. and if he have not enough, you may borrow some to make up a sufficient Quantity: To these add his last Words, dying Expressions, &c. if they are to be had; mix all these together, and be sure you strain them well. Then season all with a Handful or two of Melancholly Expressions, such as, Dreadful, Deadly, cruel cold Death, unhappy Fate, weeping Eyes, &c. *Have mixed all these Ingredients well, put them into the empty Scull of some* young Harvard; (*but in Case you have ne'er a One at Hand, you may use your own,*) *there let them Ferment for the Space of a Fortnight, and by that Time they will be incorporated into a Body, which take out, and having prepared a sufficient Quantity of double Rhimes, such as* Power, Flower; Quiver, Shiver; Grieve us, Leave us; tell you, excel you; Expeditions, Physicians; Fatigue him, Intrigue him; &c. *you must spread all upon Paper, and if you can procure a Scrap of Latin to put at the End, it will garnish it mightily; then having affixed your Name at the Bottom, with a* Mœstus Composuit, *you will have an Excellent Elegy.*

N. B. *This Receipt will serve when a Female is the Subject of your Elegy, provided you borrow a greater Quantity of Virtues, Excellencies, &c.*

SIR,

Your Servant,

SILENCE DOGOOD.

P. S. I shall make no other Answer to *Hypercarpus's* Criticism on my last Letter than this, *Mater me genuit, peperit mox filia matrem.**

---

* "My mother begat me, soon the daughter will give birth to a mother."

THE NEW-ENGLAND COURANT.

From Monday September 17. to Monday
September 24. 1722.

To the Author of the *New-England Courant*.

SIR,   **No. XIII**

IN Persons of a contemplative Disposition, the most indifferent
Things provoke the Exercise of the Imagination; and the Satisfac-
tions which often arise to them thereby, are a certain Relief to the
Labour of the Mind (when it has been intensely fix'd on more sub-
stantial Subjects) as well as to that of the Body.

IN one of the late pleasant Moon-light Evenings, I so far indulg'd
in my self the Humour of the Town in walking abroad, as to continue from my Lodgings two or three Hours later than usual, & was
pleas'd beyond Expectation before my Return. Here I found various
Company to observe, and various Discourse to attend to. I met
indeed with the common Fate of *Listeners*, who *hear no good of themselves*, but from a Consciousness of my Innocence, receiv'd it with a
Satisfaction beyond what the Love of Flattery and the Daubings of a
Parasite could produce. The Company who rally'd me were about
Twenty in Number, of both Sexes; and tho' the *Confusion of Tongues*
(like that of *Babel*) which always happens among so many impetuous
Talkers, render'd their Discourse not so intelligible as I could wish,
I learnt thus much, That one of the Females pretended to know me,
from some Discourse she had heard at a certain House before the
Publication of one of my Letters; adding, *That I was a Person of an ill
Character, and kept a criminal Correspondence with a Gentleman who
assisted me in Writing*. One of the Gallants clear'd me of this random
Charge, by saying, *That tho' I wrote in the Character of a Woman, he
knew me to be a Man; But,* continu'd he, *he has more need of endeavouring
a Reformation in himself, than spending his Wit in satyrizing others*.

I HAD no sooner left this Set of Ramblers, but I met a Crowd of

Tarpolins and their Doxies, link'd to each other by the Arms, who ran (by their own Account) after the Rate of *Six Knots an Hour,* and bent their Course towards the *Common.* Their eager and amorous Emotions of Body, occasion'd by taking their Mistresses *in Tow,* they call'd *wild Steerage:* And as a Pair of them happen'd to trip and come to the Ground, the Company were call'd upon to *bring to,* for that *Jack* and *Betty* were *founder'd.* But this Fleet were not less comical or irregular in their Progress than a Company of Females I soon after came up with, who, by throwing their Heads to the Right and Left, at every one who pass'd by them, I concluded came out with no other Design than to revive the Spirit of Love in Disappointed Batchelors, and expose themselves to Sale to the first Bidder.

BUT it would take up too much Room in your Paper to mention all the Occasions of Diversion I met with in this Night's Ramble. As it grew later, I observed, that many pensive Youths with down looks and a slow Pace, would be ever now and then crying out on the Cruelty of their Mistresses; others with a more rapid Pace and chearful Air, would be swinging their Canes, and clapping their Cheeks, and whispering at certain Intervals, *I'm certain I shall have her! This is more than I expected! How charmingly she talks!* &c.

UPON the whole I conclude, That our *Night-Walkers* are a Set of People, who contribute very much to the Health and Satisfaction of those who have been fatigu'd with Business or Study, and occasionally observe their pretty Gestures and Impertinencies. But among Men of Business, the *Shoemakers,* and other Dealers in Leather, are doubly oblig'd to them, inasmuch as they exceedingly promote the Consumption of their Ware: And I have heard of a *Shoemaker,* who being ask'd by a noted Rambler, *Whether he could tell how long her Shoes would last;* very prettily answered, *That he knew how many Days she might wear them, but not how many Nights; because they were then put to a more violent and irregular Service than when she employ'd her self in the common Affairs of the House.*

> I am, SIR,
> Your Humble Servant,
> SILENCE DOGOOD.

From *The Pennsylvania Gazette,* October 22, 1730.

A WITCH TRIAL AT MOUNT HOLLY

"SATURDAY last, at Mount-Holly, about 8 Miles from this Place*
near 300 People were gathered together to see an Experiment or two
tried on some Persons accused of Witchcraft. It seems the Accused
had been charged with making their Neighbours' Sheep dance in an
uncommon Manner, and with causing Hogs to speak and sing
Psalms, etc., to the great Terror and Amazement of the king's good
and peaceable Subjects in this Province; and the Accusers, being very
positive that if the Accused were weighed in Scales against a Bible,
the Bible would prove too heavy for them; or that, if they were
bound and put into the River they would swim; the said Accused,
desirous to make Innocence appear, voluntarily offered to undergo
the said Trials if 2 of the most violent of their Accusers would be
tried with them. Accordingly the Time and Place was agreed on and
advertised about the Country; The Accusers were 1 Man and 1
Woman: and the Accused the same. The Parties being met and the
People got together, a grand Consultation was held, before they
proceeded to Trial; in which it was agreed to use the Scales first;
and a Committee of Men were appointed to search the Men, and a
Committee of Women to search the Women, to see if they had any
Thing of Weight about them, particularly Pins. After the Scrutiny
was over a huge great Bible belonging to the Justice of the Place was
provided, and a Lane through the Populace was made from the
Justice's House to the Scales, which were fixed on a Gallows erected
for that Purpose opposite to the House, that the Justice's Wife and
the rest of the Ladies might see the Trial without coming amongst
the Mob, and after the Manner of Moorfields a large Ring was also
made. Then came out of the House a grave, tall Man carrying the

* Burlington, New Jersey.

Holy Writ before the supposed Wizard etc, (as solemnly as the
Sword-bearer of London before the Lord Mayor) the Wizard was
first put in the Scale, and over him was read a Chapter out of the
Books of Moses, and then the Bible was put in the other Scale,
(which, being kept down before) was immediately let go; but, to
the great Surprize of the Spectators, Flesh and Bones came down
plump, and outweighed that great good Book by abundance. After
the same Manner the others were served, and their Lumps of Mortality severally were too heavy for Moses and all the Prophets and
Apostles. This being over, the Accusers and the rest of the Mob, not
satisfied with this Experiment, would have the Trial by Water.
Accordingly a most solemn Procession was made to the Mill-pond,
where both Accused and Accusers being stripped (saving only to
the Women their Shifts) were bound Hand and Foot and severally
placed in the Water, lengthways, from the Side of a Barge or Flat,
having for Security only a Rope about the Middle of each, which was
held by some in the Flat. The accused man being thin and spare with
some Difficulty began to sink at last; but the rest, every one of them,
swam very light upon the Water. A Sailor in the Flat jump'd out
upon the Back of the Man accused thinking to drive him down to
the Bottom; but the Person bound, without any Help, came up some
time before the other. The Woman Accuser being told that she did
not sink, would be duck'd a second Time; when she swam again as
light as before. Upon which she declared, That she believed the
Accused had bewitched her to make her so light, and that she would
be duck'd again a Hundred Times but she would duck the Devil out
of her. The Accused Man, being surpriz'd at his own Swimming,
was not so confident of his Innocence as before, but said, 'If I am a
Witch, it is more than I know.' The more thinking Part of the Spectators were of Opinion that any Person so bound and placed in the
Water (unless they were mere Skin and Bones) would swim, till
their Breath was gone, and their Lungs fill'd with Water. But it
being the general Belief of the Populace that the Women's shifts
and the Garters with which they were bound help'd to support
them, it is said they are to be tried again the next warm Weather,
naked."

ADVICE TO A YOUNG MAN

Philadelphia, 25 June, 1745.

To My Dear Friend: I know of no Medicine fit to diminish the violent natural Inclinations you mention; and if I did, I think I should not communicate it to you. Marriage is the proper remedy. It is the most natural state of Man, and therefore the State in which you are most likely to find solid Happiness. Your reasons against entering into it at present appear to me to be not well founded. The Circumstantial Advantages you have in View by postponing it, are not only uncertain, but they are small in comparison with that of the Thing itself, the being married and settled. It is the Man and Woman united that makes the complete human Being. Separate, she wants his force of Body and Strength of Reason; he her Softness, Sensibility and acute Discernment. Together they are more likely to succeed in the World. A single Man has not nearly the Value he would have in the State of Union. He is an incomplete Animal. He resembles the odd Half of a pair of Scissors.

If you get a prudent, healthy Wife, your Industry in your Profession, with her good Economy, will be a Fortune sufficient.

But if you will not take this Counsel, and persist in thinking a Commerce with the Sex inevitable, then I repeat my former Advice that in all your Amours you should prefer old Women to young ones. You call this a Paradox, and demand my reasons. They are these:

1. Because they have more Knowledge of the World, and their minds are better stored with Observations, their Conversation is more improving and more lastingly agreeable.

2. Because when Women cease to be handsome, they study to be good. To maintain their Influence over Men, they supply the Diminution of Beauty by an Augmentation of Utility. They learn to do a thousand Services, small and great; and are the most tender and useful of all Friends when you are sick. Thus they continue amiable. And hence there is hardly such a thing to be found as an old Woman who is not a good Woman.

3. Because there is no Hazard of Children, which irregularly produced may be attended with much Inconvenience.

4. Because through more Experience they are more prudent and discreet in conducting an Intrigue to prevent Suspicion. The Commerce with them is therefore safer with regard to your reputation. And with regard to theirs, if the Affair should happen to be known, considerate People might be rather inclined to excuse an old Woman, who would kindly take care of a young Man, form his manners by her good Counsels, and prevent his ruining his Health and Fortune among mercenary Prostitutes.

5. Because in every Animal that walks upright, the Deficiency of the Fluids that fill the Muscles appears first in the highest Part. The Face first grows lank and wrinkled, then the neck, then the Breast and Arms, the lower Parts continuing to the last as plump as ever; so that covering all above with a Basket, and regarding only what is below the Girdle, it is impossible of two Women to know an old one from a young one. And as in the Dark all Cats are grey, the Pleasure of Corporal Enjoyment with an old Woman is at least equal and frequently superior; every Knack being by Practice capable of Improvement.

6. Because the sin is less. The Debauching a Virgin may be her Ruin, and make her for Life unhappy.

7. Because the Compunction is less. The having made a young girl miserable may give you frequent bitter Reflections; none of which can attend making an old Woman happy.

8th, and lastly. They are so grateful!

Thus much for my Paradox. But still I advise you to marry immediately; being sincerely,

Your affectionate Friend,
BENJAMIN FRANKLIN.

From *The Gentleman's Magazine,* April, 1747.

THE SPEECH OF POLLY BAKER

The Speech of Miss Polly Baker before a Court of Judicature, at Connecticut near Boston in New-England; where she was prosecuted the fifth time, for having a Bastard Child: Which influenced the Court to dispense with her Punishment, and which induced one of her Judges to marry her the next Day—by whom she had fifteen Children.

"May it please the honorable bench to indulge me in a few words: I am a poor, unhappy woman, who have no money to fee lawyers to plead for me, being hard put to it to get a living. I shall not trouble your honors with long speeches; for I have not the presumption to expect that you may, by any means, be prevailed on to deviate in your Sentence from the law, in my favor. All I humbly hope is, that your honors would charitably move the governor's goodness on my behalf, that my fine may be remitted. This is the fifth time, gentlemen, that I have been dragg'd before your court on the same account; twice I have paid heavy fines, and twice have been brought to publick punishment, for want of money to pay those fines. This may have been agreeable to the laws, and I don't dispute it; but since laws are sometimes unreasonable in themselves, and therefore repealed; and others bear too hard on the subject in particular circumstances, and therefore there is left a power somewhere to dispense with the execution of them; I take the liberty to say, that I think this law, by which I am punished, both unreasonable in itself, and particularly severe with regard to me, who have always lived an inoffensive life in the neighborhood where I was born, and defy my enemies (if I have any) to say I ever wrong'd any man, woman, or child. Abstracted from the law, I cannot conceive (may it please your honors) what the nature of my offense is. I have brought five fine children into the world, at the risque of my life; I have maintain'd them well by my own industry, without burthening the township, and would have done it better, if it had not been for the heavy charges and fines I have paid. Can it be a crime (in the nature of things, I mean) to add to the king's subjects, in a new country, that really wants people? I own it, I should think it rather a praiseworthy than a punishable action. I have debauched no other woman's husband, nor enticed any other youth; these things I never was charg'd with; nor has any one the least cause of complaint against me, unless, perhaps, the ministers of justice, because I have had children without being married, by which they have missed a wedding fee. But can this be a fault of mine? I appeal to your honors. You are pleased to allow I don't want sense; but I must be stupefied to the last degree, not to prefer the honorable state of wedlock to the condition I have lived in. I always was, and still am willing to enter into it; and doubt not my behaving well in it, having all the industry, frugality, fertility, and skill in economy appertaining to a good wife's character. I defy any one to say I ever refused an offer of that sort: on the contrary, I readily consented to the only proposal of marriage that ever was made me, which was when I was a virgin, but too easily confiding in the person's sincerity that made it, I unhappily lost my honor by trusting his; for he got me with child, and then forsook me.

"That very person, you all know, he is now become a magistrate of this country; and I had hopes he would have appeared this day on the bench, and have endeavored to moderate the Court in my favor; then I should have scorn'd to have mentioned it; but I must now complain of it, as unjust and unequal, that my betrayer and undoer, the first cause of all my faults and miscarriages (if they must be deemed such), should be advanced to honor and power in this government that punishes my misfortune with stripes and infamy. I should be told, 'tis like, that were there no act of Assembly in the case, the precepts of religion are violated by my transgressions. If mine is a religious offense, leave it to religious punishments. You have already excluded me from the comforts of your church communion. Is not that sufficient? You believe I have offended heaven, and must suffer eternal fire: Will not that be sufficient? What need is there then of your additional fines and whipping? I own I do not think as you do, for, if I thought what you call a sin was really such, I could not presumptuously commit it. But, how can it be believed that heaven is angry at my having children, when to the little done by me towards it, God has been pleased to add his divine skill and admirable workmanship in the formation of their bodies, and crowned the whole by furnishing them with rational and immortal souls?

"Forgive me, gentlemen, if I talk a little extravagantly on these matters; I am no divine, but if you, gentlemen, must be making laws, do not turn natural and useful actions into crimes by your prohibitions. But take into your wise consideration the great and growing number of bachelors in the country, many of whom, from the mean fear of the expenses of a family, have never sincerely and honorably courted a woman in their lives; and by their manner of living leave unproduced (which is little better than murder) hundreds of their posterity to the thousandth generation. Is not this a greater offense against the publick good than mine? Compel them, then, by law, either to marriage, or to pay double the fine of fornication every year. What must poor young women do, whom customs and nature forbid to solicit the men, and who cannot force themselves upon husbands, when the laws take no care to provide them any, and yet severely punish them if they do their duty without them; the duty of the first and great command of nature and nature's God, *encrease and multiply;* a duty, from the steady performance of which nothing has been able to deter me, but for its sake I have hazarded the loss of the publick esteem, and have frequently endured publick disgrace and punishment; and therefore ought, in my humble opinion, instead of a whipping, to have a statue erected to my memory."

TO PETER COLLINSON*

[Philadelphia,] July 11, 1747.

SIR,

In my last I informed you that, in pursuing our electrical enquiries, we had observed some particular phænomena, which we looked upon to be new, and of which I promised to give you some account, though I apprehended they might possibly not be new to you, as so many hands are daily employed in electrical experiments on your side the water, some or other of which would probably hit on the same observations.

The first is the wonderful effect of pointed bodies, both in *drawing off* and *throwing off* the electrical fire.† For example,

Place an iron shot of three or four inches diameter on the mouth of a clean dry glass bottle. By a fine silken thread from the cieling, right over the mouth of the bottle, suspend a small cork ball, about the bigness of a marble; the thread of such a length, as that the cork ball may rest against the side of the shot. Electrify the shot, and the ball will be repelled to the distance of four or five inches, more or less, according to the quantity of Electricity. When in this state, if you present to the shot the point of a long slender sharp bodkin, at six or eight inches distance, the repellency is instantly destroy'd, and the cork flies to the shot. A blunt body must be brought within an inch, and draw a spark, to produce the same effect. To prove that the electrical fire is *drawn off* by the point, if you take the blade of the bodkin out of the wooden handle, and fix it in a stick of sealing-wax, and then present it at the distance aforesaid, or if you bring it very near, no such effect follows; but sliding one finger along the

---

* Peter Collinson (1694-1768), antiquarian, botanist, and member of the Royal Society, was a Quaker merchant whose firm had a large business with the American colonies. As part of this business he corresponded with Franklin, but the interchange soon developed into scientific discussions, Collinson passing on news of recent European electrical experiments and Franklin responding with reports of his own activities.

† One practical result of this observation was Franklin's invention of the lightning rod.

wax till you touch the blade, and the ball flies to the shot immediately. If you present the point in the dark, you will see, sometimes at a foot distance, and more, a light gather upon it, like that of a fire-fly, or glow-worm; the less sharp the point, the nearer you must bring it to observe the light; and, at whatever distance you see the light, you may draw off the electrical fire, and destroy the repellency. If a cork ball so suspended be repelled by the tube, and a point be presented quick to it, tho' at a considerable distance, 'tis surprizing to see how suddenly it flies back to the tube. Points of wood will do near as well as those of iron, provided the wood is not dry; for perfectly dry wood will no more conduct Electricity than sealing-wax.

To shew that points will *throw off* as well as *draw off* the electrical fire; lay a long sharp needle upon the shot, and you cannot electrise the shot so as to make it repel the rock ball.* Or fix a needle to the end of a suspended gun-barrel, or iron rod, so as to point beyond it like a little bayonet; and while it remains there, the gun-barrel, or rod, cannot by applying the tube to the other end be electrised so as to give a spark, the fire continually running out silently at the point. In the dark you may see it make the same appearance as it does in the case before mentioned.

The repellency between the cork ball and the shot is likewise destroyed. 1, by sifting fine sand on it; this does it gradually. 2, by breathing on it. 3, by making a smoke about it from burning wood. 4, by candle-light, even though the candle is at a foot distance: these do it suddenly. The light of a bright coal from a wood fire; and the light of red-hot iron do it likewise; but not at so great a distance. Smoke from dry rosin dropt on hot iron, does not destroy the repellency; but is attracted by both shot and cork ball, forming proportionable atmospheres round them, making them look beautifully, somewhat like some of the figures in *Burnet's* or *Whiston's Theory of the Earth.*

* In his notes, Franklin credits the late Thomas Hopkinson, president of the American Philosophical Society, with having first called his attention to this phenomenon and having contrived the experiment for its demonstration. He credits Phillip Syng, silversmith of Philadelphia, with having developed the experiments with wheels which he describes below.

N. B. This experiment should be made in a closet, where the air is very still, or it will be apt to fail.

The light of the sun thrown strongly on both cork and shot by a looking-glass for a long time together, does not impair the repellency in the least. This difference between fire-light and sun-light is another thing that seems new and extraordinary to us.

We had for some time been of opinion, that the electrical fire was not created by friction, but collected, being really an element diffus'd among, and attracted by other matter, particularly by water and metals. We had even discovered and demonstrated its afflux to to the electrical sphere, as well as its efflux, by means of little light windmill-wheels made of stiff paper vanes, fixed obliquely and turning freely on fine wire axes; also by little wheels of the same matter, but formed like water-wheels. Of the disposition and application of which wheels, and the various phænomena resulting, I could, if I had time, fill you a sheet. The impossibility of electrising one's self (though standing on wax) by rubbing the tube, and drawing the fire from it; and the manner of doing it, by passing the tube near a person or thing standing on the floor, &c., had also occurred to us some months before Mr. *Watson's* ingenious *Sequel* came to hand, and these were some of the new things I intended to have communicated to you. But now I need only mention some particulars not hinted in that piece, with our reasonings thereupon; though perhaps the latter might well enough be spared.

1. A person standing on wax, and rubbing the tube, and another person on wax drawing the fire, they will both of them, (provided they do not stand so as to touch one another) appear to be electrised, to a person standing on the floor; that is, he will perceive a spark on approaching each of them with his knuckle.

2. But, if the persons on wax touch one another during the exciting of the tube, neither of them will appear to be electrised.

3. If they touch one another after exciting the tube, and drawing the fire as aforesaid, there will be a stronger spark between them, than was between either of them and the person on the floor.

4. After such strong spark, neither of them discover any electricity.

These appearances we attempt to account for thus: We suppose, as aforesaid, that electrical fire is a common element, of which every one of the three persons above mentioned has his equal share, before any operation is begun with the tube. *A,* who stands on wax and rubs the tube, collects the electrical fire from himself into the glass; and his communication with the common stock being cut off by the wax, his body is not again immediately supply'd. *B,* (who stands on wax likewise) passing his knuckle along near the tube, receives the fire which was collected by the glass from *A;* and his communication with the common stock being likewise cut off, he retians the additional quantity received. To *C,* standing on the floor, both appear to be electrised: for he having only the middle quantity of electrical fire, receives a spark upon approaching *B,* who has an over quantity; but gives one to *A,* who has an under quantity. If *A* and *B* approach to touch each other, the spark is stronger, because the difference between them is greater: After such touch there is no spark between either of them and *C,* because the electrical fire in all is reduced to the original equality. If they touch while electrising, the equality is never destroy'd, the fire only circulating. Hence have arisen some new terms among us: we say, *B,* (and bodies like circumstanced) is electrised *positively; A, negatively.** Or rather, *B* is electrised *plus; A, minus.* And we daily in our experiments electrise bodies *plus or minus,* as we think proper. To electrise *plus* or *minus,* no more needs to be known than this, that the parts of the tube or sphere that are rubbed, do, in the instant of the friction, attract the electrical fire, and therefore take it from the thing rubbing: the same parts immediately, as the friction upon them ceases, are disposed to give the fire they have received, to any body that has less. Thus you may circulate it, as Mr. *Watson* has shewn; you may also accumulate or subtract it upon, or from any body, as you connect that body with the rubber or with the receiver, the communication with the common stock being cut off. We think that ingenious gentleman was deceived when he imagined (in his *Sequel*) that the electrical fire came down the wire from the cieling to the gun-barrel, thence to the

---

* Franklin thus introduces these terms into the vocabulary of science; previously, experimenters had talked of "vitreous" and "resinous" electricity.

sphere, and so electrised the machine and the man turning the wheel, &c. We suppose it was *driven off,* and not brought on through that wire; and that the machine and man, &c., were electrised *minus, i.e.* had less electrical fire in them than things in common.

As the vessel is just upon sailing, I cannot give you so large an account of *American* electricity as I intended: I shall only mention a few particulars more. We find granulated lead better to fill the phial with, than water, being easily warmed, and keeping warm and dry in damp air. We fire spirits with the wire of the phial. We light candles, just blown out, by drawing a spark among the smoke, between the wire and snuffers. We represent lightning, by passing the wire in the dark, over a China plate, that has gilt flowers, or applying it to gilt frames of looking-glasses, &c. We electrise a person twenty or more times running, with a touch of the finger on the wire, thus: He stands on wax. Give him the electrised bottle in his hand. Touch the wire with your finger, and then touch his hand or face; there are sparks every time. We increase the force of the electrical kiss vastly, thus: Let *A* and *B* stand on wax; or *A* on wax, and *B* on the floor; give one of them the electrised phial in hand; let the other take hold of the wire; there will be a small spark; but when their lips approach, they will be struck and shock'd. The same if another gentleman and lady, *C* and *D,* standing also on wax, and joining hands with *A* and *B,* salute or shake hands. We suspend by fine silk thread a counterfeit spider, made of a small piece of burnt cork, with legs of linnen thread, and a grain or two of lead stuck in him, to give him more weight. Upon the table, over which he hangs, we stick a wire upright, as high as the phial and wire, two or three inches from the spider: then we animate him, by setting the electrified phial at the same distance on the other side of him; he will immediately fly to the wire of the phial, bend his legs in touching it; then spring off, and fly to the wire on the table; thence again to the wire of the phial, playing with his legs against both, in a very entertaining manner, appearing perfectly alive to persons unacquainted. He will continue this motion an hour or more in dry weather. We electrify, upon wax in the dark, a book that has a double line of gold round upon the covers, and then apply a knuckle to the gilding; the fire appears everywhere upon the gold like a flash of lightning: not upon the leather, nor, if you touch the leather instead of the gold. We rub our tubes with buckskin, and observe always to keep the same side to the tube, and never to sully the tube by handling; thus they work readily and easily, without the least fatigue, especially if kept in tight pasteboard cases, lined with flannel, and sitting close to the tube. This I mention, because the *European* papers on Electricity, frequently speak of rubbing the tube, as a fatiguing exercise. Our spheres are fixed on iron axes, which pass through them. At one end of the axis there is a small handle, with which you turn the sphere like a common grindstone. This we find very commodious, as the machine takes up but little room, is portable, and may be enclosed in a tight box, when not in use. 'Tis true, the sphere does not turn so swift as when the great wheel is used: but swiftness we think of little importance, since a few turns will charge the phial, &c., sufficiently.

I am, &c.

B. FRANKLIN.

PROPOSALS RELATING TO THE EDUCATION OF YOUTH IN PENSILVANIA, PHILADELPHIA: PRINTED IN THE YEAR, MDCCXLIX*

ADVERTISEMENT TO THE READER.

It has long been regretted as a Misfortune to the Youth of this Province, that we have no ACADEMY, in which they might receive the Accomplishments of a regular Education. The following Paper of Hints towards forming a Plan for that Purpose, is so far approv'd by some publick-spirited Gentleman, to whom it has been privately communicated, that they have directed a Number of Copies to be made by the Press, and properly distributed, in order to obtain the Sentiments and Advice of Men of Learning, Understanding, and Experience in these Matters; and have determined to use their Interest and best Endeavours, to have the Scheme, when compleated, carried gradually into Execution; in which they have Reason to believe they shall have the hearty Concurrence and Assistance of many who are Well-wishers to their Country. Those who incline to favour the Design with their Advice, either as to the Parts of Learning to be taught, the Order of Study, the Method of Teaching, the Œconomy of the School, or any other Matter of Importance to the Success of the Undertaking, are desired to communicate their Sentiments as

* Franklin illustrated this tract with copious notes from pedagogical writers and with a special note on "Authors quoted in this Paper." His proposal resulted in an academy, opened January 7, 1751, of which he was president until 1756.

soon as may be, by Letter directed to B. Franklin, *Printer,* in Philadelphia."

PROPOSALS

The good Education of Youth has been esteemed by wise Men in all Ages, as the surest Foundation of the Happiness both of private Families and of Commonwealths. Almost all Governments have therefore made it a principal Object of their Attention, to establish and endow with proper Revenues, such Seminaries of Learning, as might supply the succeeding Age with Men qualified to serve the Publick with Honour to themselves, and to their Country.

Many of the first Settlers of these Provinces were Men who had received a good Education in *Europe,* and to their Wisdom and good Management we owe much of our present Prosperity. But their Hands were full, and they could not do all Things. The present Race are not thought to be generally of equal Ability: For though the *American* Youth are allow'd not to want Capacity; yet the best Capacities require Cultivation, it being truly with them, as with the best Ground, which unless well tilled and sowed with profitable Seed, produces only ranker Weeds.

That we may obtain the Advantages arising from an Increase of Knowledge, and prevent as much as may be the mischievous Consequences that would attend a general Ignorance among us, the following *Hints* are offered towards forming a Plan for the Education of the Youth of *Pennsylvania*, viz.

It is propos'd,

That some Persons of Leisure and publick Spirit apply for a Charter, by which they may be incorporated, with Power to erect an Academy for the Education of Youth, to govern the same, provide Masters, make Rules, receive Donations, purchase Lands, etc., and to add to their Number, from Time to Time such other Persons as they shall judge suitable.

That the Members of the Corporation make it their Pleasure, and in some Degree their Business, to visit the Academy often, encourage and countenance the Youth, countenance and assist the

Masters, and by all Means in their Power advance the Usefulness and
Reputation of the Design; that they look on the Students as in some
Sort their Children, treat them with Familiarity and Affection, and,
when they have behav'd well, and gone through their Studies, and
are to enter the World, zealously unite, and make all the Interest that
can be made to establish them, whether in Business, Offices, Marriages, or any other Thing for their Advantage, preferably to all
other Persons whatsoever even of equal Merit.

And if Men may, and frequently do, catch such a Taste for cultivating Flowers, for Planting, Grafting, Inoculating, and the like,
as to despise all other Amusements for their Sake, why may not we
expect they should acquire a Relish for that *more useful* Culture of
young Minds. *Thompson* says,

> " 'T is Joy to see the human Blossoms blow,
> When infant Reason grows apace, and calls
> For the kind Hand of an assiduous Care.
> Delightful Task! to rear the tender Thought,
> To teach the young Idea how to shoot;
> To pour the fresh Instruction o'er the Mind,
> To breathe th' enliv'ning Spirit, and to fix
> The generous Purpose in the glowing Breast."

That a House be provided for the ACADEMY, if not in the Town,
not many Miles from it; the Situation high and dry, and if it may be,
not far from a River, having a Garden, Orchard, Meadow, and a
Field or two.

That the House be furnished with a Library (if in the Country, if
in the Town, the Town Libraries may serve) with Maps of all
Countries, Globes, some mathematical Instruments, an Apparatus
for Experiments in Natural Philosophy, and for Mechanics; Prints,
of all Kinds, Prospects, Buildings, Machines, &c.

That the Rector be a Man of good Understanding, good Morals,
diligent and patient, learn'd in the Languages and Sciences, and a
correct pure Speaker and Writer of the *English* Tongue; to have such
Tutors under him as shall be necessary.

That the boarding Scholars diet together, plainly, temperately, and frugally.

That, to keep them in Health, and to strengthen and render active their Bodies, they be frequently exercis'd in Running, Leaping, Wrestling, and Swimming, &c.

That they have peculiar Habits to distinguish them from other Youth, if the Academy be in or near the Town; for this, among other Reasons, that their Behaviour may be the better observed.

As to their STUDIES, it would be well if they could be taught *every Thing* that is useful, and *every Thing* that is ornamental: But Art is long, and their Time is short. It is therefore propos'd that they learn those Things that are likely to be *most useful* and *most ornamental*. Regard being had to the several Professions for which they are intended.

All should be taught to write a *fair Hand,* and swift, as that is useful to All. And with it may be learnt something of *Drawing,* by Imitation of Prints, and some of the first Principles of Perspective.

Arithmetick, Accounts, and some of the first Principles of *Geometry* and *Astronomy*.

The *English* Language might be taught by Grammar; in which some of our best Writers, as *Tillotson, Addison, Pope, Algernoon Sidney, Cato's Letters,* &c., should be Classicks: the *Stiles* principally to be cultivated, being the *clear* and the *concise*. Reading should also be taught; and pronouncing, properly, distinctly, emphatically; not with an even Tone, which *under-does,* nor a theatrical, which *over-does* Nature.

To form their Stile they should be put on Writing Letters to each other, making Abstracts of what they read; or writing the same Things in their own Words; telling or writing Stories lately read, in their own Expressions. All to be revis'd and corrected by the Tutor, who should give his Reasons, and explain the Force and Import of Words, &c.

To form their Pronunciation, they may be put on making Declamations, repeating Speeches, delivering Orations &c.; The Tutor assisting at the Rehearsals, teaching, advising, correcting their Accent, &c.

But if History be made a constant Part of their Reading, such as the Translations of the *Greek* and *Roman* Historians, and the modern Histories of ancient *Greece* and *Rome,* &c. may not almost all Kinds of useful Knowledge be that Way introduc'd to Advantage, and with Pleasure to the Student? As

GEOGRAPHY, by reading with Maps, and being required to point out the Places *where* the greatest Actions were done, to give their old and new Names, with the Bounds, Situation, Extent of the Countries concern'd, &c.

CHRONOLOGY, by the Help of *Helvicus* or some other Writer of the Kind, who will enable them to tell *when* those Events happened; what Princes were Cotemporaries, what States or famous Men flourish'd about that Time, &c. The several principal Epochas to be first well fix'd in their Memories.

ANTIENT CUSTOMS, religious and civil, being frequently mentioned in History, will give Occasion for explaining them; in which the Prints of Medals, Basso-Relievos, and antient Monuments will greatly assist.

MORALITY, by descanting and making continual Observations on the Causes of the Rise or Fall of any Man's Character, Fortune, Power &c. mention'd in History; the Advantages of Temperance, Order, Frugality, Industry, Perseverance &c. &c. Indeed the general natural Tendency of Reading good History must be, to fix in the Minds of Youth deep Impressions of the Beauty and Usefulness of Virtue of all Kinds, Publick Spirit, Fortitude, &c.

History will show the wonderful Effects of ORATORY, in governing, turning and leading great Bodies of Mankind, Armies, Cities, Nations. When the Minds of Youth are struck with Admiration at this, then is the Time to give them the Principles of that Art, which they will study with Taste and Application. Then they may be made acquainted with the best Models among the antients, their Beauties being particularly pointed out to them. Modern Political Oratory being chiefly performed by the Pen and Press, its Advantages over the Antient in some Respects are to be shown; as that its Effects are more extensive, more lasting, &c.

History will also afford frequent Opportunities of showing the Necessity of a *Publick Religion,* from its Usefulness to the Publick; the Advantage of a Religious Character among private Persons; the Mischiefs of Superstition, &c. and the Excellency of the CHRISTIAN RELIGION above all others antient or modern.

History will also give Occasion to expatiate on the Advantage of Civil Orders and Constitutions; how Men and their Properties are protected by joining in Societies and establishing Government; their Industry encouraged and rewarded, Arts invented, and Life made more comfortable: The Advantages of *Liberty,* Mischiefs of *Licentiousness,* Benefits arising from good Laws and a due Execution of Justice, &c. Thus may the first Principles of sound *Politicks* be fix'd in the Minds of Youth.

On *Historical* Occasions, Questions of Right and Wrong, Justice and Injustice, will naturally arise, and may be put to Youth, which they may debate in Conversation and in Writing. When they ardently desire Victory, for the Sake of the Praise attending it, they will begin to feel the Want, and be sensible of the Use of *Logic,* or the Art of Reasoning to *discover* Truth, and of Arguing to *defend* it, and *convince* Adversaries. This would be the Time to acquaint them with the Principles of that Art. Grotius, Puffendorff, and some other Writers of the same Kind, may be used on these Occasions to decide their Disputes. Publick Disputes warm the Imagination, whet the Industry, and strengthen the natural Abilities.

When Youth are told, that the Great Men whose Lives and Actions they read in History, spoke two of the best Languages that ever were, the most expressive, copious, beautiful; and that the finest Writings, the most correct Compositions, the most perfect Productions of human Wit and Wisdom, are in those Languages, which have endured Ages, and will endure while there are Men; that no Translation can do them Justice, or give the Pleasure found in Reading the Originals; that those Languages contain all Science; that one of them is become almost universal, being the Language of Learned Men in all Countries; that to understand them is a distinguishing Ornament, &c. they may be thereby made desirous of learning those Languages, and their Industry sharpen'd in the Acquisition of them. All intended for Divinity, should be taught the *Latin* and *Greek;* for Physick, the *Latin, Greek,* and *French;* for Law, the *Latin* and *French;* Merchants, the *French, German,* and *Spanish:* And though all should not be compell'd to learn *Latin, Greek,* or the modern foreign Languages; yet none that have an ardent Desire to learn them should be refused; their *English,* Arithmetick and other Studies absolutely necessary, being at the same Time not neglected.

If the new *Universal History* were also read, it would give a *connected* Idea of human Affairs, so far as it goes, which should be follow'd by the best modern Histories, particularly of our Mother Country; then of these Colonies; which should be accompanied with Observations on their Rise, Encrease, Use to *Great Britain,* Encouragements, Discouragements, etc. the Means to make them flourish, secure their Liberties, &c.

With the History of Men, Times, and Nations, should be read at proper Hours or Days, some of the best *Histories of Nature,* which would not only be delightful to Youth, and furnish them with Matter for their Letters, &c. as well as other History; but afterwards of great Use to them, whether they are Merchants, Handicrafts, or Divines; enabling the first the better to understand many Commodities, Drugs, &c.; the second to improve his Trade or Handicraft by new Mixtures, Materials, &c., and the last to adorn his Discourses by beautiful Comparisons, and strengthen them by new Proofs of Divine Providence. The Conversation of all will be improved by it, as Occasions frequently occur of making Natural Observations, which are instructive, agreeable, and entertaining in almost all Companies. *Natural History* will also afford Opportunities of introducing many Observations, relating to the Preservation of Health, which may be afterwards of great Use. *Arbuthnot* on Air and *Aliment, Sanctorius* on Perspiration, *Lemery* on Foods, and some others, may now be read, and a very little Explanation will make them sufficiently intelligible to Youth.

While they are reading Natural History, might not a little *Gardening,*

Planting, Grafting, Inoculating, etc., be taught and practised; and now and then Excursions made to the neighbouring Plantations of the best Farmers, their Methods observ'd and reason'd upon for the Information of Youth? The Improvement of Agriculture being useful to all, and Skill in it no Disparagement to any.

The History of *Commerce,* of the Invention of Arts, Rise of Manufactures, Progress of Trade, Change of its Seats, with the Reasons, Causes, &c., may also be made entertaining to Youth, and will be useful to all. And this, with the Accounts in other History of the prodigious Force and Effect of Engines and Machines used in War, will naturally introduce a Desire to be instructed in *Mechanicks,* and to be inform'd of the Principles of that Art by which weak Men perform such Wonders, Labour is sav'd, Manufactures expedited, &c. This will be the Time to show them Prints of antient and modern Machines, to explain them, to let them be copied, and to give Lectures in Mechanical Philosophy.

With the whole should be constantly inculcated and cultivated, that *Benignity of Mind,* which shows itself in *searching for* and *seizing* every Opportunity *to serve* and *to oblige;* and is the Foundation of what is called GOOD BREEDING; highly useful to the Possessor, and most agreeable to all.

The Idea of what is *true Merit* should also be often presented to Youth, explain'd and impress'd on their Minds, as consisting in an *Inclination* join'd with an *Ability* to serve Mankind, one's Country, Friends and Family; which *Ability* is (with the Blessing of God) to be acquir'd or greatly encreas'd by *true Learning;* and should indeed be the great *Aim* and *End* of all Learning.

From *The Pennyslvania Gazette*. May 9, 1751.

EXPORTING OF FELONS
TO THE COLONIES

TO THE PRINTERS OF THE GAZETTE

By a Passage in one of your late Papers, I understand that the Government at home will not suffer our mistaken Assemblies to make any Law for preventing or discouraging the Importation of Convicts from Great Britain, for this kind Reason, '*That such Laws are against the Publick Utility, as they tend to prevent the* IMPROVEMENT *and* WELL PEOPLING *of the Colonies.*'

Such a tender *parental* Concern in our *Mother Country* for the *Welfare* of her *Children,* calls aloud for the highest *Returns* of Gratitude and Duty. This every one must be sensible of: But 'tis said, that in our present Circumstances it is absolutely impossible for us to make *such* as are adequate to the Favour. I own it; but nevertheless let us do our Endeavour. 'Tis something to show a grateful Disposition.

In some of the uninhabited Parts of these Provinces, there are Numbers of these venomous Reptiles we call RATTLE-SNAKES; Felons-convict from the Beginning of the World: These, whenever we meet with them, we put to Death, by Virtue of an old Law, *Thou shalt bruise his Head.* But as this is a sanguinary Law, and may seem too cruel; and as however mischievous those Creatures are with us, they may possibly change their Natures, if they were to change the Climate; I would humbly propose, that this general Sentence of *Death* be changed for *Transportation.*

In the Spring of the Year, when they first creep out of their Holes, they are feeble, heavy, slow, and easily taken; and if a small Bounty were allow'd *per* Head, some Thousands might be collected annually, and *transported* to *Britain.* There I would propose to have them carefully distributed in *St. James's Park,* in the *Spring-Gardens* and other

Places of Pleasure about *London;* in the Gardens of all the Nobility and Gentry throughout the Nation; but particularly in the Gardens of the *Prime Ministers,* the *Lords of Trade* and *Members of Parliament;* for to them we are *most particularly* obliged.

There is no human Scheme so perfect, but some Inconveniencies may be objected to it: Yet when the Conveniencies far exceed, the Scheme is judg'd rational, and fit to be executed. Thus Inconveniencies have been objected to that *good* and *wise* Act of Parliament, by virtue of which all the *Newgates* and *Dungeons* in *Britain* are emptied into the Colonies. It has been said, that these Thieves and Villains introduc'd among us, spoil the Morals of Youth in the Neighbourhoods that entertain them, and perpetrate many horrid Crimes: But let not *private Interests* obstruct *publick* Utility. Our *Mother* knows what is best for us. What is a little *Housebreaking, Shoplifting,* or *Highway Robbing;* what is a *Son* now and then *corrupted* and *hang'd,* a Daughter *debauch'd* and *pox'd,* a Wife *stabb'd,* a Husband's *Throat cut,* or a Child's *Brains beat out* with an Axe, compar'd with this 'IM-PROVEMENT and WELL PEOPLING of the Colonies!'

Thus it may perhaps be objected to my Scheme, that the *Rattle-Snake* is a mischievous Creature, and that his changing his Nature with the Clime is a mere Supposition, not yet confirm'd by sufficient Facts. What then? Is not Example more prevalent than Precept? And may not the honest rough British Gentry, by a Familiarity with these Reptiles, learn to *creep,* and to *insinuate,* and to *slaver,* and to *wriggle* into Place (and perhaps to *poison* such as stand in their Way) Qualities of no small Advantage to Courtiers! In comparison of which 'IMPROVEMENT and PUBLICK UTILITY,' what is a *Child* now and then kill'd by their venomous Bite, . . . or even a favourite *Lap Dog?*

I would only add, that this exporting of Felons to the Colonies, may be consider'd as a *Trade,* as well as in the Light of a *Favour,* Now all Commerce implies Returns: Justice requires them: There can be no Trade without them. And *Rattle-Snakes* seem the most *suitable Returns* for the *Human Serpents* sent us by our *Mother* Country. In this, however, as in every other Branch of Trade, she will have the Advantage of us. She will reap *equal* Benefits without equal

Risque of the Inconveniencies and Dangers. For the *Rattle-Snake* gives Warning before he attempts his Mischief; which the Convict does not. I am

Yours, &c.

AMERICANUS.

OBSERVATIONS

CONCERNING THE INCREASE OF MANKIND, PEOPLING OF COUNTRIES, ETC.

Written in Pensilvania, 1751.

1. TABLES of the Proportion of Marriages to Births, of Deaths to Births, of Marriages to the Numbers of Inhabitants, &c., form'd on Observaions (sic) made upon the Bills of Mortality, Christnings, &c., of populous Cities, will not suit Countries; nor will Tables form'd on Observations made on full-settled old Countries, as *Europe,* suit new Countries, as *America.*

2. For People increase in Proportion to the Number of Marriages, and that is greater in Proportion to the Ease and Convenience of supporting a Family. When families can be easily supported, more Persons marry, and earlier in Life.

3. In Cities, where all Trades, Occupations, and Offices are full, many delay marrying till they can see how to bear the Charges of a Family; which Charges are greater in Cities, as Luxury is more common: many live single during Life, and continue Servants to Families, Journeymen to Trades; &c. hence Cities do not by natural Generation supply themselves with Inhabitants; the Deaths are more than the Births.

4. In Countries full settled, the Case must be nearly the same; all Lands being occupied and improved to the Heighth; those who cannot get Land, must Labour for others that have it; when

Labourers are plenty, their Wages will be low; by low Wages a family is supported with Difficulty; this Difficulty deters many from Marriage, who therefore long continue Servants and single. Only as the Cities take Supplies of People from the Country, and thereby make a little more Room in the Country; Marriage is a little more encourag'd there, and the Births exceed the Deaths.

5. *Europe* is generally full settled with Husbandmen, Manufacturers, &c., and therefore cannot now much increase in People: *America* is chiefly occupied by Indians, who subsist mostly by Hunting. But as the Hunter, of all Men, requires the greatest Quantity of Land from whence to draw his Subsistence, (the Husbandman subsisting on much less, the Gardner on still less, and the Manufacturer requiring least of all), the *Europeans* found *America* as fully settled as it well could be by Hunters; yet these, having large Tracks, were easily prevail'd on to part with Portions of Territory to the new Comers, who did not much interfere with the Natives in Hunting, and furnish'd them with many Things they wanted.

6. Land being thus plenty in *America,* and so cheap as that a labouring man, that understands Husbandry, can in a short Time save Money enough to purchase a Piece of new Land sufficient for a Plantation, whereon he may subsist a Family, such are not afraid to marry; for, if they even look far enough forward to consider how their Children, when grown up, are to be provided for, they see that more Land is to be had at rates equally easy, all Circumstances considered.

7. Hence Marriages in *America* are more general, and more generally early, than in *Europe.* And if it is reckoned there, that there is but one Marriage per Annum among 100 persons, perhaps we may here reckon two; and if in *Europe* they have but 4 Births to a Marriage (many of their Marriages being late), we may here reckon 8, of which if one half grow up, and our Marriages are made, reckoning one with another at 20 Years of Age, our People must at least be doubled every 20 Years.

8. But notwithstanding this Increase, so vast is the Territory of *North America,* that it will require many Ages to settle it fully; and, till it is fully settled, Labour will never be cheap here, where no

Man continues long a Labourer for others, but gets a Plantation of his own, no Man continues long a Journeyman to a Trade, but goes among those new Settlers, and sets up for himself, &c. Hence Labour is no cheaper now in *Pennsylvania,* than it was 30 Years ago, tho' so many Thousand labouring People have been imported.

9. The Danger therefore of these Colonies interfering with their Mother Country in Trades that depend on Labour, Manufactures, &c., is too remote to require the attention of *Great-Britain.*

10. But in Proportion to the Increase of the Colonies, a vast Demand is growing for British Manufactures, a glorious Market wholly in the Power of *Britain,* in which Foreigners cannot interfere, which will increase in a short Time even beyond her Power of supplying, tho' her whole Trade should be to her Colonies: Therefore *Britain* should not too much restrain Manufactures in her Colonies. A wise and good Mother will not do it. To distress, is to weaken, and weakening the Children weakens the whole Family.

11. Besides if the Manufactures of *Britain* (by reason of the *American* Demands) should rise too high in Price, Foreigners who can sell cheaper will drive her Merchants out of Foreign Markets; Foreign Manufactures will thereby be encouraged and increased, and consequently foreign Nations, perhaps her Rivals in Power, grow more populous and more powerful; while her own Colonies, kept too low, are unable to assist her, or add to her Strength.

12. 'Tis an ill-grounded Opinion that by the Labour of slaves, *America* may possibly vie in Cheapness of Manufactures with *Britain.* The Labour of Slaves can never be so cheap here as the Labour of working Men is in *Britain.* Any one may compute it. Interest of Money is in the Colonies from 6 to 10 per Cent. Slaves one with another cost 30£ Sterling per Head. Reckon then the Interest of the first Purchase of a Slave, the Insurance or Risque on his Life, his Cloathing and Diet, Expences in his Sickness and Loss of Time, Loss by his Neglect of Business (Neglect is natural to the Man who is not to be benefited by his own Care or Diligence), Expence of a Driver to keep him at Work, and his Pilfering from

Time to Time, almost every Slave being *by Nature* a Thief, and compare the whole Amount with the Wages of a Manufacturer of Iron or Wool in *England,* you will see that Labour is much cheaper there than it ever can be by Negroes here. Why then will *Americans* purchase Slaves? Because Slaves may be kept as long as a *Man* pleases, or has Occasion for their Labour; while hired Men are continually leaving their masters (often in the midst of his Business,) and setting up for themselves.—Sec. 8.

13. As the Increase of People depends on the Encouragement of Marriages, the following Things must diminish a Nation, viz. 1. *The being conquered;* for the Conquerors will engross as many Offices, and exact as much Tribute or Profit on the Labour of the conquered, as will maintain them in their new Establishment, and this diminishing the Subsistence of the Natives, discourages their Marriages, and so gradually diminishes them, while the foreigners increase. 2. *Loss of Territory.* Thus, the *Britons* being driven into *Wales,* and crowded together in a barren Country insufficient to support such great Numbers, diminished 'till the People bore a Proportion to the Produce, while the *Saxons* increas'd on their abandoned lands; till the Island became full of *English.* And, were the *English* now driven into *Wales* by some foreign Nation, there would in a few Years, be no more Englishmen in *Britain,* than there are now people in *Wales.* 3. *Loss of Trade.* Manufactures exported, draw Subsistence from Foreign Countries for Numbers; who are thereby enabled to marry and raise Families. If the Nation be deprived of any Branch of Trade, and no new Employment is found for the People occupy'd in that Branch, it will also be soon deprived of so many People. 4. *Loss of Food.* Suppose a Nation has a Fishery, which not only employs great Numbers, but makes the Food and Subsistence of the People cheaper. If another Nation becomes Master of the Seas, and prevents the Fishery, the People will diminish in Proportion as the Loss of Employ and Dearness of Provision, makes it more difficult to subsist a Family. 5. *Bad Government and insecure Property.* People not only leave such a Country, and settling Abroad incorporate with other Nations, lose their native Language, and become Foreigners, but, the Industry of those that remain being discourag'd, the Quantity

of Subsistence in the Country is lessen'd, and the Support of a Family becomes more difficult. So heavy Taxes tend to diminish a People. 6. *The Introduction of Slaves.* The Negroes brought into the *English* Sugar *Islands* have greatly diminish'd the Whites there; the Poor are by this Means deprived of Employment, while a few Families acquire vast Estates; which they spend on Foreign Luxuries, and educating their Children in the Habit of those Luxuries; the same Income is needed for the Support of one that might have maintain'd 100. The Whites who have Slaves, not labouring, are enfeebled, and therefore not so generally prolific; the Slaves being work'd too hard, and ill fed, their Constitutions are broken, and the Deaths among them are more than the Births; so that a continual Supply is needed from *Africa.* The Northern Colonies, having few Slaves, increase in Whites. Slaves also pejorate* the Families that use them; the white Children become proud, disgusted with Labour,

---

* Writing to David Hume, September 27, 1760, Franklin discussed the style as well as the content of this pamphlet and said:

"I thank you for your friendly admonition relating to some unusual words in the pamphlet. It will be of service to me. The *'pejorate'* and the *'colonize,'* since they are not in common use here, I give up as bad; for certainly in writings intended for persuasion and for general information, one cannot be too clear; and every expression in the least obscure is a fault. The *'unshakeable'* too, though clear, I give up as rather low. The introducing new words, where we are already possessed of old ones sufficiently expressive, I confess must be generally wrong, as it tends to change the language; yet, at the same time, I cannot but wish the usage of our tongue permitted making new words, when we want them, by composition of old ones whose meanings are already well understood. The Germans allow of it, and it is a common practice with their writers. Many of our present English words were originally so made; and many of the Latin words. In point of clearness, such compound words would have the advantage of any we can borrow from the ancient or from foreign languages. For instance, the word *inaccessible,* though long in use among us, is not yet, I dare say, so universally understood by our people, as the word *uncomeatable* would immediately be, which we are not allowed to write. But I hope with you, that we shall always in America make the best English of this Island our standard, and I believe it will be so. I assure you it often gives me pleasure to reflect, how greatly the *audience* (if I may so term it) of a good English writer will, in another century or two, be increased by the increase of English people in our colonies."

and being educated in Idleness, are rendered unfit to get a Living by Industry.

14. Hence the Prince that acquires new Territory, if he finds it vacant, or removes the Natives to give his own People Room; the Legislator that makes effectual Laws for promoting of Trade, increasing Employment, improving Land by more or better Tillage, providing more Food by Fisheries; securing Property, &c. and the Man that invents new Trades, Arts, or Manufactures, or new Improvements in Husbandry, may be properly called *Fathers* of their Nation, as they are the Cause of the Generation of Multitudes, by the Encouragement they afford to Marriage.

15. As to Privileges granted to the married, (such as the *Jus trium Liberorum* among the *Romans,*) they may hasten the filling of a Country that has been thinned by War or Pestilence, or that has otherwise vacant Territory; but cannot increase a People beyond the Means provided for their Subsistence.

16. Foreign Luxuries and needless Manufactures, imported and used in a Nation, do, by the same Reasoning, increase the People of the Nation that furnishes them, and diminish the People of the Nation that uses them. Laws, therefore, that prevent such Importations, and on the contrary promote the Exportation of Manufactures to be consumed in Foreign Countries, may be called (with Respect to the People that make them) *generative Laws,* as, by increasing Subsistence they encourage Marriage. Such Laws likewise strengthen a Country, doubly, by increasing its own People and diminishing its Neighbours.

17. Some *European* Nations prudently refuse to consume the Manufactures of *East-India:*—They should likewise forbid them to their Colonies; for the Gain to the Merchant is not to be compar'd with the Loss, by this Means, of People to the Nation.

18. Home Luxury in the Great increases the Nation's Manufacturers employ'd by it, who are many, and only tends to diminish the Families that indulge in it, who are few. The greater the common fashionable Expence of any Rank of People, the more cautious they are of Marriage. Therefore Luxury should never be suffer'd to become common.

19. The great Increase of Offspring in particular Families is not always owing to greater Fecundity of Nature, but sometimes to Examples of Industry in the Heads, and industrious Education; by which the Children are enabled to provide better for themselves, and their marrying early is encouraged from the Prospect of good Subsistence.

20. If there be a Sect, therefore, in our Nation, that regard Frugality and Industry as religious Duties, and educate their Children therein, more than others commonly do; such Sect must consequently increase more by natural Generation, than any other sect in *Britain*.

21. The Importation of Foreigners into a Country, that has as many Inhabitants as the present Employments and Provisions for Subsistence will bear, will be in the End no Increase of People; unless the New Comers have more Industry and Frugality than the Natives, and then they will provide more Subsistence, and increase in the Country; but they will gradually eat the Natives out. Nor is it necessary to bring in Foreigners to fill up any occasional Vacancy in a Country; for such Vacancy (if the Laws are good, sec. 14, 16,) will soon be filled by natural Generation. Who can now find the Vacancy made in *Sweden, France,* or other Warlike Nations, by the Plague of Heroism, 40 years ago; in *France,* by the Expulsion of the Protestants; in *England,* by the Settlement of her Colonies; or in *Guinea,* by 100 Years Exportation of Slaves, that has blacken'd half *America?* The thinness of Inhabitants in *Spain* is owing to National Pride and Idleness, and other Causes, rather than to the Expulsion of the Moors, or to the making of new Settlements.

22. There is, in short, no Bound to the prolific Nature of Plants or Animals, but what is made by their crowding and interfering with each other's means of Subsistence. Was the Face of the Earth vacant of other Plants, it might be gradually sowed and overspread with one Kind only; as, for Instance, with Fennel; and were it empty of other Inhabitants, it might in a few Ages be replenish'd from one Nation only; as, for Instance, with *Englishmen.* Thus there are suppos'd to be now upwards of One Million *English* Souls in *North-America,* (tho' 'tis thought scarce 80,000 have been brought over

Sea,) and yet perhaps there is not one the fewer in *Britain,* but rather many more, on Account of the Employment the Colonies afford to Manufacturers at Home. This Million doubling, suppose but once in 25 Years, will, in another Century, be more than the People of *England,* and the greatest Number of *Englishmen* will be on this Side the Water. What an Accession of Power to the *British* Empire by Sea as well as Land! What Increase of Trade and Navigation! What Numbers of Ships and Seamen! We have been here but little more than 100 years, and yet the Force of our Privateers in the late War, united, was greater, both in Men and Guns, than that of the whole *British* Navy in Queen *Elizabeth's* Time. How important an Affair then to *Britain* is the present Treaty for settling the Bounds between her Colonies and the *French,* and how careful should she be to secure Room enough, since on the Room depends so much the Increase of her People.

23. In fine, a Nation well regulated is like a Polypus; take away a Limb, its Place is soon supply'd; cut it in two, and each deficient Part shall speedily grow out of the Part remaining. Thus if you have Room and Subsistence enough, as you may by dividing, make ten Polypes out of one, you may of one make ten Nations, equally populous and powerful; or rather increase a Nation ten fold in Numbers and Strength.*

And since Detachments of *English* from *Britain,* sent to *America,* will have their Places at Home so soon supply'd and increase so largely here; why should the *Palatine Boors* be suffered to swarm into our Settlements and, by herding together, establish their Language and Manners, to the Exclusion of ours? Why should *Pennsylvania,* founded by the *English,* become a Colony of *Aliens,* who will shortly be so numerous as to Germanize us instead of our Anglifying them, and will never adopt our Language or Customs any more than they can acquire our Complexion?

24. Which leads me to add one Remark, that the Number of purely white People in the World is proportionably very small. All *Africa* is black or tawny; *Asia* chiefly tawny; *America* (exclusive of

---

* The essay ended here in all editions during Franklin's lifetime but the first.

the new Comers) wholly so. And in *Europe*, the *Spaniards*, *Italians*, *French*, *Russians*, and *Swedes*, are generally of what we call a swarthy Complexion; as are the *Germans* also, the *Saxons* only excepted, who, with the *English*, make the principal Body of White People on the Face of the Earth. I could wish their Numbers were increased. And while we are, as I may call it, *Scouring* our Planet, by *clearing America* of Woods, and so making this Side of our Globe reflect a brighter Light to the Eyes of Inhabitants in *Mars* or *Venus*, why should we, in the Sight of Superior Beings, darken its People? Why increase the Sons of *Africa*, by planting them in *America*, where we have so fair an Opportunity, by excluding all Blacks and Tawneys, of increasing the lovely White and Red? But perhaps I am partial to the Complexion of my Country, for such Kind of Partiality is natural to Mankind.

TO PETER COLLINSON

Philadelphia, Aug. 25, 1755.

DEAR SIR,—

As you have my former papers on Whirlwinds, &c., I now send you an account of one which I had lately an opportunity of seeing and examining myself.

Being in *Maryland*, riding with Colonel *Tasker*, and some other gentlemen to his country-seat, where I and my son were entertained by that amiable and worthy man with great hospitality and kindness, we saw in the vale below us, a small whirlwind beginning in the road, and shewing itself by the dust it raised and contained. It appeared in the form of a sugar-loaf, spinning on its point, moving up the hill towards us, and enlarging as it came forward. When it passed by us, its smaller part near the ground, appeared no bigger than a common barrel, but widening upwards, it seemed, at 40 or 50 feet high, to be 20 or 30 feet in diameter. The rest of the company stood looking after it, but my curiosity being stronger, I followed it, riding close by its side, and observed its licking up, in its progress, all the dust that was under its smaller part. As it is a common opinion that a shot, fired through a water-spout, will break it, I tried to break this little whirlwind, by striking my whip frequently through it, but without any effect. Soon after, it quitted the road and took into the woods, growing every moment larger and stronger, raising, instead of dust, the old dry leaves with which the ground was thick covered, and making a great noise with them and the branches of the trees, bending some tall trees round in a circle swiftly and very surprizingly, though the progressive motion of the whirl was not so swift but that a man on foot might have kept pace with it; but the circular motion was amazingly rapid. By the leaves it was now filled with, I could plainly perceive that the current of air they were driven by, moved upwards in a spiral line; and when I saw the trunks and bodies of large trees invelop'd in the passing whirl, which continued intire after it had left them I no longer wondered that my whip had no effect on it in its smaller state. I accompanied it about three quarters of a mile, till some limbs of dead trees, broken off by the whirl, flying about and falling near me, made me more apprehensive of danger; and then I stopped, looking at the top of it as it went on, which was visible, by means of the leaves contained in it, for a very great height above the trees. Many of the leaves, as they got loose from the upper and widest part, were scattered in the wind; but so great was their height in the air, that they appeared no bigger than flies. My son, who was by this time come up with me, followed the whirlwind till it left the woods, and crossed an old tobacco-field, where, rinding neither dust nor leaves to take up, it gradually became invisible below as it went away over that field. The course of the general wind then blowing was along with us as we travelled, and the progressive motion of the whirlwind was in a direction nearly opposite, though it did not keep a strait line, nor was its progressive motion uniform, it making little sallies on either hand as it went, proceeding sometimes faster and sometimes slower, and seeming sometimes for a few seconds almost stationary, then starting forward pretty fast again. When we rejoined the company, they were admiring the vast height of the leaves now brought by the common wind, over our heads. These leaves accompanied us as we travelled, some falling now and then round about us, and some not reaching the ground till we had gone near three miles from the place where we first saw the whirlwind begin. Upon my asking Colonel *Tasker* if such whirlwinds were common in *Maryland,* he answered pleasantly, "No, not at all common; but we got this on purpose to treat Mr. Franklin." And a very high treat it was, to

Dear Sir,

Your affectionate friend and humble servant,

B. F[RANKLIN].

From *Poor Richard Improved: 1757.*

A STRIKING SUN DIAL

How to make a STRIKING SUN DIAL, by which not only a Man's own Family, but all his Neighbours for ten Miles round, may know what a Clock it is, when the Sun shines, without seeing the Dial.

Chuse an open Place in your Yard or Garden, on which the Sun may shine all Day without any Impediment from Trees or Buildings.

On the Ground mark out your Hour Lines, as for a horizontal Dial, according to Art, taking Room enough for the Guns. On the Line for One o'Clock, place one Gun; on the Two o'Clock Line two Guns, and so of the rest. The Guns must all be charged with Powder, but Ball is unnecessary. Your Gnomon or Style must have twelve burning Glasses annex'd to it, and be so placed that the Sun shining through the Glasses, one after the other, shall cause the Focus or burning Spot to fall on the Hour Line of One, for Example, at One a Clock, and there kindle a Train of Gunpowder that shall fire one Gun. At Two a clock, a Focus shall fall on the Hour Line of Two, and kindle another Train that shall discharge Two Guns successively: and so of the rest.

Note, There must be 78 Guns in all. Thirty-two Pounders will be best for this Use; but 18 Pounders may do, and will cost less, as well as use less Powder, for nine Pounds of Powder will do for one Charge of each eighteen Pounder, whereas the Thirty-two Pounders would require for each Gun 16 Pounds.

Note also, That the chief Expense will be the Powder, for the Cannon once bought, will, with Care, last 100 Years.

Note moreover, that there will be a great Saving of Powder in Cloudy Days.

Kind Reader, Methinks I hear thee say, That is indeed a good Thing to know how the Time passes, but this Kind of Dial, notwithstanding the mentioned Savings, would be very Expensive; and the Cost greater than the Advantage, Thou art wise, my Friend, to be so considerate beforehand; some Fools would not have found out so much, till thay had made the Dial and try'd it. . . . Let all such learn that many a private and many a publick Project, are like this Striking Dial, great Cost for little Profit.

THE WAY TO WEALTH

PREFACE TO POOR RICHARD IMPROVED: 1758

COURTEOUS READER

I have heard that nothing gives an Author so great Pleasure, as to find his Works respectfully quoted by other learned Authors. This Pleasure I have seldom enjoyed; for tho' I have been, if I may say it without Vanity, an *eminent Author* of Almanacks annually now a full Quarter of a Century, my Brother Authors in the same Way, for what Reason I know not, have ever been very sparing in their Applauses, and no other Author has taken the least

Notice of me, so that did not my Writings produce me some solid *Pudding,* the great Deficiency of *Praise* would have quite discouraged me.

I concluded at length, that the People were the best Judges of my Merit; for they buy my Works; and besides, in my Rambles, where I am not personally known, I have frequently heard one or other of my Adages repeated, with, *as Poor Richard says,* at the End on 't; this gave me some Satisfaction, as it showed not only that my Instructions were regarded, but discovered likewise some Respect for my Authority; and I own, that to encourage the Practice of remembering and repeating those wise Sentences, I have sometimes *quoted myself* with great Gravity.

Judge, then how much I must have been gratified by an Incident I am going to relate to you. I stopt my Horse lately where a great Number of People were collected at a Vendue of Merchant Goods. The Hour of Sale not being come, they were conversing on the Badness of the Times and one of the Company call'd to a plain clean old Man, with white Locks, "Pray, Father Abraham, what think you of the Times? Won't these heavy Taxes quite ruin the Country? How shall we be ever able to pay them? What would you advise us to?" Father *Abraham* stood up, and reply'd, "If you'd have my Advice, I'll give it you in short, for *A Word to the Wise is enough,* and *many Words won't fill a Bushel,* as *Poor Richard* says." They join'd in desiring him to speak his Mind, and gathered round him, he proceeded as follows;

"Friends," says he, and Neighbours, "the Taxes are indeed very heavy, and if those laid on by the Government were the only Ones we had to pay, we might more easily discharge them; but we have many others, and much more grievous to some of us. We are taxed twice as much by our *Idleness,* three times as much by our *Pride,* and four times as much by our *Folly;* and from these Taxes the Commissioners cannot ease or deliver us by allowing an Abatement. However let us hearken to good Advice, and something may be done for us; *God helps them that help themselves,* as *Poor Richard* says, in his Almanack of 1733.

It would be thought a hard Government that should tax its

People one-tenth Part of their *Time,* to be employed in its Service. But *Idleness* taxes many of us much more, if we reckon all that is spent in absolute *Sloth,* or doing of nothing, with that which is spent in idle Employments or Amusements, that amount to nothing. *Sloth,* by bringing on Diseases, absolutely shortens Life. *Sloth, like Rust, consumes faster than Labour wears; while the used Key is always bright,* as Poor Richard says. *But dost thou love Life, then do not squander Time, for that's the stuff Life is made of,* as Poor Richard says. How much more than is necessary do we spend in sleep, forgetting that *The sleeping Fox catches no Poultry,* and that *There will be sleeping enough in the Grave,* as Poor Richard says.

If Time be of all Things the most precious, wasting Time must be, as Poor Richard says, *the greatest Prodigality;* since, as he elsewhere tells us, *Lost Time is never found again; and what we call Time enough, always proves little enough:* Let us then up and be doing, and doing to the Purpose; so by Diligence shall we do more with less Perplexity. *Sloth makes all Things difficult, but Industry all easy,* as Poor Richard says; and *He that riseth late must trot all Day, and shall scarce overtake his Business at Night;* while *Laziness travels so slowly, that Poverty soon overtakes him,* as we read in *Poor Richard,* who adds, *Drive thy Business, let not that drive thee;* and *Early to Bed, and early to rise, makes a Man healthy, wealthy, and wise.*

So what signifies *wishing* and *hoping* for better Times. We may make these Times better, if we bestir ourselves. *Industry need not wish,* as Poor Richard says, *and he that lives upon Hope will die fasting. There are no Gains without Pains; then Help Hands, for I have no Lands,* or if I have, they are smartly taxed. And, as *Poor Richard* likewise observes, *He that hath a Trade hath an Estate; and he that hath a Calling, hath an Office of Profit and Honour;* but then the *Trade* must be worked at, and the *Calling* well followed, or neither the *Estate* nor the *Office* will enable us to pay our Taxes. If we are industrious, we shall never starve; for, as *Poor Richard* says, *At the working Man's House Hunger looks in, but dares not enter.* Nor will the Bailiff or the Constable enter, for *Industry pays Debts, while Despair encreaseth them,* says *Poor Richard.* What though you have found no Treasure, nor has any rich Relation left you a Legacy, *Diligence is the Mother of*

Good-luck as *Poor Richard* says *and God gives all Things to Industry. Then plough deep, while Sluggards sleep, and you shall have Corn to sell and to keep,* says *Poor Dick.* Work while it is called To-day, for you know not how much you may be hindered To-morrow, which makes *Poor Richard* say, *One to-day is worth two To-morrows,* and farther, *Have you somewhat to do To-morrow, do it To-day.* If you were a Servant, would you not be ashamed that a good Master should catch you idle? Are you then your own Master, *be ashamed to catch yourself idle,* as *Poor Dick* says. When there is so much to be done for yourself, your Family, your Country, and your gracious King, be up by Peep of Day; *Let not the Sun look down and say, Inglorious here he lies.* Handle your Tools without Mittens; remember that *The Cat in Gloves catches no Mice,* as *Poor Richard* says. 'Tis true there is much to be done, and perhaps you are weak-handed, but stick to it steadily; and you will see great Effects, for *Constant Dropping wears away Stones,* and by *Diligence and Patience the Mouse ate in two the Cable;* and *Little Strokes fell great Oaks,* as *Poor Richard* says in his Almanack, the Year I cannot just now remember.

Methinks I hear some of you say, *Must a Man afford himself no Leisure?* I will tell thee, my friend, what *Poor Richard* says, *Employ thy Time well, if thou meanest to gain Leisure; and, since thou art not sure of a Minute, throw not away an Hour.* Leisure, is Time for doing something useful; this Leisure the diligent Man will obtain, but the lazy Man never; so that, as *Poor Richard* says *A Life of Leisure and a Life of Laziness are two Things.* Do you imagine that Sloth will afford you more Comfort than Labour? No, for as *Poor Richard* says, *Trouble springs from Idleness, and grievous Toil from needless Ease. Many without Labour, would live by their Wits only, but they break for want of Stock.* Whereas Industry gives Comfort, and Plenty, and Respect: *Fly Pleasures, and they'll follow you. The diligent Spinner has a large Shift; and now I have a Sheep and a Cow, everyBody bids me good Morrow;* all which is well said by *Poor Richard.*

But with our Industry, we must likewise be *steady, settled,* and *careful,* and oversee our own Affairs *with our own Eyes,* and not trust too much to others; for, as *Poor Richard* says

> *I never saw an oft-removed Tree,*
> *Nor yet an oft-removed Family,*
> *That throve so well as those that settled be.*

And again, *Three Removes is as bad as a Fire;* and again, *Keep thy Shop, and thy Shop will keep thee;* and again, *If you would have your Business done, go; if not, send.* And again,

> *He that by the Plough would thrive,*
> *Himself must either hold or drive.*

And again, *The Eye of a Master will do more Work than both his Hands;* and again, *Want of Care does us more Damage than Want of Knowledge;* and again, *Not to oversee Workmen, is to leave them your Purse open.* Trusting too much to others' Care is the Ruin of many; for, as the Almanack says, *In the Affairs of this World, Men are saved, not by Faith, but by the Want of it;* but a Man's own Care is profitable; for, saith *Poor Dick, Learning is to the Studious,* and *Riches to the Careful,* as well as *Power to the Bold,* and *Heaven to the Virtuous,* And farther, *If you would have a faithful Servant, and one that you like, serve yourself.* And again, he adviseth to Circumspection and Care, even in the smallest Matters, because sometimes *A little Neglect may breed great Mischief;* adding, *for want of a Nail the Shoe was lost; for want of a Shoe the Horse was lost: and for want of a Horse the Rider was lost, being overtaken and slain by the Enemy; all for want of Care about a Horse-shoe Nail.*

So much for Industry, my Friends, and Attention to one's own Business; but to these we must add *Frugality,* if we would make our *Industry* more certainly successful. A Man may, if he knows not how to save as he gets, *keep his Nose all his Life to the Grindstone,* and die not worth a *Groat* at last. *A fat Kitchen makes a lean Will,* as *Poor Richard* says; and

> *Many Estates are spent in the Getting,*
> *Since Women for Tea forsook Spinning and Knitting,*
> *And men for Punch forsook Hewing and Splitting.*

If you would be wealthy, says he, in another Almanack, *think of Saving as well as of Getting: The Indies have not made Spain rich, because her Outgoes are greater than her Incomes.*

Away then with your expensive Follies, and you will not then have so much Cause to complain of hard Times, heavy Taxes, and chargeable Families; for, as *Poor Dick* says,

> *Women and Wine, Game and Deceit,*
> *Make the Wealth small and the Wants great.*

And farther, *What maintains one Vice, would bring up two Children.* You may think perhaps, that a *little* Tea, or a *little* Punch now and then, Diet a *little* more costly, Clothes a *little* finer, and a *little* Entertainment now and then, can be no *great* Matter; but remember what *Poor Richard* says, *Many a Little makes a Mickle;* and farther, Beware of little *Expences; A small Leak will sink a great Ship;* and again, *Who Dainties love, shall Beggars prove;* and moreover, *Fools make Feasts, and wise Men eat them.*

Here you are all got together at this Vendue of *Fineries* and *Knicknacks.* You call them *Goods;* but if you do not take Care, they will prove *Evils* to some of you. You expect they will be sold *cheap,* and perhaps they may for less than they cost; but if you have no Occasion for them, they must be *dear* to you. Remember what *Poor Richard* says; *Buy what thou hast no Need of, and ere long thou shalt sell thy Necessaries.* And again, *At a great Pennyworth pause a while:* He means, that perhaps the Cheapness is *apparent* only, and not *Real;* or the bargain, by straitening thee in thy Business, may do thee more Harm than Good. For in another Place he says, *Many have been ruined by buying good Pennyworths.* Again, *Poor Richard* says, 'tis *foolish to lay out Money in a Purchase of Repentance;* and yet this Folly is practised every Day at Vendues, for want of minding the Almanack. *Wise Men,* as *Poor Dick* says, *learn by others Harms, Fools scarcely by their own;* but *felix quem faciunt aliena pericula cautum.* Many a one, for the Sake of Finery on the Back, have gone with a hungry Belly, and half-starved their Families. *Silks and Sattins, Scarlet and Velvets,* as *Poor Richard* says, *puts out the Kitchen Fire.*

These are not the *Necessaries* of Life; they can scarcely be called the *Conveniences;* and yet only because they look pretty, how many *want* to *have* them! The *artificial* Wants of Mankind thus become more numerous that the *Natural;* and, as *Poor Dick* says, *for one Poor Person, there are an hundred indigent.* By these, and other Extravagancies, the Genteel are reduced to poverty, and forced to borrow of those whom they formerly despised, but who through Industry and Frugality have maintained their Standing; in which Case it appears plainly, that *A Ploughman on his Legs is higher than a Gentleman on his Knees,* as *Poor Richard* says. Perhaps they have had a small Estate left them, which they knew not the Getting of; they think, *'tis Day, and will never be Night;* that a little to be spent out of *so much,* is not worth minding; *a Child and a Fool,* as *Poor Richard* says, *imagine Twenty shillings and Twenty Years can never be spent* but, *always taking out of the Meal-tub, and never putting in, soon comes to the Bottom;* as *Poor Dick* says, *When the Well's dry, they know the Worth of Water.* But this they might have known before, if they had taken his Advice; *If you would know the Value of Money, go and try to borrow some; for, he that goes a borrowing goes a sorrowing;* and indeed so does he that lends to such People, when he goes *to get it in again.* *Poor Dick* farther advises, and says,

> *Fond Pride of Dress is sure a very Curse;*
> *E'er Fancy you consult, consult your Purse.*

And again, *Pride is as loud a Beggar as Want, and a great deal more saucy.* When you have bought one fine Thing, you must buy ten more, that your Appearance may be all of a Piece; but *Poor Dick* says, *'Tis easier to suppress the first Desire, than to satisfy all that follow it.* And 'tis as truly Folly for the Poor to ape the Rich, as for the Frog to swell, in order to equal the ox.

> *Great Estates may venture more,*
> *But little Boats should keep near Shore.*

Tis, however, a Folly soon punished; for *Pride that dines on Vanity, sups on Contempt,* as *Poor Richard* says. And in another Place, *Pride*

breakfasted with Plenty, dined with Poverty, and supped with Infamy.
And after all, of what Use is this *Pride of Appearance,* for which so
much is risked so much is suffered? It cannot promote Health, or
ease Pain; it makes no Increase of Merit in the Person, it creates
Envy, it hastens Misfortune.

> *What is a Butterfly? At best*
> *He's but a Caterpillar drest*
> *The gaudy Fop's his Picture just,*

as *Poor Richard* says.

But what Madness must it be to *run in Debt* for these Super-
fluities! We are offered, by the Terms of this Vendue, *Six Months'
Credit;* and that perhaps has induced some of us to attend it, because
we cannot spare the ready Money, and hope now to be fine without
it. But, ah, think what you do when you run in Debt; *you give to
another Power over your Liberty.* If you cannot pay at the Time, you
will be ashamed to see your Creditor; you will be in Fear when you
speak to him; you will make poor pitiful sneaking Excuses, and
by Degrees come to lose your Veracity, and sink into base downright
lying; for, as *Poor Richard* says *The second Vice is Lying, the first is
running in Debt.* And again, to the same Purpose, *Lying rides upon
Debt's Back.* Whereas a free-born *Englishman* ought not to be ashamed
or afraid to see or speak to any Man living. But Poverty often
deprives a Man of all Spirit and Virtue: *'Tis hard for an empty Bag to
stand upright,* as *Poor Richard* truly says.

What would you think of that Prince, or that Government, who
should issue an Edict forbidding you to dress like a Gentleman or a
Gentlewoman, on Pain of Imprisonment or Servitude? Would you
not say, that you were free, have a Right to dress as you please, and
that such an Edict would be a Breach of your Privileges, and such a
Government tyrannical? And yet you are about to put yourself
under that Tyranny, when you run in Debt for such Dress! Your
Creditor has Authority, at his Pleasure to deprive you of your
Liberty, by confining you in Gaol for Life, or to sell you for a
Servant, if you should not be able to pay him! When you have got

your Bargain, you may, perhaps, think little of Payment; but *Creditors, Poor Richard* tells us, *have better Memories than Debtors;* and in another Place says, *Creditors are a superstitious Sect, great Observers of set Days and Times.* The Day comes round before you are aware, and the Demand is made before you are prepared to satisfy it, Or if you bear your Debt in Mind, the Term which at first seemed so long, will, as it lessens, appear extreamly short. *Time* will seem to have added Wings to his Heels as well as Shoulders. *Those have a short Lent,* saith *PoorRichard, who owe Money to be paid at Easter.* Then since, as he says, *The Borrower is a Slave to the Lender, and the Debtor to the Creditor,* disdain the Chain, preserve your Freedom; and maintain your Independency: Be *industrious* and *free;* be *frugal* and *free.* At present, perhaps, you may think yourself in thriving Circumstances, and that you can bear a little Extravagance without Injury; but,

> *For Age and Want, save while you may;*
> *No Morning Sun lasts a whole Day,*

as *Poor Richard* says. Gain may be temporary and uncertain, but ever while you live, Expence is constant and certain; and *'tis easier to build two Chimnies, than to keep one in Fuel,* as Poor Richard says. So, *Rather go to Bed supperless than rise in Debt.*

> *Get what you can, and what you get hold;*
> *'Tis the Stone that will turn all your lead into Gold,*

as *Poor Richard* says. And when you have got the Philosopher's Stone, sure you will no longer complain of bad Times, or the Difficulty of paying Taxes.

This Doctrine, my Friends, is *Reason* and *Wisdom;* but after all, do not depend too much upon your own *Industry,* and *Frugality,* and *Prudence,* though excellent Things, for they may all be blasted without the Blessing of Heaven; and therefore, ask that Blessing humbly, and to be not uncharitable to those that at present seem to want it, but comfort and help them. Remember, *Job* suffered, and was afterwards prosperous.

And now to conclude, *Experience keeps a dear School, but Fools will learn in no other, and scarce in that;* for it is true, *we may give Advice, but we cannot give Conduct,* as *Poor Richard* says: However, remember this, *They that won't be counselled, can't be helped,* as *Poor Richard* says: and farther, That, *if you will not hear Reason, she'll surely rap your Knuckles.*"

Thus the old Gentleman ended his Harangue. The People heard it, and approved the Doctrine, and immediately practised the contrary, just as if it had been a common Sermon; for the Vendue opened, and they began to buy extravagantly, notwithstanding, his Cautions and their own Fear of Taxes. I found the good Man had thoroughly studied my Almanacks, and digested all I had dropt on these Topicks during the Course of Five and twenty Years. The frequent Mention he made of me must have tired any one else, but my Vanity was wonderfully delighted with it; though I was conscious not that a tenth Part of the Wisdom was my own, which he ascribed to me, but rather the *Gleanings* I had made of the Sense of all Ages and Nations. However, I resolved to be the better for the Echo of it; and though I had at first determined to buy Stuff for a new Coat, I went away resolved to wear my old One a little longer. *Reader,* if thou wilt do the same, thy Profit will be as great as mine. I *am, as ever, thine to serve thee,*

RICHARD SAUNDERS.
July 7, 1757.

TO THE EDITOR OF A NEWSPAPER*

Monday, May 20, [1765].

SIR,

In your Paper of Wednesday last, an ingenious Correspondent that calls himself THE SPECTATOR, and dates from *Pimlico,* under the Guise of Good Will to the News-writers, whom he calls an

* It is not known for which newspaper Franklin intended this letter.

"useful Body of Men in this great City," has, in my Opinion, art-fully attempted to turn them & their Works into Ridicule, wherein if he could succeed, great Injury might be done to the Public as well as to those good People.

Supposing, Sir, that the *"We hears"* they give us of this & t'other intended Voyage or Tour of this & t'other great Personage, were mere Inventions, yet they at least offer us an innocent Amusement while we read, and useful Matter of Conversation when we are dispos'd to converse.

Englishmen, Sir, are too apt to be silent when they have nothing to say; too apt to be sullen when they are silent; and, when they are sullen, to hang themselves. But, by these *We hears,* we are supplied with abundant funds of Discourse, we discuss the Motives for such Voyages, the Probability of their being undertaken, and the Practicability of their Execution. Here we display our Judgment in Politics, our Knowledge of the Interests of Princes, and our Skill in Geography, and (if we have it) show our Dexterity moreover in Argumentation. In the mean time, the tedious Hour is kill'd, we go home pleas'd with the Applauses we have receiv'd from others, or at least with those we secretly give to ourselves: We sleep soundly, & live on, to the Comfort of our Families. But, Sir, I beg leave to say, that all the Articles of News that seem improbable are not mere Inventions. Some of them, I can assure you on the Faith of a Traveller, are serious Truths. And here, quitting Mr. Spectator of Pimlico, give me leave to instance the various number-less Accounts the Newswriters have given us, with so much honest Zeal for the welfare of *Poor Old England,* of the establishing Manufactures in the Colonies to the Prejudice of those of this King-dom. It is objected by superficial Readers, who yet pretend to some Knowledge of those Countries, that such Establishments are not only improbable, but impossible, for that their Sheep have but little Wooll, not in the whole sufficient for a Pair of Stockings a Year to each Inhabitant; and that, from the Universal Dearness of Labour among them, the Working of Iron and other Materials, except in some few coarse Instances, is impracticable to any Ad-vantage.

Dear Sir, do not let us suffer ourselves to be amus'd with such groundless Objections. The very Tails of the American Sheep are so laden with Wooll, that each has a little Car or Waggon on four little Wheels, to support & keep it from trailing on the Ground. Would they caulk their Ships, would they fill their Beds, would they even litter their Horses with Wooll, if it were not both plenty and cheap? And what signifies Dearness of Labour, when an English Shilling passes for five and Twenty? Their engaging 300 Silk Throwsters here in one Week, for New York, was treated as a Fable, because, forsooth, they have "no Silk there to throw." Those, who made this Objection, perhaps did not know, that at the same time the Agents from the King of Spain were at Quebec to contract for 1000 Pieces of Cannon to be made there for the Fortification of Mexico, and at N York engaging the annual Supply of woven Floor-Carpets for their West India Houses, other Agents from the Emperor of China were at Boston treating about an Exchange of raw Silk for Wooll, to be carried in Chinese Junks through the Straits of Magellan.

And yet all this is as certainly true, as the Account said to be from Quebec, in all the Papers of last Week, that the Inhabitants of Canada are making Preparations for a Cod and Whale Fishery this "Summer in the upper Lakes." Ignorant People may object that the upper Lakes are fresh, and that Cod and Whale are Salt Water Fish: But let them know, Sir, that Cod, like other Fish when attack'd by their Enemies, fly into any Water where they can be safest; that Whales, when they have a mind to eat Cod, pursue them wherever they fly: and that the grand Leap of the Whale in that Chase up the Fall of Niagara is esteemed, by all who have seen it, as one of the finest Spectacles in Nature. Really, Sir, the World is grown too incredulous. It is like the Pendulum ever swinging from one Extream to another. Formerly every thing printed was believed, because it was in print. Now Things seem to be disbelieved for just the very same Reason. Wise Men wonder at the present Growth of Infidelity. They should have consider'd, when they taught People to doubt the Authority of Newspapers and the Truth of Predictions in Almanacks, that the next Step might be a

Disbelief in the well vouch'd Accts of Ghosts Witches, and Doubts even of the Truths of the Creed!

Thus much I thought it necessary to say in favour of an honest Set of Writers, whose comfortable Living depends on collecting & supplying the Printers with News at the small Price of Sixpence an Article, and who always show their Regard to Truth, by contradicting in a subsequent Article such as are wrong,—for another Sixpence,—to the great Satisfaction & Improvement of us Coffeehouse Students in History & Politics, and the infinite Advantage of all future Livies, Rapins, Robertsons, Humes, and McAulays, who may be sincerely inclin'd to furnish the World with that *rara Avis,* a true History. I am, Sir, your humble Servant,

A Traveller.

ON THE PRICE OF CORN, AND MANAGEMENT OF THE POOR

TO THE PUBLIC.

I am one of that class of people, that feeds you all, and at present is abused by you all; in short I am a *farmer*.

By your newspapers we are told, that God had sent a very short harvest to some other countries of Europe. I thought this might be in favour of Old England; and that now we should get a good price for our grain, which would bring millions among us, and make us flow in money; that to be sure is scarce enough.

But the wisdom of government forbade the exportation.

"Well," says I, "then we must be content with the market price at home."

"No;" say my lords the mob, "you sha'nt have that. Bring your corn to market if you dare; we'll sell it for you for less money, or take it for nothing."

Being thus attacked by both ends *of the constitution,* the head and tail *of government,* what am I to do?

Must I keep my corn in the barn, to feed and increase the breed of rats? Be it so; they cannot be less thankful than those I have been used to feed.

Are we farmers the only people to be grudged the profits of our honest labour? And why? One of the late scribblers against us gives a bill of fare of the provisions at my daughter's wedding, and proclaims to all the world, that we had the insolence to eat beef and pudding! Has he not read the precept in the good Book, *Thou shalt not muzzle the mouth of the ox that treadeth out the corn;* or does he think us less worthy of good living than our oxen?

"O, but the manufacturers! the manufacturers! they are to be favoured, and they must have bread at a cheap rate!"

Hark ye, Mr. Oaf; the farmers live splendidly, you say. And pray, would you have them hoard the money they get? Their fine clothes and furniture, do they make them themselves, or for one another, and so keep the money among them? Or do they employ these your darling manufacturers, and so scatter it again all over the nation?

The wool would produce me a better price, it it were suffered to go to foreign markets; but that, Messieurs the Public, your laws will not permit. It must be kept all at home, that our *dear* manufacturers may have it the cheaper. And then, having yourselves thus lessened our encouragement for raising sheep, you curse us for the scarcity of mutton!

I have heard my grandfather say, that the farmers submitted to the prohibition on the exportation of wool, being made to expect and believe, that, when the manufacturer bought his wool cheaper, they should also have their cloth cheaper. But the deuce a bit. It has been growing dearer and dearer from that day to this. How so? Why, truly, the cloth is exported; and that keeps up the price.

Now, if it be a good principle, that the exportation of a commodity is to be restrained, that so our people at home may have it the cheaper, stick to that principle, and go thorough-stitch with it. Prohibit the exportation of your cloth, your leather, and shoes, your iron ware, and your manufactures of all sorts, to make them all cheaper at home. And cheap enough they will be, I will warrant you; till people leave off making them.

Some folks seem to think they ought never to be easy till England becomes another Lubberland, where it is fancied that streets are paved with penny-rolls, the houses tiled with pancakes, and chickens, ready roasted, cry, "Come eat me."

I say, when you are sure you have got a good principle, stick to it, and carry it through. I hear it is said, that though it was *necessary and right* for the ministry to advise a prohibition of the exportation of corn, yet it was *contrary to law;* and also, that though it was *contrary to law* for the mob to obstruct wagons, yet it was *necessary and right*. Just the same thing to a tittle. Now they tell me, an act of indemnity ought to pass in favour of the ministry, to secure them from the consequences of having acted illegally. If so, pass another in favour of the mob. Others say, some of the mob ought to be hanged, by way of example, If so,—but I say no more than I have said before, *when you are sure that you have a good principle, go through with it.*

You say, poor labourers cannot afford to buy bread at a high price, unless they had higher wages. Possibly. But how shall we farmers be able to afford our labourers higher wages, if you will not allow us to get, when we might have it, a higher price for our corn?

By all that I can learn, we should at least have had a guinea a quarter more, if the exportation had been allowed. And this money England would have got from foreigners.

But, it seems, we farmers must take so much less, that the poor may have it so much cheaper.

This operates, then, as a tax for the maintenance of the poor. A very good thing you will say. But I ask, Why a partial tax? why laid on us farmers only? If it be a good thing, pray,

Messieurs the Public, take your share of it, by indemnifying us a little out of your public treasury. In doing a good thing, there is both honour and pleasure; you are welcome to your share of both.

For my own part, I am not so well satisfied of the goodness of this thing. I am for doing good to the poor, but I differ in opinion about the means. I think the best way of doing good to the poor, is, not making them easy *in* poverty, but leading or driving them *out* of it. In my youth, I travelled much, and I observed in different countries, that the more public provisions were made for the poor, the less they provided for themselves, and of course became poorer. And, on the contrary, the less was done for them, the more they did for themselves, and became richer. There is no country in the world where so many provisions are established for them; so many hospitals to receive them when they are sick or lame, founded and maintained by voluntary charities; so many almshouses for the aged of both sexes, together with a solemn general law made by the rich to subject their estates to a heavy tax for the support of the poor. Under all these obligations, are our poor modest, humble, and thankful? And do they use their best endeavours to maintain themselves, and lighten our shoulders of this burthen? On the contrary, I affirm, that there is no country in the world in which the poor are more idle, dissolute, drunken, and insolent. The day you passed that act, you took away from before their eyes the greatest of all inducements to industry, frugality, and sobriety, by giving them a dependence on somewhat else than a careful accumulation during youth and health, for support in age or sickness.

In short, you offered a premium for the encouragement of idleness, and you should not now wonder, that it has had its effect in the increase of poverty. Repeal that law, and you will soon see a change in their manners. *Saint Monday* and *Saint Tuesday* will soon cease to be holidays. Six *days shalt thou labour,* though one of the old commandments long treated as out of date, will again be looked upon as a respectable precept; industry will increase, and with it plenty among the lower people; their circumstances will mend, and more will be done for their happiness by inuring them to provide for themselves, than could be done by dividing all your estates among them.

Excuse me, Messieurs the Public, if, upon this *interesting* subject, I put you to the trouble of reading a little of *my* nonsense. I am sure I have lately read a great deal of *yours*, and therefore from you (at least from those of you who are writers) I deserve a little indulgence.

I am yours, &c.
ARATOR.

From *The Gentleman's Magazine*, October, 1773, p. 513.

AN EDICT
BY THE KING OF PRUSSIA

Dantzic, Sept. 5, [1773].

We have long wondered here at the supineness of the English nation, under the Prussian impositions upon its trade entering our port. We did not, till lately, know the claims, ancient and modern, that hang over that nation; and therefore could not, suspect that it might submit to those impositions from a sense of duty or from principles of equity. The following Edict, just made publick, may, if serious, throw some light upon this matter.

"FREDERIC, by the grace of God, King of Prussia, &c. &c. &c., to all present and to come, (*à tous présens et à venir,*) Health. The peace now enjoyed throughout our dominions, having afforded us leisure to apply ourselves to the regulation of commerce, the improvement of our finances, and at the same time the easing our domestic subjects in their taxes: For these causes, and other good considerations us thereunto moving, we hereby make known, that, after having deliberated these affairs in our council, present our dear brothers, and other great officers of the state, members of the same, we, of our certain knowledge, full power, and authority royal, have made and issued this present Edict, viz.

"Whereas it is well known to all the world, that the first German settlements made in the Island of Britain, were by colonies of people, subject to our renowned ducal ancestors, and drawn from their dominions, under the conduct of Hengist, Horsa, Hella, Uff, Cerdicus, Ida, and others; and that the said colonies have flourished under the protection of our august house for ages past; have never been emancipated therefrom; and yet have hitherto yielded little profit to the same: And whereas we ourselves have in the last war fought for and defended the said colones, against the power of France, and thereby enabled them to make conquests from the said power in America, for which we have not yet received adequate compensation: And whereas it is just and expedient that a revenue should be raised from the said colonies in Britain, towards our indemnification; and that those who are descendants of our ancient subjects, and thence still owe us due obedience, should contribute to the replenishing of our royal coffers as they must have done, had their ancestors remained in the territories now to us appertaining: We do therefore hereby ordain and command, that, from and after the date of these presents, there shall be levied and paid to our officers of the *customs,* on all goods, wares, and merchandizes, and on all grain and other produce of the earth, exported from the said Island of Britain, and on all goods of whatever kind imported into the same, a duty of four and a half per cent *ad valorem,* for the use of us and our successors. And that the said duty may more effectually be collected, we do hereby ordain, that all ships or vessels bound from Great Britain to any other part of the world, or from any other part of the world to Great Britain, shall in their respective voyages touch at our port of Koningsberg, there to be unladen, searched, and charged with the said duties.

"And whereas there hath been from time to time discovered

in the said island of Great Britain, by our colonists there, many mines or beds of iron-stone; and sundry subjects, of our ancient dominion, skilful in converting the said stone into metal, have in time past transported themselves thither, carrying with them and communicating that art; and the inhabitants of the said island, presuming that they had a natural right to make the best use they could of the natural productions of their country for their own benefit, have not only built furnaces for smelting the said stone into iron, but have erected plating-forges, slitting-mills, and steel-furnaces, for the more convenient manufacturing of the same; thereby endangering a diminution of the said manufacture in our ancient dominion;—we do therefore hereby farther ordain, that, from and after the date hereof, no mill or other engine for slitting or rolling of iron, or any plating-forge to work with a tilt-hammer, or any furnace for making steel, shall be erected or continued in the said island of Great Britain: and the Lord Lieutenant of every county in the said island is hereby commanded, on information of any such erection within his county, to order and by force to cause the same to be abated and destroyed; as he shall answer the neglect thereof to us at his peril. But we are nevertheless graciously pleased to permit the inhabitants of the said island to transport their iron into Prussia, there to be manufactured, and to them returned; they paying our Prussian subjects for the workmanship, with all the costs of commission, freight, and risk, coming and returning; any thing herein contained to the contrary notwithstanding.

"We do not, however, think fit to extend this our indulgence to the article of wool; but, meaning to encourage, not only the manufacturing of woollen cloth, but also the raising of wool, in our ancient dominions, and to prevent both, as much as may be, in our said island, we do hereby absolutely forbid the transportation of wool from thence, even to the mother country, Prussia; and that those islanders may be farther and more effectually restrained in making any advantage of their own wool in the way of manufacture, we command that none shall be carried out of one county into another; nor shall any worsted, bay, or woollen yarn, cloth, says, bays, kerseys, serges, frizes, druggets, cloth-serges, shalloons, or any other drapery stuffs, or woollen manufactures whatsoever, made up or mixed with wool in any of the said counties, be carried into any other county, or be waterborne even across the smallest river or creek, on penalty of forfeiture of the same, together with the boats, carriages, horses, &c., that shall be employed in removing them. Nevertheless, our loving subjects there are hereby permitted (if they think proper) to use all their wool as manure for the improvement of their lands.

"And whereas the art and mystery of making hats hath arrived at great perfection in Prussia, and the making of hats by our remoter subjects ought to be as much as possible restrained: and forasmuch as the islanders before mentioned, being in possession of wool, beaver and other furs, have presumptuously conceived they had a right to make some advantage thereof, by manufacturing the same into hats, to the prejudice of our domestic manufacture: We do therefore hereby strictly command and ordain, that no hats or felts whatsoever, dyed or undyed, finished or unfinished, shall be loaded or put into or upon any vessel, cart, carriage, or horse, to be transported or conveyed out of one county in the said island into another county, or to any other place whatsoever, by any person or persons whatsoever; on pain of forfeiting the same, with a penalty of five hundred pounds sterling for every offence. Nor shall any hatmaker, in any of the said counties, employ more than two apprentices, on penalty of five pounds sterling per month; we intending hereby that such hatmakers, being so restrained, both in the production and sale of their commodity, may find no advantage in continuing their business. But, lest the said islanders should suffer inconveniency by the want of hats, we are farther graciously pleased to permit them to send their beaver furs to Prussia; and we also permit hats made thereof to be exported from Prussia to Britain; the people thus favoured to pay all costs and charges of manufacturing, interest, commission to our merchants, insurance and freight going and returning, as in the case of iron.

"And, lastly, being willing farther to favour our said colonies in Britain, we do hereby also ordain and command, that all the *thieves,* highway and street robbers, housebreakers, forgerers, murderers, s—d—tes, and villains of every denomination, who have forfeited their lives to the law in Prussia; but whom we, in our great clemency, do not think fit here to hang, shall be emptied out of our gaols into the said island of Great Britain, for the better peopling of that country.

"We flatter ourselves, that these our royal regulations and commands will be thought just and reasonable by our much-favoured colonists in England; the said regulations being copied from their statutes of 10 and 11 William III. c. 10, 5 Geo. II. c. 22, 23, Geo. II, c. 29, 4 Geo. I. c. 11, and from other equitable laws made by their parliaments; or from instructions given by their Princes; or from resolutions of both Houses, entered into for the good government of their *own colonies in Ireland and America.*

"And all persons in the said island are hereby cautioned not to oppose in any wise the execution of this our Edict, or any part thereof, such opposition being high treason; of which all who are suspected shall be transported in fetters from Britain to Prussia, there to be tried and executed according to the Prussian law.

"Such is our pleasure.

"Given at Potsdam, this twenty-fifth day of the month of August, one thousand seven hundred and seventy-three, and in the thirty-third year of our reign.

"By the King, in his Council.
"RECHTMAESSIG, *Sec.*"

Some take this Edict to be merely one of the King's *Jeux d'Esprit:* others suppose it serious, and that he means a quarrel with England; but all here think the assertion it concludes with, "that these regulations are copied from acts of the English parliament respecting their colonies," a very injurious one; it being impossible to believe, that a people distinguished for their love of liberty, a nation so wise, so liberal in its sentiments, so just and equitable towards its neighbours, should, from mean and injudicious views of petty immediate profit, treat its own children in a manner so arbitrary and tyrannical!*

From *The Gentleman's Magazine,* September, 1773.

RULES

BY WHICH
A GREAT EMPIRE MAY BE REDUCED TO A SMALL ONE;

PRESENTED TO A LATE MINISTER,†
WHEN HE ENTERED UPON HIS ADMINISTRATION.

An ancient Sage boasted, that, tho' he could not fiddle, he knew how to make a *great city* of a *little one.* The science that I, a modern simpleton, am about to communicate, is the very reverse.

---

* Writing to his son from London, October 6, 1773, Franklin reported on the reception of this satire: "I was down at Lord Le Despencer's when the post brought that day's papers. Mr. Whitehead was there, too, (Paul Whitehead the author of 'Manners,') who runs early through all the papers and tells the company what he finds remarkable. He had them in another room, and we were chatting in the breakfast parlour, when he came running in to us, out of breath with the paper in his hand. Here! says he, here's news for ye! *Here's the King of Prussia, claiming a right to this kingdom!* All stared, and I as much as anybody; and he went on to read it. When he had read two or three paragraphs, a gentleman present said, *Damn his impudence, I dare say, we shall hear by next post that he is upon his march with one hundred thousand men to back this.* Whitehead, who is very shrewd, soon after began to smoke it, and looking in my face said, *I'll be hanged if this is not some of your American jokes upon us.* The reading went on, and ended with abundance of laughing, and a general verdict that it was a fair hit: and the piece was cut out of the paper and preserved in my Lord's collection."

† The Earl of Hillsborough.

I address myself to all ministers who have the management of extensive dominions, which from their very greatness are become troublesome to govern, because the multiplicity of their affairs leaves no time for *fiddling*.

I. In the first place, gentlemen, you are to consider, that a great empire, like a great cake, is most easily diminished at the edges. Turn your attention, therefore, first to your *remotest* provinces; that, as you get rid of them, the next may follow in order.

II. That the possibility of this separation may always exist, take special care the provinces are never incorporated with the mother country; that they do not enjoy the same common rights, the same privileges in commerce; and that they are governed by *severer* laws, all of *your enacting,* without allowing them any share in the choice of the legislators. By carefully making and preserving such distinctions, you will (to keep to my simile of the cake) act like a wise gingerbread-baker, who, to facilitate a division, cuts his dough half through in those places where, when baked, he would have it *broken to pieces.*

III. Those remote provinces have perhaps been acquired, purchased, or conquered, at the *sole expence* of the settlers, or their ancestors, without the aid of the mother country. If this should happen to increase her *strength,* by their growing numbers, ready to join in her wars; her *commerce,* by their growing demand for her manufactures; or her *naval power,* by greater employment for her ships and seamen, they may probably suppose some merit in this, and that it entitles them to some favour; you are therefore to *forget it all, or resent it,* as if they had done you injury. If they happen to be zealous whigs, friends of liberty, nurtured in revolution principles, *remember all that* to their prejudice, and resolve to punish it; for such principles, after a revolution is thoroughly established, are of *no more use;* they are even *odius* and *abominable.*

IV. However peaceably your colonies have submitted to your government, shewn their affection to your interests, and patiently borne their grievances; you are to *suppose* them always inclined to revolt, and treat them accordingly. Quarter troops among them, who by their insolence may *provoke* the rising of mobs, and by their bullets and bayonets *suppress* them. By this means, like the husband who uses his wife ill *from suspicion,* you may in time convert your *suspicions* into *realities.*

V. Remote provinces must have *Governors* and *Judges,* to represent the Royal Person, and execute everywhere the delegated parts of his office and authority. You ministers know, that much of the strength of government depends on the *opinion* of the people; and much of that opinion on the *choice of rulers* placed immediately over them. If you send them wise and good men for governors, who study the interest of the colonists, and advance their prosperity, they will think their King wise and good, and that he wishes the welfare of his subjects. If you send them learned and upright men for Judges, they will think him a lover of justice. This may attach your provinces more to his government. You are therefore to be careful whom you recommend for those offices. If you can find prodigals, who have ruined their fortunes, broken gamesters or stockjobbers, these may do well as *governors;* for will they probably be rapacious, and provoke the people by their extortions. Wrangling proctors and pettifogging lawyers, too, are not amiss; for they will be for ever disputing and quarrelling with their little parliaments. If withal they should be ignorant, wrongheaded, and insolent, so much the better. Attornies' clerks and Newgate solicitors will do for *Chief Justices,* especially if they hold their places *during your pleasure;* and all will contribute to impress those ideas of your government, that are proper for a people *you would wish to renounce it.*

VI. To confirm these impressions, and strike them deeper, whenever the injured come to the capital with complaints of mal-administration, oppression, or injustice, punish such suitors with long delay, enormous expence, and a final judgment in favour of the oppressor. This will have an admirable effect every way. The trouble of future complaints will be prevented, and Governors and Judges will be encouraged to farther acts of oppression and injustice; and thence the people may become more disaffected, and at length desperate.

VII. When such Governors have crammed their coffers, and made themselves so odious to the people that they can no longer remain among them, with safety to their persons, *recall and reward* them with pensions. You may make them *baronets* too, if that respectable order should not think fit to resent it. All will contribute to encourage new governors in the same practice, and make the supreme government, *detestable*.

VIII. If, when you are engaged in war, your colonies should vie in liberal aids of men and money against the common enemy, upon your simple requisition, and give far beyond their abilities, reflect that a penny taken from them by your power is more honourable to you, than a pound presented by their benevolence; despise therefore their voluntary grants, and resolve to harass them with novel taxes. They will probably complain to your parliaments, that they are taxed by a body in which they have no representative, and that is contrary to common right. They will petition for redress. Let the Parliaments flout their claims, reject their petitions, refuse even to suffer the reading of them, and treat the petitioners with the utmost contempt. Nothing can have a better effect in producing the alienation proposed; for though many can forgive injuries, *none ever forgave contempt*.

IX. In laying these taxes, never regard the heavy burthens those remote people already undergo, in defending their own frontiers, supporting their own provincial governments, making new roads, building bridges, churches, and other public edifices, which in old countries have been done to your hands by your ancestors, but which occasion constant calls and demands on the purses of a new people. Forget the *restraints* you lay on their trade for *your own* benefit, and the advantage a *monopoly* of this trade gives your exacting merchants. Think nothing of the wealth those merchants and your manufacturers acquire by the colony commerce; their encreased ability thereby to pay taxes at home; their accumulating, in the price of their commodities, most of those taxes, and so levying them from their consuming customers; all this, and the employment and support of thousands of your poor by the colonists, you are *intirely to forget*. But remember to make your arbitrary tax more grievous to your provinces, by public declarations importing that your power of taxing them has *no limits;* so that when you take from them without their consent one shilling in the pound, you have a clear right to the other nineteen. This will probably weaken every idea of *security in their property,* and convince them, that under such a government they *have nothing they can call their own;* which can scarce fail of producing the *happiest consequences!*

X. Possibly, indeed, some of them might still comfort themselves, and say, "Though we have no property, we have yet *something* left that is valuable; we have constitutional *liberty,* both of person and of conscience. This King, these Lords, and these Commons, who it seems are too remote from us to know us, and feel for us, cannot take from us our *Habeas Corpus* right, or our right of trial *by a jury of our neighbours;* they cannot deprive us of the exercise of our religion, alter our ecclesiastical constitution, and compel us to be Papists, if they please, or Mahometans." To annihilate this comfort, begin by laws to perplex their commerce with infinite regulations, impossible to be remembered and observed; ordain seizures of their property for every failure; take away the trial of such property by Jury, and give it to arbitrary Judges of your own appointing, and of the lowest characters in the country, whose salaries and emoluments are to arise out of the duties or condemnations, and whose appointments are *during pleasure.* Then let there be a formal declaration of both Houses, that opposition to your edicts is *treason,* and that any person suspected of treason in the provinces may, according to some obsolete law, be seized and sent to the metropolis of the empire for trial; and pass an act, that those there charged with certain other offences, shall be sent away in chains from their friends and country to be tried in the same manner for felony. Then erect a new Court of Inquisition among them, accompanied by an armed force, with instructions to transport all such suspected persons; to be ruined by the expence, if they bring over evidences to prove their innocence, or be found guilty and hanged, if they cannot afford it. And, lest the people should think you cannot possibly go any farther, pass another solemn declaratory act, "that King, Lords, Commons had, hath, and of right ought to have, full power and authority to make statutes of sufficient force and validity to bind the unrepresented provinces IN ALL CASES WHATSOEVER." This will include *spiritual* with temporal, and, taken together, must operate wonderfully to your purpose; by convincing them, that they are at present under a power something like that spoken of in the scriptures, which can not only *kill their bodies,* but *damn their souls* to all eternity, by compelling them, if it pleases, *to worship the Devil.*

XI. To make your taxes more odious, and more likely to procure resistance, send from the capital a board of officers to superintend the collection, composed of the most *indiscreet, ill-bred,* and *insolent* you can find. Let these have large salaries out of the extorted revenue, and live in open, grating luxury upon the sweat and blood of the industrious; whom they are to worry continually with groundless and expensive prosecutions before the abovementioned arbitrary revenue Judges; *all at the cost of the party prosecuted,* tho' acquitted, because *the King is to pay no costs.* Let these men, *by your order,* be exempted from all the common taxes and burthens of the province, though they and their property are protected by its laws. If any revenue officers are *suspected* of the least tenderness for the people, discard them. If others are justly complained of, protect and reward them. If any of the under officers behave so as to provoke the people to drub them, promote those to better offices: this will encourage others to procure for themselves such profitable drubbings, by multiplying and enlarging such provocations, and *all will work towards the end you aim at.*

XII. Another way to make your tax odious, is to misapply the produce of it. If it was originally appropriated for the *defence* of the provinces, the better support of government, and the administration of justice, where it may be *necessary,* then apply none of it to that *defence,* but bestow it where it is *not necessary,* in augmented salaries or pensions to every governor, who has distinguished himself by his enmity to the people, and by calumniating them to their sovereign. This will make them pay it more unwillingly, and be more apt to quarrel with those that collect it and those that imposed it, who will quarrel again with them, and all shall contribute to your *main purpose,* of making them *weary of your government.*

XIII. If the people of any province have been accustomed to support their own Governors and Judges to satisfaction, you are to apprehend that such Governors and Judges may be thereby influenced to treat the people kindly, and to do them justice. This is another reason for applying part of that revenue in larger salaries to such Governors and Judges, given, as their commissions are, *during your pleasure* only; forbidding them to take any salaries from their provinces; that thus the people may no longer hope any kindness from their Governors, or (in Crown cases) any justice from their Judges. And, as the money thus misapplied in one province is extorted from all, probably *all will resent the misapplication*.

XIV. If the parliaments of your provinces should dare to claim rights, or complain of your administration, order them to be harrassed with *repeated dissolutions*. If the same men are continually returned by new elections, adjourn their meetings to some country village, where they cannot be accommodated, and there keep them *during pleasure;* for this, you know, is your PREROGATIVE; and an excellent one it is, as you may manage it to promote discontents among the people, diminish their respect, and *increase their disaffection*.

XV. Convert the brave, honest officers of your *navy* into pimping tide-waiters and colony officers of the *customs*. Let those, who in time of war fought gallantly in defence of the commerce of their countrymen, in peace be taught to prey upon it. Let them learn to be corrupted by great and real smugglers; but (to shew their diligence) scour with armed boats every bay, harbour, river, creek, cove, or nook throughout the coast of your colonies; stop and detain every coaster, every wood-boat, every fisherman, tumble their cargoes and even their ballast inside out and upside down; and, if a penn'orth of pins is found un-entered, let the whole be seized and confiscated. Thus shall the trade of your colonists suffer more from their friends in time of peace, than it did from their enemies in war. Then let these boats crews land upon every farm in their way, rob the orchards, steal the pigs and the poultry, and insult the inhabitants. If the injured and exasperated farmers, unable to procure other justice, should attack the aggressors, drub them, and burn their boats; you are to call this *high treason and rebellion,* order fleets and armies into their country, and threaten to carry all the offenders three thousand miles to be hanged, drawn, and quartered. *O! this will work admirably!*

XVI. If you are told of discontents in your colonies, never believe that they are general, or that you have given occasion for them; therefore do not think of applying any remedy, or of changing any offensive measure. Redress no grievance, lest they should be encouraged to demand the redress of some other grievance. Grant no request that is just and reasonable, lest they should make another that is unreasonable. Take all your informations of the state of the colonies from your Governors and officers in enmity with them. Encourage and reward these *leasing-makers;* secrete their lying accusations, lest they should be confuted; but act upon them as the clearest evidence; and believe nothing you hear from the friends of the people: suppose all *their* complaints to be invented and promoted by a few factious demagogues, whom if you could catch and hang, all would be quiet. Catch and hang a few of them accordingly; and the *blood of the Martyrs* shall *work miracles* in favour of your purpose.

XVII. If you see *rival nations* rejoicing at the prospect of your disunion with your provinces, and endeavouring to promote it; if they translate, publish, and applaud all the complaints of your discontented colonists, at the same time privately stimulating you to severer measures, let not that *alarm* or offend you. Why should it, since you all mean *the same thing?*

XVIII. If any colony should at their own charge erect a fortress to secure their port against the fleets of a foreign enemy, get your Governor to betray that fortress into your hands. Never think of paying what it cost the country, for that would look, at least, like some regard for justice; but turn it into a citadel to awe the inhabitants and curb their commerce. If they should have lodged in such fortress the very arms they bought and used to aid you in your conquests, seize them all; it will provoke like *ingratitude* added to *robbery*. One admirable effect of these operations will be, to discourage every other colony from erecting such defences, and so your enemies may more easily invade them; to the great disgrace of your government, and of course *the furtherance of your project*.

XIX. Send armies into their country under pretence of protecting the inhabitants; but, instead of garrisoning the forts on their frontiers with those troops, to prevent incursions, demolish those forts, and order the troops into the heart of the country, that the savages may be encouraged to attack the frontiers, and that the troops may be protected by the inhabitants. This will seem to proceed from your ill will or your ignorance, and contribute farther to produce and strengthen an opinion among them, *that you are no longer fit to govern them*.

XX. Lastly, invest the General of your army in the provinces, with great and unconstitutional powers, and free him from the controul of even your own Civil Governors. Let him have troops enow under his command, with all the fortresses in his possession; and who knows but (like some provincial Generals in the Roman empire, and encouraged by the universal discontent you have produced) he may take it into his head to set up for himself? If he should, and you have carefully practised these few *excellent rules* of mine, take my word for it, all the provinces will immediately join him; and you will that day (if you have not done it sooner) get rid of the trouble of governing them, and all the *plagues* attending their *commerce* and connection from henceforth and for ever.

Q. E. D.

THE SALE OF THE HESSIANS

FROM THE COUNT DE SCHAUMBERGH TO THE BARON HOHENDORF, COMMANDING THE HESSIAN TROOPS IN AMERICA

Rome, February 18, 1777.

MONSIEUR LE BARON:

On my return from Naples, I received at Rome your letter of the 27th December of last year. I have learned with unspeakable pleasure the courage our troops exhibited at Trenton, and you cannot imagine my joy on being told that of the 1,950 Hessians engaged in the fight, but 345 escaped. There were just 1,605 men killed, and I cannot sufficiently commend your prudence in sending an exact list of the dead to my minister in London. This precaution was the more necessary, as the report sent to the English ministry does not give but 1,455 dead. This would make 483,450 florins instead of 643,500 which I am entitled to demand under our convention. You will comprehend the prejudice which such an error would work in my finances, and I do not doubt you will take the necessary pains to prove that Lord North's list is false and yours correct.

The court of London objects that there were a hundred wounded who ought not to be included in the list, nor paid for as dead; but I trust you will not overlook my instructions to you on quitting Cassel, and that you will not have tried by human succor to recall the life of the unfortunates whose days could not be lengthened but by the loss of a leg or an arm. That would be making them a pernicious present, and I am sure they would rather die than live in a condition no longer fit for my service. I do not mean by this that you should assassinate them; we should be humane, my dear Baron, but you may insinuate to the surgeons with entire propriety that a crippled man is a reproach to their profession, and that there is no wiser course than to let every one of them die when he ceases to be fit to fight.

I am about to send to you some new recruits. Don't economize them. Remember glory before all things. Glory is true wealth. There is nothing degrades the soldier like the love of money. He must care only for honour and reputation, but this reputation must be acquired in the midst of dangers. A battle gained without costing the conqueror any blood is an inglorious success, while the conquered cover themselves with glory by perishing with their arms in their hands. Do you remember that of the 300 Lacedæmonians who defended the defile of Thermopylæ, not one returned? How happy should I be could I say the same of my brave Hessians!

It is true that their king, Leonidas, perished with them: but things have changed, and it is no longer the custom for princes of the empire to go and fight in America for a cause with which they have no concern. And besides, to whom should they pay the thirty guineas per man if I did not stay in Europe to receive them? Then, it is necessary also that I be ready to send recruits to replace the men you lose. For this purpose I must return to Hesse. It is true, grown men are becoming scarce there, but I will send you boys. Besides, the scarcer the commodity the higher the price. I am assured that the women and little girls have begun to till our lands, and they get on not badly. You did right to send back to Europe that Dr. Crumerus who was so successful in curing dysentery. Don't bother with a man who is subject to looseness of the bowels. That disease makes bad soldiers. One coward will do more mischief in an engagement than ten brave men will do good. Better that they burst in their barracks than fly in a battle, and tarnish the glory of our arms. Besides, you know that they pay me as killed for all who die from disease, and I don't get a farthing for runaways. My trip to Italy, which has cost me enormously, makes it desirable that there should be a great mortality among them. You will therefore promise promotion to all who expose themselves; you will exhort them to seek glory in the midst of dangers; you will say to Major Maundorff that I am not at all content with his saving the 345 men who escaped the massacre of Trenton. Through the whole campaign he has not had ten men killed in consequence of his orders. Finally, let it be your principal object to prolong the war and avoid a decisive engagement on either side, for I have made arrangements for a grand Italian opera, and I do not wish to be obliged to give it up. Meantime I pray God, my dear Baron de Hohendorf, to have you in his holy and gracious keeping.

THE EPHEMERA*

An Emblem of Human Life

You may remember, my dear friend, that when we lately spent that happy day in the delightful garden and sweet society of the Moulin Joly, I stopt a little in one of our walks, and staid some time behind the company. We had been shown numberless skeletons of a kind of little fly, called an ephemera, whose successive generations, we were told, were bred and expired within the day. I happened to see a living company of them on a leaf, who appeared to be engaged in conversation. You know I understand all the inferior animal tongues: my too great application to the study of them is the best excuse I can give for the little progress I have made in your charming language. I listened through curiosity to the discourse of these little creatures; but as they, in their national vivacity, spoke three or four together, I could make but little of their conversation. I found, however, by some broken expressions that I heard now and then, they were disputing warmly on the merit of two foreign musicians, one a *cousin,* the other a *moscheto;* in which dispute they spent their time, seemingly as regardless of the shortness of life as if they had been sure of

* This bagatelle was addressed to Madame Brillon, then in her thirties, the wife of a French treasury official. Franklin met her shortly after he arrived in Paris as the American minister, and the two developed a warm friendship with Franklin becoming a frequent visitor at her home, *Moulin Joly.*

living a month. Happy people! thought I, you live certainly under a wise, just, and mild government, since you have no public grievances to complain of, nor any subject of contention but the perfections and imperfections of foreign music. I turned my head from them to an old grey-headed one, who was single on another leaf, and talking to himself. Being amused with his soliloquy, I put it down in writing; in hopes it will likewise amuse her to whom I am so much indebted for the most pleasing of all amusements, her delicious company and heavenly harmony.

"It was," said he, "the opinion of learned philosophers of our race, who lived and flourished long before my time, that this vast world, the Moulin Joly, could not itself subsist more than eighteen hours; and I think there was some foundation for that opinion, since, by the apparent motion of the great luminary that gives life to all nature, and which in my time has evidently declined considerably towards the ocean at the end of our earth, it must then finish its course, be extinguished in the waters that surround us, and leave the world in cold and darkness, necessarily producing universal death and destruction. I have lived seven of those hours, a great age, being no less than four hundred and twenty minutes of time. How very few of us continue so long! I have seen generations born, flourish, and expire. My present friends are the children and grandchildren of the friends of my youth, who are now, alas, no more! And I must soon follow them; for, by the course of nature, though still in health, I cannot expect to live above seven or eight minutes longer. What now avails all my toil and labor, in amassing honey-dew on this leaf, which I cannot live to enjoy! What the political struggles I have been engaged in, for the good of my compatriot inhabitants of this bush, or my philosophical studies for the benefit of our race in general! for, in politics, what can laws do without morals? Our present race of ephemeræ will in a course of minutes become corrupt, like those of other and older bushes, and consequently as wretched. And in philosophy how small our progress! Alas! art is long, and life is short! My friends would comfort me with the idea of a name, they say, I shall leave behind me; and they tell me I have lived long enough to nature and to glory. But what will fame be to an ephemera who no longer exists? And what will become of all history in the eighteenth hour, when the world itself, even the whole Moulin Joly, shall come to its end, and be buried in universal ruin?"

To me, after all my eager pursuits, no solid pleasures now remain, but the reflection of a long life spent in meaning well, the sensible conversation of a few good lady ephemeræ, and now and then a kind smile and a tune from the ever amiable *Brillante*.

B. FRANKLIN.

THE LEVÉE

IN the first chapter of Job we have an account of a transaction said to have arisen in the court, or at the *levée,* of the best of all possible princes, or of governments by a single person, viz. that of God himself.

At this *levée,* in which the sons of God were assembled, Satan also appeared.

It is probable the writer of that ancient book took his idea of this *levée* from those of the eastern monarchs of the age he lived in.

It is to this day usual at the *levées* of princes, to have persons assembled who are enemies to each other, who seek to obtain favor by whispering calumny and detraction, and thereby ruining those that distinguish themselves by their virtue and merit. And kings frequently ask a familiar question or two, of every one in the circle, merely to show their benignity. These circumstances are particularly exemplified in this relation.

If a modern king, for instance, finds a person in the circle who has not lately been there, he naturally asks him how he has passed his time since he last had the pleasure of seeing him? the gentleman perhaps replies that he has been in the country to view his estates, and visit some friends. Thus Satan being asked whence he cometh?

answers, "From going to and fro in the earth, and walking up and down in it." And being further asked, whether he had considered the uprightness and fidelity of the prince's servant Job, he immediately displays all the malignance of the designing courtier, by answering with another question: "Doth Job serve God for naught? Hast thou not given him immense wealth, and protected him in the possession of it? Deprive him of that, and he will curse thee to thy face." In modern phrase, Take away his places and his pensions, and your Majesty will soon find him in the opposition.

This whisper against Job had its effect. He was delivered into the power of his adversary, who deprived him of his fortune, destroyed his family, and completely ruined him.

The book of Job is called by divines a sacred poem, and, with the rest of the Holy Scriptures, is understood to be written for our instruction.

What then is the instruction to be gathered from this supposed transaction?

Trust not a single person with the government of your state. For if the Deity himself, being the monarch may for a time give way to calumny, and suffer it to operate the destruction of the best of subjects; what mischief may you not expect from such power in a mere man, though the best of men, from whom the truth is often industriously hidden, and to whom falsehood is often presented in its place, by artful, interested, and malicious courtiers?

And be cautious in trusting him even with limited powers, lest sooner or later he sap and destroy those limits, and render himself absolute.

For by the disposal of places, he attaches to himself all the place-holders, with their numerous connexions, and also all the expecters and hopers of places, which will form a strong party in promoting his views. By various political engagements for the interest of neighbouring states or princes, he procures their aid in establishing his own personal power. So that, through the hopes of emolument in one part of his subjects, and the fear of his resentment in the other, all opposition falls before him.

DIALOGUE BETWEEN
FRANKLIN AND THE GOUT

Midnight, October 22, 1780.

FRANKLIN. Eh! Oh! Eh! What have I done to merit these cruel sufferings?

GOUT. Many things; you have ate and drank too freely, and too much indulged those legs of yours in their indolence.

FRANKLIN. Who is it that accuses me?

GOUT. It is I, even I, the Gout.

FRANKLIN. What! my enemy in person?

GOUT. No, not your enemy.

FRANKLIN. I repeat it; my enemy; for you would not only torment my body to death, but ruin my good name; you reproach me as a glutton and a tippler; now all the world, that knows me, will allow that I am neither the one nor the other.

GOUT. The world may think as it pleases; it is always very complaisant to itself, and sometimes to its friends; but I very well know that the quantity of meat and drink proper for a man, who takes a reasonable degree of exercise, would be too much for another, who never takes any.

FRANKLIN. I take—Eh! Oh!—as much exercise—Eh! as—I can, Madam Gout. You know my sedentary state, and on that account, it would seem, Madam Gout, as if you might spare me a little, seeing it is not altogether my own fault.

GOUT. Not a jot; your rhetoric and your politeness are thrown away; your apology avails nothing. If your situation in life is a sedentary one, your amusements, your recreations, at least, should be active. You ought to walk or ride; or, if the weather prevents that play at billiards. But let us examine your course of life. While the mornings are long, and you have leisure to go abroad, what do you do? Why, instead of gaining an appetite for breakfast, by salutary exercise, you amuse yourself, with books, pamphlets, or newspapers, which commonly are not worth the reading. Yet you eat an inordinate breakfast, four dishes of tea, with cream, and one or two buttered toasts, with slices of hung beef, which I fancy are not things the most easily digested. Immediately afterward you sit down to write at your desk, or converse with persons who apply to you on business. Thus the time passes till one, without any kind of bodily exercise. But all this I could pardon, in regard, as you say, to your sedentary condition. But what is your practice after dinner? Walking in the beautiful gardens of those friends, with whom you have dined, would be the choice of men of sense; yours is to be fixed down to chess, where you are found engaged for two or three hours! This is your perpetual recreation, which is the least eligible of any for a sedentary man, because, instead of accelerating the motion of the fluids, the rigid attention it requires helps to retard the circulation and obstruct internal secretions. Wrapt in the speculations of this wretched game, you destroy your constitution. What can be expected from such a course of living, but a body replete with stagnant humours, ready to fall a prey to all kinds of dangerous maladies, if I, the Gout, did not occasionally bring you relief by agitating those humours, and so purifying or dissipating them? If it was in some nook or alley in Paris, deprived of walks, that you played awhile at chess after dinner, this might be excusable; but the same taste prevails with you in Passy, Auteuil, Montmartre, or Sanoy, places where there are the finest gardens and walks, a pure air, beautiful women, and most agreeable and instructive conversation; all which you might enjoy by frequenting the walks. But these are rejected for this abominable game of chess. Fie, then Mr. Franklin! But amidst my instructions, I had almost forgot to administer my wholesome corrections; so take that twinge,—and that.

FRANKLIN. Oh! Eh! Oh! Ohhh! As much instruction as you please, Madam Gout, and as many reproaches; but pray, Madam, a truce with your corrections!

GOUT. No, Sir, no,—I will not abate a particle of what is so much for your good,—therefore—

FRANKLIN. Oh! Ehhh!—It is not fair to say I take no exercise, when I do very often, going out to dine and returning in my carriage.

GOUT. That, of all imaginable exercises, is the most slight and insignificant, if you allude to the motion of a carriage suspended on springs. By observing the degree of heat obtained by different kinds of motion, we may form an estimate of the quantity of exercise given by each. Thus, for example, if you turn out to walk in winter with cold feet, in an hour's time you will be in a glow all over; ride on horseback, the same effect will scarcely be perceived by four hours' round trotting; but if you loll in a carriage, such as you have mentioned, you may travel all day, and gladly enter the last inn to warm your feet by a fire. Flatter yourself then no longer, that half an hour's airing in your carriage deserves the name of exercise. Providence has appointed few to roll in carriages, while he has given to all a pair of legs, which are machines infinitely more commodious and serviceable. Be grateful, then, and make a proper use of yours. Would you know how they forward the circulation of your fluids, in the very action of transporting you from place to place; observe when you walk, that all your weight is alternately thrown from one leg to the other; this occasions a great pressure on the vessels of the foot, and repels their contents; when relieved, by the weight being thrown on the other foot, the vessels of the first are allowed to replenish, and, by a return of this weight, this repulsion again succeeds; thus accelerating the circulation of the blood. The heat produced in any given time, depends on the degree of this acceleration; the fluids are shaken, the humours attenuated, the secretions facilitated, and all goes well; the cheeks are ruddy, and health is established. Behold your fair friend at Auteuil;* a lady who received from bounteous nature more really useful science, than half a dozen such pretenders to philosophy as you have been able to extract from all your books. When she honours you with a visit, it is on foot. She walks all hours of the day, and leaves indolence, and its concomitant maladies, to be endured by her horses. In this see at once the preservative of her health and personal charms. But when you go to Auteuil, you must

* Madame Helvetius, to whom Franklin unsuccessfully proposed marriage in 1780, was the widow of the philosopher. She lived at Auteuil while Franklin lived at nearby Passy.

have your carriage, though it is no further from Passy to Auteuil than from Auteuil to Passy.

FRANKLIN. Your reasonings grow very tiresome.

GOUT. I stand corrected. I will be silent and continue my office; take that, and that.

FRANKLIN. Oh! Ohh! Talk on, I pray you!

GOUT. No, no; I have a good number of twinges for you tonight, and you may be sure of some more to-morrow.

FRANKLIN. What, with such a fever! I shall go distracted. Oh! Eh! Can no one bear it for me?

GOUT. Ask that of your horses; they have served you faithfully.

FRANKLIN. How can you so cruelly sport with my torments?

GOUT. Sport! I am very serious. I have here a list of offences against your own health distinctly written, and can justify every stroke inflicted on you.

FRANKLIN. Read it then.

GOUT. It is too long a detail; but I will briefly mention some particulars.

FRANKLIN. Proceed. I am all attention.

GOUT. Do you remember how often you have promised yourself, the following morning, a walk in the grove of Boulogne, in the garden de la Muette, or in your own garden, and have violated your promise, alleging, at one time, it was too cold, at another too warm, too windy, too moist, or what else you pleased; when in truth it was too nothing, but your insuperable love of ease?

FRANKLIN. That I confess may have happened occasionally, probably ten times in a year.

GOUT. Your confession is very far short of the truth; the gross amount is one hundred and ninety-nine times.

FRANKLIN. Is it possible?

GOUT. So possible, that it is fact; you may rely on the accuracy of my statement. You know M. Brillon's gardens, and what fine walks they contain; you know the handsome flight of an hundred steps, which lead from the terrace above to the lawn below. You have been in the practice of visiting this amiable family twice a week, after dinner, and it is a maxim of your own, that "a man may take as much exercise in walking a mile, up and down stairs, as in ten on level ground." What an opportunity was here for you to have had exercise in both these ways! Did you embrace it, and how often?

FRANKLIN. I cannot immediately answer that question.

GOUT. I will do it for you; not once.

FRANKLIN. Not once?

GOUT. Even so. During the summer you went there at six o'clock. You found the charming lady, with her lovely children and friends, eager to walk with you, and entertain you with their agreeable conversation; and what has been your choice? Why to sit on the terrace satisfying yourself with the fine prospect, and passing your eye over the beauties of the garden below, without taking one step to descend and walk about in them. On the contrary, you call for tea and the chess-board; and lo! you are occupied in your seat till nine o'clock, and that besides two hours' play after dinner; and then, instead of walking home, which would have bestirred you a little, you step into your carriage. How absurd to suppose that all this carelessness can be reconcilable with health, without my interposition!

FRANKLIN. I am convinced now of the justness of poor Richard's remark, that "Our debts and our sins are always greater than we think for."

GOUT. So it is. You philosophers are sages in your maxims, and fools in your conduct.

FRANKLIN. But do you charge among my crimes, that I return in a carriage from Mr. Brillon's?

GOUT. Certainly; for, having been seated all the while, you cannot object the fatigue of the day, and cannot want therefore the relief of a carriage.

FRANKLIN. What then would you have me do with my carriage?

GOUT. Burn it if you choose; you would at least get heat out of it once in this way; or, if you dislike that proposal, here's another for you; observe the poor peasants, who work in the vineyards and grounds about the villages of Passy, Auteuil, Chaillot, &c.; you may find every day, among these deserving creatures, four or five old men and women, bent and perhaps crippled by weight of years, and too long and too great labour. After a most fatiguing day, these people have to trudge a mile or two to their smoky huts. Order your coachman to set them down. This is an act that will be good for your soul; and, at the same time, after your visit to the Brillons, if you return on foot, that will be good for your body.

FRANKLIN. Ah! how tiresome you are!

GOUT. Well, then, to my office; it should not be forgotten that I am your physician. There.

FRANKLIN. Ohhh! what a devil of a physician!

GOUT. How ungrateful you are to say so! Is it not I who, in the character of your physician, have saved you from the palsy, dropsy, and apoplexy? one or other of which would have done for you long ago, but for me.

FRANKLIN. I submit, and thank you for the past, but entreat the discontinuance of your visits for the future; for, in my mind one had better die than be cured so dolefully. Permit me just to hint, that I have also not been unfriendly to *you*. I never feed physician or quack of any kind, to enter the list against you; if then you do not leave me to my repose, it may be said you are ungrateful too.

GOUT. I can scarcely acknowledge that as any objection. As to quacks, I despise them; they may kill you indeed, but cannot injure me. And, as to regular physicians, they are at last convinced that the gout, in such a subject as you are, is no disease, but a remedy; and wherefore cure a remedy?—but to our business,—there.

FRANKLIN. Oh! oh!—for Heaven's sake leave me! and I promise faithfully never more to play at chess, but to take exercise daily, and live temperately.

GOUT. I know you too well. You promise fair; but, after a few months of good health, you will return to your old habits; your fine promises will be forgotten like the forms of last year's clouds. Let us then finish the account, and I will go. But I leave you with an assurance of visiting you again at a proper time and place; for my object is your good, and you are sensible now that I am your *real friend*.

INFORMATION FOR THOSE
WHO WOULD REMOVE TO
AMERICA

Many Persons in Europe, having directly or by Letters, express'd to the Writer of this, who is well acquainted with North America, their Desire of transporting and establishing themselves in that Country; but who appear to have formed, thro' Ignorance, mistaken Ideas and Expectations of what is to be obtained there; he thinks it may be useful, and prevent inconvenient, expensive, and fruitless Removals and Voyages of improper Persons, if he gives some clearer and truer Notions of that part of the World, than appear to have hitherto prevailed.

He finds it is imagined by Numbers, that the Inhabitants of North America are rich, capable of rewarding, and dispos'd to reward, all sorts of Ingenuity; that they are at the same time ignorant of all the Sciences, and, consequently, that Strangers, prossessing Talents in the Belles-Lettres, fine Arts, &c., must be highly esteemed, and so well paid, as to become easily rich themselves; that there are also abundance of profitable Offices to be disposed of, which the Natives are not qualified to fill; and that, having few Persons of Family among them, Strangers of Birth must be greatly respected, and of course easily obtain the best of those Offices, which will make all their Fortunes; that the Governments too, to encourage Emigrations from Europe, not only pay the Expence of personal Transportation, but give Lands gratis to Strangers, with Negroes to work for them, Utensils of Husbandry and Stocks of Cattle. These are all wild Imaginations; and those who go to America with Expectations founded upon them will surely find themselves disappointed.

The Truth is, that though there are in that Country few People so miserable as the Poor of Europe, there are also very few that in Europe would be called rich; it is rather a general happy Mediocrity that prevails. There are few great Proprietors of the Soil, and few

Tenants; most People cultivate their own Lands, or follow some Handicraft or Merchandise; very few rich enough to live idly upon their Rents or Incomes, or to pay the high Prices given in Europe for Paintings, Statues, Architecture, and the other Works of Art, that are more curious than useful. Hence the natural Geniuses, that have arisen in America with such Talents, have uniformly quitted that Country for Europe, where they can be more suitably rewarded. It is true, that Letters and Mathematical Knowledge are in Esteem there, but they are at the same time more common than is apprehended; there being already existing nine Colleges or Universities, viz. four in New England, and one in each of the Provinces of New York, New Jersey, Pensilvania, Maryland, and Virginia, all furnish'd with learned Professors; besides a number of smaller Academies; these educate many of their Youth in the Languages, and those Sciences that qualify men for the Professions of Divinity, Law, or Physick. Strangers indeed are by no means excluded from exercising those Professions; and the quick Increase of Inhabitants everywhere gives them a Chance of Employ, which they have in common with the Natives. Of civil Offices, or Employments, there are few; no superfluous Ones, as in Europe; and it is a Rule establish'd in some of the States, that no Office should be so profitable as to make it desirable. The 36th Article of the Constitution of Pennsilvania, runs expressly in these Words; "As every Freeman, to preserve his Independence, (if he has not a sufficient Estate) ought to have some Profession, Calling, Trade, or Farm, whereby he may honestly subsist, there can be no Necessity for, nor Use in, establishing Offices of Profit; the usual Effects of which are Dependance and Servility, unbecoming Freemen, in the Possessors and Expectants; Faction, Contention, Corruption, and Disorder among the People. Wherefore, whenever an Office, thro' Increase of Fees or otherwise, becomes so profitable, as to occasion many to apply for it, the Profits ought to be lessened by the Lagislature."

These Ideas prevailing more or less in all the United States, it cannot be worth any Man's while, who has a means of Living at home, to expatriate himself, in hopes of obtaining a profitable civil Office in America; and, as to military Offices, they are at an End with the War, the Armies being disbanded. Much less is it adviseable for a Person to go thither, who has no other Quality to recommend him but his Birth. In Europe it has indeed its Value; but it is a Commodity that cannot be carried to a worse Market than that of America, where people do not inquire concerning a Stranger, *What is he?* but, *What can he do?* If he has any useful Art, he is welcome; and if he exercises it, and behaves well, he will be respected by all that know him; but a mere Man of Quality, who, on that Account, wants to live upon the Public, by some Office or Salary, will be despis'd and disregarded. The Husbandman is in honor there, and even the Mechanic, because their Employments are useful. The People have a saying, that God Almighty is himself a Mechanic, the greatest in the Univers; and he is respected and admired more for the Variety, Ingenuity, and Utility of his Handyworks, than for the Antiquity of his Family. They are pleas'd with the Observation of a Negro, and frequently mention it, that *Boccarorra* (meaning the White men) *make de black man workee, make de Horse workee, made de Ox workee, make ebery ting workee; only de Hog. He, de hog, no workee; he eat, he drink, he walk about, he go to sleep when he please, he libb like a Gentleman.* According to these Opinions of the Americans, one of them would think himself more oblig'd to a Genealogist, who could prove for him that his Ancestors and Relations for ten Generations had been Ploughmen, Smiths, Carpenters, Turners, Weavers, Tanners, or even Shoemakers, and consequently that they were useful Members of Society; than if he could only prove that they were Gentlemen, doing nothing of Value, but living idly on the Labour of others, mere *fruges consumere nati,** and otherwise *good for nothing,* till by their Death their Estates, like the Carcass of the Negro's Gentleman-Hog, come to be *cut up.*

With regard to Encouragements for Strangers from Government, they are really only what are derived from good Laws and Liberty. Strangers are welcome, because there is room enough for them all, and therefore the old Inhabitants are not jealous of them; the Laws protect them sufficiently, so that they have no need of the Patronage

* ". . . born merely to eat up the corn."—WATTS [FRANKLIN'S NOTE.]

of Great Men; and every one will enjoy securely the Profits of his Industry. But, if he does not bring a Fortune with him, he must work and be industrious to live. One or two Years' residence gives him all the Rights of a Citizen; but the government does not at present, whatever it may have done in former times, hire People to become Settlers, by Paying their Passages, giving Land, Negroes, Utensils, Stock, or any other kind of Emolument whatsoever. In short, America is the Land of Labour, and by no means what the English call *Lubberland,* and the French *Pays de Cocagne,* where the streets are said to be pav'd with half-peck Loaves, the Houses til'd with Pancakes, and where the Fowls fly about ready roasted, crying, *Come eat me!*

Who then are the kind of Persons to whom an Emigration to America may be advantageous? And what are the Advantages they may reasonably expect?

Land being cheap in that Country, from the vast Forests still void of Inhabitants, and not likely to be occupied in an Age to come, insomuch that the Propriety of an hundred Acres of fertile Soil full of Wood may be obtained near the Frontiers, in many Places, for Eight or Ten Guineas, hearty young Labouring Men, who understand the Husbandry of Corn and Cattle, which is nearly the same in that Country as in Europe, may easily establish themselves there. A little Money sav'd of the good Wages they receive there, while they work for others, enables them to buy the Land and begin their Plantation, in which they are assisted by the Good-Will of their Neighbours, and some Credit. Multitudes of poor People from England, Ireland, Scotland, and Germany, have by this means in a few years become wealthy Farmers, who, in their own Countries, where all the Lands are fully occupied, and the Wages of Labour low, could never have emerged from the poor Condition wherein they were born.

From the salubrity of the Air, the healthiness of the Climate, the plenty of good Provisions, and the Encouragement to early Marriages by the certainty of Subsistence in cultivating the Earth, the Increase of Inhabitants by natural Generation is very rapid in America, and becomes still more so by the Accession of Strangers; hence there is a continual Demand for more Artisans of all the necessary and useful kinds, to supply those Cultivators of the Earth with Houses, and with Furniture and Utensils of the grosser sorts, which cannot so well be brought from Europe. Tolerably good Workmen in any of those mechanic Arts are sure to find Employ, and to be well paid for their Work, there being no Restraints preventing Strangers from exercising any Art they understand, nor any Permission necessary. If they are poor, they begin first as Servants or Journeymen; and if they are sober, industrious, and frugal, they soon become Masters, establish themselves in Business, marry, raise Families, and become respectable Citizens.

Also, Persons of moderate Fortunes and Capitals, who, having a Number of Children to provide for, are desirous of bringing them up to Industry, and to secure Estates for their Posterity, have Opportunities of doing it in America, which Europe does not afford. There they may be taught and practise profitable mechanic Arts, without incurring Disgrace on that Account, but on the contrary acquiring Respect by such Abilities. There small Capitals laid out in Lands, which daily become more valuable by the Increase of People, afford a solid Prospect of ample Fortunes thereafter for those Children. The Writer of this has known several Instances of large Tracts of Land, bought, on what was then the Frontier of Pensilvania, for Ten Pounds per hundred Acres, which after 20 years, when the Settlements had been extended far beyond them, sold readily, without any Improvement made upon them, for three Pounds per Acre. The Acre in America is the same with the English Acre, or the Acre of Normandy.

Those, who desire to understand the State of Government in America, would do well to read the Constitutions of the several States, and the Articles of Confederation that bind the whole together for general Purposes, under the Direction of one Assembly, called the Congress. These Constitutions have been printed, by order of Congress, in America; two Editions of them have also been printed in London; and a good Translation of them into French has lately been published at Paris.

Several of the Princes of Europe having of late years, from an Opinion of Advantage to arise by producing all Commodities and

Manufactures within their own Dominions, so as to diminish or render useless their Importations, have endeavoured to entice Workmen from other Countries by high Salaries, Privileges, &c. Many Persons, pretending to be skilled in various great Manufactures, imagining that America must be in Want of them, and that the Congress would probably be dispos'd to imitate the Princes above mentioned, have proposed to go over, on Condition of having their Passages paid, Lands given, Salaries appointed, exclusive Privileges for Terms of years, &c. Such Persons, on reading the Articles of Confederation, will find, that the Congress have no Power committed to them, or Money put into their Hands, for such purposes; and that if any such Encouragement is given, it must be by the Government of some separate State. This, however, has rarely been done in America; and, when it has been done, it has rarely succeeded, so as to establish a Manufacture, which the Country was not yet so ripe for as to encourage private Persons to set it up; Labour being generally too dear there, and Hands difficult to be kept together, every one desiring to be a Master, and the Cheapness of Lands inclining many to leave Trades for Agriculture. Some indeed have met with Success, and are carried on to Advantage; but they are generally such as require only a few Hands, or wherein great Part of the Work is performed by Machines. Things that are bulky, and of so small Value as not well to bear the Expence of Freight, may often be made cheaper in the Country than they can be imported; and the Manufacture of such Things will be profitable wherever there is a sufficient Demand. The Farmers in America produce indeed a good deal of Wool and Flax; and none is exported, it is all work'd up; but it is in the Way of domestic Manufacture, for the Use of the Family. The buying up Quantities of Wool and Flax, with the Design to employ Spinners, Weavers, &c., and form great Establishments, producing Quantities of Linen and Woollen Goods for Sale, has been several times attempted in different Provinces; but those Projects have generally failed, goods of equal Value being imported cheaper. And when the Governments have been solicited to support such Schemes by Encouragements, in Money, or by imposing Duties on Importation of such Goods, it has been generally refused, on this

Principle, that, if the Country is ripe for the Manufacture, it may be carried on by private Persons to Advantage; and if not, it is a Folly to think of forcing Nature. Great Establishments of Manufacture require great Numbers of Poor to do the Work for small Wages; these Poor are to be found in Europe, but will not be found in America, till the Lands are all taken up and cultivated, and the Excess of People, who cannot get Land, want Employment. The Manufacture of Silk, they say, is natural in France, as that of Cloth in England, because each Country produces in Plenty the first Material; but if England will have a Manufacture of Silk as well as that of Cloth, and France one of Cloth as well as that of Silk, these unnatural Operations must be supported by mutual Prohibitions, or high Duties on the Importation of each other's Goods; by which means the Workmen are enabled to tax the home Consumer by greater Prices, while the higher Wages they receive makes them neither happier nor richer, since they only drink more and work less. Therefore the Governments in America do nothing to encourage such Projects. The People, by this Means, are not impos'd on, either by the Merchant or Mechanic. If the Merchant demands too much Profit on imported Shoes, they buy of the Shoemaker; and if he asks too high a Price, they take them of the Merchant; thus the two Professions are checks on each other. The Shoemaker, however, has, on the whole, a considerable Profit upon his Labour in America, beyond what he had in Europe, as he can add to his Price a Sum nearly equal to all the Expences of Freight and Commission, Risque or Insurance, &c., necessarily charged by the Merchant. And the Case is the same with the Workmen in every other Mechanic Art. Hence it is, that Artisans generally live better and more easily in America than in Europe; and such as are good Œconomists make a comfortable Provision for Age, and for their Children. Such may, therefore, remove with Advantage to America.

In the long-settled Countries of Europe, all Arts, Trades, Professions, Farms, &c., are so full, that it is difficult for a poor Man, who has Children, to place them where they may gain, or learn to gain, a decent Livelihood. The Artisans, who fear creating future Rivals in Business, refuse to take Apprentices, but upon Conditions of Money, Maintenance, or the like, which the Parents are unable to comply with. Hence the Youth are dragg'd up in Ignorance of every gainful Art, and oblig'd to become Soldiers, or Servants, or Thieves, for a Subsistence. In America, the rapid Increase of Inhabitants takes away that Fear of Rivalship, and Artisans willingly receive Apprentices from the hope of Profit by their Labour, during the Remainder of the Time stipulated, after they shall be instructed. Hence it is easy for poor Families to get their Children instructed; for the Artisans are so desirous of Apprentices, that many of them will even give Money to the Parents, to have Boys from Ten to Fifteen Years of Age bound Apprentices to them till the Age of Twenty-one; and many poor Parents have, by that means, on their Arrival in the Country, raised Money enough to buy Land sufficient to establish themselves, and to subsist the rest of their Family by Agriculture. These Contracts for Apprentices are made before a Magistrate, who regulates the Agreement according to Reason and Justice, and, having in view the Formation of a future useful Citizen, obliges the Master to engage by a written Indenture, not only that, during the time of Service stipulated, the Apprentice shall be duly provided with Meat, Drink, Apparel, washing, and Lodging, and, at its Expiration, with a compleat new Suit of Cloaths, but also that he shall be taught to read, write, and cast Accompts; and that he shall be well instructed in the Art or Profession of his Master, or some other, by which he may afterwards gain a Livelihood, and be able in his turn to raise a Family. A Copy of this Indenture is given to the Apprentice or his Friends, and the Magistrate keeps a Record of it, to which recourse may be had, in case of Failure by the Master in any Point of Performance. This desire among the Masters, to have more Hands employ'd in working for them, induces them to pay the Passages of young Persons, of both Sexes, who, on their Arrival, agree to serve them one, two, three, or four Years; those, who have already learnt a Trade, agreeing for a shorter Term, in proportion to their Skill, and the consequent immediate Value of their Service; and those, who have none, agreeing for a longer Term, in consideration of being taught in Art their Poverty would not permit them to acquire in their own Country.

The almost general Mediocrity of Fortune that prevails in America obliging its People to follow some Business for subsistence, those Vices, that arise usually from Idleness, are in a great measure prevented. Industry and constant Employment are great preservatives of the Morals and Virtue of a Nation. Hence bad Examples to Youth are more rare in America, which must be a comfortable Consideration to Parents. To this may be truly added, that serious Religion, under its various Denominations, is not only tolerated, but respected and practised. Atheism is unknown there; Infidelity rare and secret; so that persons may live to a great Age in that Country, without having their Piety shocked by meeting with either an Atheist or an Infidel. And the Divine Being seems to have manifested his Approbation of the mutual Forbearance and Kindness with which the different Sects treat each other, by the remarkable Prosperity with which He has been pleased to favour the whole Country.

TO OLIVER NEAVE

DEAR SIR,

I cannot be of opinion with you that it is too late in life for you to learn to swim. The river near the bottom of your garden affords a most convenient place for the purpose. And as your new employment requires your being often on the water, of which you have such a dread, I think you would do well to make the trial; nothing being so likely to remove those apprehensions as the consciousness of an ability to swim to the shore, in case of an accident, or of supporting yourself in the water till a boat could come to take you up.

I do not know how far corks or bladders may be useful in learning to swim, having never seen much trial of them. Possibly they may be of service in supporting the body while you are learning what is called the stroke, or that manner of drawing in and striking out the hands and feet that is necessary to produce progressive motion. But you will be no swimmer till you can place some confidence in the power of the water to support you; I would therefore advise the acquiring that confidence in the first place; especially as I have known several, who, by a little of the practice necessary for that purpose, have insensibly acquired the stroke, taught as it were by nature.

The practice I mean is this. Choosing a place where the water deepens gradually, walk coolly into it till it is up to your breast, then turn round, your face to the shore, and throw an egg into the water between you and the shore. It will sink to the bottom, and be easily seen there, as your water is clear. It must lie in water so deep as that you cannot reach it to take it up but by diving for it. To encourage yourself in order to do this, reflect that your progress will be from deeper to shallower water, and that at any time you may, by bringing your legs under you and standing on the bottom, raise your head far above the water. Then plunge under it with your eyes open, throwing yourself towards the egg, and endeavouring by the action of your hands and feet against the water to get forward till within reach of it. In this attempt you will find, that the water buoys you up against your inclination; that it is not so easy a thing to sink as you imagined; that you cannot but by active force get down to the egg. Thus you feel the power of the water to support you, and learn to confide in that power; while your endeavours to overcome it, and to reach the egg, teach you the manner of acting on the water with your feet and hands, which action is afterwards used in swimming to support your head higher above water, or to go forward through it.

I would the more earnestly press you to the trial of this method, because, though I think I satisfied you that your body is lighter than water, and that you might float in it a long time with your mouth free for breathing, if you would put yourself in a proper posture, and would be still and forbear struggling; yet till you have obtained this experimental confidence in the water, I cannot depend on your having the necessary presence of mind to recollect that posture and the directions I gave you relating to it. The surprise may put all out of your mind. For though we value ourselves on being reasonable, knowing creatures, reason and knowledge seem on such occasions to be of little use to us; and the brutes, to whom we allow scarce a glimmering of either, appear to have the advantage of us.

I will, however, take this opportunity of repeating those particulars to you, which I mentioned in our last conversation, as, by perusing them at your leisure, you may possibly imprint them so in your memory as on occasion to be of some use to you.

1. That though the legs, arms, and head, of a human body, being solid parts, are specifically something heavier than fresh water, yet the trunk, particularly the upper part, from its hollowness, is so much lighter than water, as that the whole of the body taken together is too light to sink wholly under water, but some part will remain above, until the lungs become filled with water, which happens from drawing water into them instead of air, when a person in the fright attempts breathing while the mouth and nostrils are under water.

2. That the legs and arms are specifically lighter than salt water, and will be supported by it, so that a human body would not sink in salt water, though the lungs were filled as above, but from the greater specific gravity of the head.

3. That therefore a person throwing himself on his back in salt water, and extending his arms, may easily lie so as to keep his mouth and nostrils free for breathing; and by a small motion of his hands may prevent turning, if he should perceive any tendency to it.

4. That in fresh water, if a man throws himself on his back, near the surface, he cannot long continue in that situation but by proper action of his hands on the water. If he uses no such action, the legs and lower part of the body will gradually sink till he comes into an upright position, in which he will continue suspended, the hollow of the breast keeping the head uppermost.

5. But if, in this erect position, the head is kept upright above the shoulders, as when we stand on the ground, the immersion will, by the weight of that part of the head that is out of water, reach above the mouth and nostrils, perhaps a little above the eyes, so that a man cannot long remain suspended in water with his head in that position.

6. The body continuing suspended as before, and upright, if the head be leaned quite back, so that the face looks upwards, all the back part of the head being then under water, and its weight

consequently in a great measure supported by it, the face will remain above water quite free for breathing, will rise an inch higher every inspiration, and sink as much every expiration, but never so low as that the water may come over the mouth.

7. If therefore a person, unacquainted with swimming and falling accidentally into the water, could have presence of mind sufficient to avoid struggling and plunging, and to let the body take this natural position, he might continue long safe from drowning till perhaps help would come. For as to the clothes, their additional weight while immersed is very inconsiderable, the water supporting it, though when he comes out of the water, he would find them very heavy indeed.

But, as I said before, I would not advise you or any one to depend on having this presence of mind on such an occasion, but learn fairly to swim; as I wish all men were taught to do in their youth. They would, on many occurrences, be the safer for having that skill, and on many more the happier, as freer from painful apprehensions of danger, to say nothing of the enjoyment in so delightful and wholesome an exercise. Soldiers particularly should, methinks, all be taught to swim; it might be of frequent use either in surprising an enemy, or saving themselves. And if I had now boys to educate, I should prefer those schools (other things being equal) where an opportunity was afforded for acquiring so advantageous an art, which, once learned, is never forgotten.

I am, Sir, &c.
B. Franklin.

TO SAMUEL MATHER*

Passy, May 12, 1784.

REV^d SIR,

I received your kind letter, with your excellent advice to the people of the United States, which I read with great pleasure, and hope it will be duly regarded. Such writings, though they may be lightly passed over by many readers, yet, if they make a deep impression on one active mind in a hundred, the effects may be considerable. Permit me to mention one little instance, which, though it relates to myself, will not be quite uninteresting to you. When I was a boy, I met with a book, entitled *"Essays to do Good,"*† which I think was written by your father. It had been so little regarded by a former possessor, that several leaves of it were torn out; but the remainder gave me such a turn of thinking, as to have an influence on my conduct through life; for I have always set a greater value on the character of a *doer of good,* than on any other kind of reputation; and if I have been, as you seem to think, a useful citizen, the public owes the advantage of it to that book.

You mention your being in your 78th year; I am in my 79th; we are grown old together. It is now more than 60 years since I left Boston, but I remember well both your father and grandfather, having heard them both in the pulpit, and seen them in their houses. The last time I saw your father was in the beginning of 1724, when I visited him after my first trip to Pennsylvania. He received me in his library, and on my taking leave showed me a shorter way out of the house through a narrow passage, which was crossed by a beam over head. We were still talking as I withdrew, he accompanying me behind, and I turning partly towards him, when he said hastily, *"Stoop, stoop!"* I did not understand him, till I felt my head hit

---

* Samuel Mather (1708-1785) was the son of Cotton and the last of the "Mather dynasty" in the Boston pulpit.

† Generally known by the title that Franklin gives it, this work is Cotton Mather's *Bonifacius* (1710).

against the beam. He was a man that never missed any occasion of giving instruction, and upon this he said to me, "*You are young, and have the world before you;* STOOP *as you go through it, and you will miss many hard thumps.*" This advice, thus beat into my head, has frequently been of use to me; and I often think of it, when I see pride mortified, and misfortunes brought upon people by their carrying their heads too high.

I long much to see again my native place, and to lay my bones there. I left it in 1723; I visited it in 1733, 1743, 1753, and 1763. In 1773 I was in England; in 1775 I had a sight of it, but could not enter, it being in possession of the enemy. I did hope to have been there in 1783, but could not obtain my dismission from this employment here; and now I fear I shall never have that happiness. My best wishes however attend my dear country. *Esto perpetua.* It is now blest with an excellent constitution; may it last for ever!

This powerful monarchy continues its friendship for the United States. It is a friendship of the utmost importance to our security, and should be carefully cultivated. Britain has not yet well digested the loss of its dominion over us, and has still at times some flattering hopes of recovering it. Accidents may increase those hopes, and encourage dangerous attempts. A breach between us and France would infallibly bring the English again upon our backs; and yet we have some wild heads among our countrymen, who are endeavouring to weaken that connexion! Let us preserve our reputation by performing our engagements; our credit by fulfilling our contracts; and friends by gratitude and kindness; for we know not how soon we may again have occasion for all of them. With great and sincere esteem, I have the honour to be, &c.

B. FRANKLIN.

SPEECH IN THE CONVENTION

AT THE CONCLUSION OF ITS DELIBERATIONS

Mr. President: I confess, that I do not entirely approve of this Constitution at present; but, Sir, I am not sure I shall never approve it; for, having lived long, I have experienced many instances of being obliged, by better information or fuller consideration, to change my opinions even on important subjects, which I once thought right, but found to be otherwise. It is therefore that, the older I grow, the more apt I am to doubt my own judgment of others. Most men, indeed, as well as most sects in religion, think themselves in possession of all truth, and that wherever others differ from them, it is so far error. Steele, a Protestant, in a dedication, tells the Pope that the only difference between our two churches in their opinions of the certainty of their doctrine, is, the Romish Church is *infallible,* and the Church of England is *never in the wrong*. But, though many private Persons think almost as highly of their own infallibility as of that of their Sect, few express it so naturally as a certain French Lady, who, in a little dispute with her sister, said, "But I meet with nobody but myself that is *always* in the right." "*Je ne trouve que moi qui aie toujours raison.*"

In these sentiments, Sir, I agree to this Constitution, with all its faults,—if they are such; because I think a general Government necessary for us, and there is no *form* of government but what may be a blessing to the people, if well administered; and I believe, farther, that this is likely to be well administered for a course of years, and can only end in despotism, as other forms have done before it, when the people shall become so corrupted as to need despotic government, being incapable of any other. I doubt, too, whether any other Convention we can obtain, may be able to make a better constitution; for, when you assemble a number of men, to have the advantage of their joint wisdom, you inevitably assemble with those men all their prejudices, their passions, their errors of opinion, their local interests, and their selfish views. From such an assembly can a *perfect* production be expected? It therefore astonishes me, Sir, to find this system approaching so near to perfection as it does; and I think it will astonish our enemies, who are waiting with confidence to hear, that our councils are confounded like those of the builders of Babel, and that our States are on the point of separation, only to meet hereafter for the purpose of cutting one another's throats. Thus I consent, Sir, to this Constitution, because I expect no better, and because I am not sure that it is not the best. The opinions I have had of its *errors* I sacrifice to the public good. I have never whispered a syllable of them abroad. Within these walls they were born, and here they shall die. If every one of us, in returning to our Constituents, were to report the objections he has had to it, and endeavour to gain Partisans in support of them, we might prevent its being generally received, and thereby lose all the salutary effects and great advantages resulting naturally in our favour among foreign nations, as well as among ourselves, from our real or apparent unanimity. Much of the strength and efficiency of any government, in procuring and securing happiness to the people, depends on *opinion,* on the general opinion of the goodness of that government, as well as of the wisdom and integrity of its governors. I hope, therefore, for our own sakes, as a part of the people, and for the sake of our posterity, that we shall act heartily and unanimously in recommending this Constitution, wherever our Influence may extend, and turn our future thoughts and endeavours to the means of having it *well administered.*

On the whole, Sir, I cannot help expressing a wish, that every member of the Convention who may still have objections to it, would with me on this occasion doubt a little of his own infallibility, and, to make *manifest* our *unanimity,* put his name to this Instrument.

TO EZRA STILES*

Philad^a, **March 9. 1790.**

REVEREND AND DEAR SIR,

I received your kind Letter of Jan'y 28, and am glad you have at length received the portrait of Gov'r Yale from his Family, and deposited it in the College Library. He was a great and good Man, and had the Merit of doing infinite Service to your Country by his Munificence to that Institution. The Honour you propose doing me by placing mine in the same Room with his, is much too great for my Deserts; but you always had a Partiality for me, and to that it must be ascribed. I am however too much obliged to Yale College, the first learned Society that took Notice of me and adorned me with its Honours, to refuse a Request that comes from it thro' so esteemed a Friend. But I do not think any one of the Portraits you mention, as in my Possession, worthy of the Place and Company you propose to place it in. You have an excellent Artist lately arrived. If he will undertake to make one for you, I shall cheerfully pay the Expence; but he must not delay setting about it, or I may slip thro' his fingers, for I am now in my eighty-fifth year, and very infirm.

I send with this a very learned Work, as it seems to me, on the antient Samaritan Coins, lately printed in Spain, and at least curious for the Beauty of the Impression. Please to accept it for your College Library. I have subscribed for the Encyclopœdia now printing here, with the Intention of presenting it to the College. I shall probably depart before the Work is finished, but shall leave Directions for its Continuance to the End. With this you will receive some of the first numbers.

You desire to know something of my Religion. It is the first time

---

* Ezra Stiles (1727-1795) was a prominent Congregational minister who became president of Yale College in 1778. On January 28, 1790, he had written Franklin asking his opinion "concerning Jesus of Nazareth," and urging Franklin to disregard his request if it appeared to stem from impertinence or improper curiosity.

I have been questioned upon it. But I cannot take your Curiosity amiss, and shall endeavour in a few Words to gratify it. Here is my Creed. I believe in one God, Creator of the Universe. That he governs it by his Providence. That he ought to be worshipped. That the most acceptable Service we render to him is doing good to his other Children. That the soul of Man is immortal, and will be treated with Justice in another Life respecting its Conduct in this. These I take to be the fundamental Principles of all sound Religion, and I regard them as you do in whatever Sect I meet with them.

As to Jesus of Nazareth, my Opinion of whom you particularly desire, I think the System of Morals and his Religion, as he left them to us, the best the World ever saw or is likely to see; but I apprehend it has received various corrupting Changes, and I have, with most of the present Dissenters in England, some Doubts as to his Divinity; tho' it is a question I do not dogmatize upon, having never studied it, and think it needless to busy myself with it now, when I expect soon an Opportunity of knowing the Truth with less Trouble. I see no harm, however, in its being believed, if that Belief has the good Consequence, as probably it has, of making his Doctrines more respected and better observed; especially as I do not perceive, that the Supreme takes it amiss, by distinguishing the Unbelievers in his Government of the World with any peculiar Marks of his Displeasure.

I shall only add, respecting myself, that, having experienced the Goodness of that Being in conducting me prosperously thro' a long life, I have no doubt of its Continuance in the next, though without the smallest Conceit of meriting such Goodness. My Sentiments on this Head you will see in the Copy of an old Letter enclosed,* which I wrote in answer to one from a zealous Religionist,

* Probably a letter of June 6, 1753, to Joseph Huey in which Franklin replies, apparently, to Huey's Puritan cautioning against expecting salvation by good works rather than faith. Franklin told Huey, "He that for giving a Draught of Water to a thirsty Person, should expect to be paid with a good Plantation, would be modest in his Demands, compar'd with those who think they deserve Heaven for the little good they do on Earth." Characteristically, however, Franklin went on to say that though the faith Huey insisted upon "has doubtless its

whom I had relieved in a paralytic case by electricity, and who, being afraid I should grow proud upon it, sent me his serious though rather impertinent Caution. I send you also the Copy of another Letter, which will shew something of my Disposition relating to Religion. With great and sincere Esteem and Affection, I am, Your obliged old Friend and most obedient humble Servant

B. FRANKLIN.

P. S. Had not your College some Present of Books from the King of France? Please to let me know, if you had an Expectation given you of more, and the Nature of that Expectation? I have a Reason for the Enquiry.

I confide, that you will not expose me to Criticism and censure by publishing any part of this Communication to you. I have ever let others enjoy their religious Sentiments, without reflecting on them for those that appeared to me unsupportable and even absurd. All Sects here, and we have a great Variety, have experienced my good will in assisting them with Subscriptions for building their new Places of Worship; and, as I have never opposed any of their Doctrines, I hope to go out of the World in Peace with them all.

---

use in the World," he, nevertheless, wished it were more productive of good works than he had observed it to be. He told Huey that Christ "prefer'd the *Doers* of the Word to the meer *Hearers*."

The letter alluded to in the next sentence cannot be identified with certainty.

Rinehart Editions